THE FAITHFUL EXECUTIONER

THE FAITHFUL EXECUTIONER

Life and Death, Honor and Shame in the

Turbulent Sixteenth Century

✝

JOEL F. HARRINGTON

FARRAR, STRAUS AND GIROUX

NEW YORK

Farrar, Straus and Giroux
18 West 18th Street, New York 10011

Illustration credits appear on page 285.

Library of Congress Cataloging-in-Publication Data
Harrington, Joel F. (Joel Francis)
    The faithful executioner : life and death, honor and shame in the turbulent
sixteenth century / Joel F. Harrington.
        p.   cm.
    Includes index.
    ISBN 978-0-8090-4992-9 (hardback)
    1. Schmidt, Franz, d. 1634.   2. Executions and executioners—Germany—
Nuremberg—Biography.   3. Criminal procedure—Germany—Nuremberg—
History.   4. Crime—Germany—Nuremberg—History.   I. Title.

HV8551 .H374 2013
364.66092—dc23
[B]
                                                            2012029017

Designed by Jonathan D. Lippincott

www.fsgbooks.com
www.twitter.com/fsgbooks • www.facebook.com/fsgbooks

1   3   5   7   9   10   8   6   4   2

Frontispiece: Albrecht Dürer, *Saint Catherine [of Alexandria] and the Hangman* (1517).
Note that the executioner holds the kneeling saint steady before administering his blow.

For my father, John E. Harrington, Jr.

Contents

THE WORLD OF FRANTZ SCHMIDT

Inset map labels:
North Sea
Baltic Sea
Elbe
Rhine
FRANCONIA
Danube
A L P S
Main

SAXONY
Saale
Gräfenthal
Steinach
Hof
Kronach
Presseck
Lichtenfels
Main
Kulmbach
Weyer
(Bad) Staffelstein
Weismain
BOHEMIA
Main
Eschenau
Hollfeld
Bayreuth
BAMBERG
F R A N C O N I A
WÜRZBURG
Forchheim
Pegnitz
Betzenstein
Neustadt an
der Aisch
Regnitz
Gräfenberg
Velden
Herzogenaurach
Hersbruck
Langenzenn
Fürth
Pegnitz
Lauf
Amberg
MARGRAVATE OF
BRANDENBERG-
ANSBACH
NUREMBERG
Altdorf bei
Nürnberg
UPPER
PALATINATE
Ansbach
Feucht
Schwabach
Pyrbaum
Lichtenau
Roth
Heilbronn
Regnitz
Sulzbürg
Hilpoltstein
Heideck
Altmühl
Danube
Scale of miles
DUCHY OF BAVARIA
10   20   30   40
Map by Gene Thorp

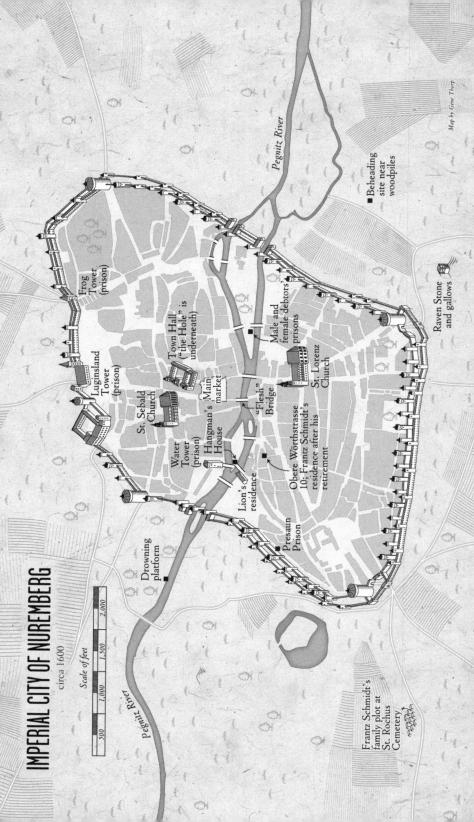

IMPERIAL CITY OF NUREMBERG

circa 1600

Scale of feet

500 1,000 1,500 2,000

Map by Gene Thorp

Pegnitz River

Pegnitz River

Pegnitz River

Beheading site near woodpiles

Raven Stone and gallows

Frog Tower (prison)

Luginsland Tower (prison)

Water Tower (prison)

St. Sebald Church

Town Hall "the Hole" is underneath

Hangman's House

Main market

"Flesh" Bridge

Male and female debtors prisons

St. Lorenz Church

Obere Wörthstrasse 10; Franz Schmidt's residence after his retirement

Lion's residence

Presaun Prison

Drowning platform

Franz Schmidt's family plot at St. Rochus Cemetery

Preface

Every useful person is respectable.

—Julius Krautz, executioner of Berlin (1889)[1]

The sun has barely cleared the horizon when a crowd begins to form on the chilly Thursday morning of November 13, 1617. Yet another public execution awaits the free city of Nuremberg, renowned throughout Europe as a bastion of law and order, and spectators from all ranks of society are eager to secure a good viewing spot before the main event gets under way. Vendors have already set up makeshift stands to hawk Nuremberger sausages, fermented cabbage, and salted herrings, lining the entire route of the death procession, from the town hall to the gallows just outside the city walls. Other adults and children roam the crowd, selling bottles of beer and wine. By midmorning the throng has grown to a few thousand spectators and the dozen or so town constables on duty, known as archers, are visibly uneasy at the prospect of maintaining order. Drunken young men jostle one another and grow restless, filling the air with their ribald ditties. Pungent wafts of vomit and urine mix with the fragrant smoke from grilling sausages and roasting chestnuts.

Rumors about the condemned prisoner, traditionally referred to as the "poor sinner," circulate through the crowd at a dizzying pace. The basics are quickly conveyed: his name is Georg Karl Lambrecht, age thirty, formerly of the Franconian village of Mainberheim. Though he had trained and worked for many years as a miller, he most recently toiled in the more menial position of wine carrier. Everyone knows that he has been sentenced to death for counterfeiting prolific amounts of gold and silver coins with his brother and other nefarious figures, all of whom successfully got away. More intriguing to the anxious spectators, he is widely reputed to be skilled in magic, having divorced his first wife for adultery and "whored around the countryside" with an infamous sorceress known as the Iron Biter. On one recent occasion, according to several witnesses, Lambrecht threw a black hen in the air and cried, "See, devil, you have here your morsel, now give me mine!" upon which he cursed to death one of his many enemies. His late mother is also rumored to have been a witch and his father was long ago hanged as a thief, thereby validating the prison chaplain's assessment that "the apple did not fall far from the tree with this one."

Shortly before noon, the bells of nearby Saint Sebaldus begin to ring solemnly, joined in quick succession by Our Lady's Church on the main market, then Saint Lorenz on the other side of the Pegnitz River. Within a few minutes, the poor sinner is led out of a side door of the stately town hall, his ankles shackled and wrists bound tightly with sturdy rope. Johannes Hagendorn, one of the criminal court's two chaplains, later writes in his journal that at this moment Lambrecht turns to him and fervently asks for forgiveness from his many sins. He also makes one last futile plea to be dispatched with a sword stroke to the neck, a quicker and more honorable death than being burned alive, the prescribed punishment for counterfeiting. His request denied, Lambrecht is expertly shepherded to the adjoining market square by the city's longtime executioner, Frantz Schmidt. From there a slow procession of local dignitaries moves toward the site of execution, a mile away. The judge of the "blood court," dressed in red and black patrician finery, leads the solemn cortege on horseback, followed on foot by the condemned man, two chaplains, and the executioner, better known to residents, like all men of his craft, by the honorific of Meister (Master) Frantz. Behind him walk darkly clad representatives from the Nuremberg city council, scions of the city's wealthy leading families, followed by the heads of several local craftsmen's guilds, thus signaling a genuinely civic occasion. As he passes the spectators lining his way, the visibly weeping Lambrecht calls out blessings to those he recognizes, asking their pardon. Upon exiting the city's formidable walls through the southern Ladies' Gate (Frauentor), the procession approaches its destination: a solitary raised platform popularly known as the Raven Stone, in reference to the birds that come to feast on the corpses left to rot after execution. The poor sinner climbs a few stone steps with the executioner and turns to address the crowd from the platform, unable to avoid a glance at the neighboring gallows. He makes one more public confession and a plea for divine forgiveness, then drops to his knees and recites the Lord's Prayer, the chaplain murmuring words of consolation in his ear.

Upon the prayer's conclusion, Meister Frantz sits Lambrecht down in the "judgment chair" and drapes a fine silk cord around his neck so that he might be discreetly strangled before being set on fire—a final act of mercy on the part of the executioner. He also binds the condemned tightly with a chain around his chest, then hangs a small sack of gunpowder from his neck and places wreaths covered in pitch between Lambrecht's arms and legs, all designed to accelerate the body's burning. The chaplain continues to pray with the poor sinner while Meister Frantz adds several bushels of straw around the chair, fixing them in place with small pegs. Just before the executioner tosses a torch at Lambrecht's feet, his assistant surreptitiously tightens the cord around the condemned man's neck, presumably garroting him to death. Once the flames begin licking the chair, however, it is immediately clear that this effort has been botched, with the condemned man pathetically crying out "Lord, into your hands I commend my spirit." As the fire burns on, there are a few more shrieks of "Lord Jesus, take my spirit," then only the crackles of the flames are heard and the stench of burnt flesh fills the air. Later that day, Chaplain Hagendorn, now fully sympathetic, confides to his journal, based on the clear evidence of pious contrition at the end, "I have no doubt whatsoever that he came through this terrible and pitiful death to eternal life and has become a child and heir of eternal life."[2]

One outcast departs this life; another remains behind, sweeping up his victim's charred bones and embers. Professional killers like Frantz Schmidt have long been feared, despised, and even pitied, but rarely considered as genuine individuals, capable—or worthy—of being known to posterity. But what is going through the mind of this sixty-three-year-old veteran executioner as he brushes clean the stone where the convicted man's last gasps of desperate piety so recently pierced the thickening smoke? Certainly not any doubts about Lambrecht's guilt, which he himself helped establish during two lengthy interrogations of the accused, as well as the depositions of several witnesses—not to mention the counterfeiting tools and other incontrovertible evidence found in the condemned's residence. Is Meister Frantz perhaps reenvisioning and ruing the bungled strangulation that made such an embarrassing scene possible? Has his professional pride been wounded, his reputation besmirched? Or has he simply been hardened to insensitivity by nearly five decades in what everyone considered a singularly unsavory occupation?[3]

Normally, answering any of these questions would remain a speculative endeavor, a guessing game without any chance of a satisfactory resolution. But in the case of Meister Frantz Schmidt of Nuremberg, we have a rare and distinct advantage. Like his chaplain colleague, Meister Frantz kept a personal journal of the executions and other criminal punishments he administered throughout his exceptionally long career. This remarkable document covers forty-five years, from Schmidt's first execution at the age of nineteen, in 1573, to his retirement in 1618. As it turned out, his gruesome dispatch of the penitent counterfeiter would be his final execution, the culmination of a career during which, by his own estimate, he personally killed 394 people and flogged or disfigured hundreds more.

So what was going through Meister Frantz's mind? Astonishingly, although his journal has in fact long been well-known to historians of early modern Germany (c. 1500 to 1800), very few, if any, readers have attempted to answer this question. At least five manuscript copies of the since-lost original circulated privately during the nearly two centuries after its author's death, with printed versions appearing in 1801 and 1913. An abridged English translation of the 1913 edition appeared in 1928, followed by mere facsimiles of the two German editions, both issued in small print runs.[4]

My own first encounter with Meister Frantz's journal occurred some years ago in the local history corner of a Nuremberg bookstore. While considerably less dramatic than, say, the discovery of a long-lost manuscript in a sealed vault that opens only after you solve a series of ancient riddles, it was nonetheless a eureka moment. The very idea that a professional executioner from four centuries ago might be fully literate, let alone somehow motivated to record his own thoughts and deeds in this manner, struck me as a fascinating prospect. How could it be that no one to this date had made significant use of this remarkable source to reconstruct this man's life and the world in which he lived? Here, consigned to a back shelf as a mere antiquarian curiosity, was an amazing story begging to be told.

I purchased the slim volume, took it home to read, and made a few important discoveries. First, Frantz Schmidt was by no means unique among executioners in his self-chronicling—although he remains unsurpassed for his era in both the length of time covered and the detail conveyed in most entries. While the majority of German men in his day remained illiterate, some contemporary executioners could write well enough to keep simple, formulaic execution lists, a few of which have even survived to the present day.[5] By the beginning of the modern era, the executioner's memoir had become a popular genre in itself, the most famous being the chronicles of the Sanson family, an executioner dynasty that presided in Paris from the mid-seventeenth to the mid-nineteenth centuries. The subsequent decline of capital punishment across Europe prompted a final wave of published reminiscences from "last executioners," some of which became bestsellers.[6]

Still, the continued obscurity of this fascinating figure remained puzzling until I examined the journal more closely and made a second, more daunting discovery. Although Meister Frantz is undeniably riveting in his portrayals of the diverse criminals he encounters, he consistently keeps himself tantalizingly in the background—a shadowy and taciturn observer despite his vital role in many of the events he describes. In this respect, the journal itself reads less as a diary in any modern sense and more as a chronicle of a professional life. Its 621 entries, ranging in length from a few lines to a few pages, are indeed written in chronological order, but in the form of two lists, the first comprising all Meister Frantz's capital punishments from 1573 on, and the second covering all the corporal punishments he administered from 1578 on—floggings, brandings, and the chopping of fingers, ears, and tongues. Each entry contains the name, profession, and hometown of the culprit, as well as the crimes in question, the form of punishment, and where it was administered. Over time, Meister Frantz adds more background information about the culprits and their victims, more details about the immediate crimes and previous offenses, and occasionally fuller descriptions of the last hours or moments before an execution. In a few dozen longer entries, he provides still more information about the deviants in question and even re-creates certain key scenes, with colorful descriptions and occasional lines of dialogue.

Many historians would not even consider Schmidt's journal a proper "ego document"—the kind of source, such as a diary or personal correspondence, that scholars look to for evidence of a person's thoughts, feelings, and interior struggles. There are no accounts of moral crises brought on by long sessions of torture, no lengthy philosophical discourses about justice, not even any pithy speculations on the meaning of life. In fact, there are strikingly few personal references at all. In over forty-five years of entries, Schmidt only writes the words "I" and "my" fifteen times each and "me" only once. The majority of instances refer to professional milestones (e.g., *my first execution with the sword*), without expressing an opinion or emotion, and the remainder appear as random insertions (e.g., *I whipped her out of town three years ago*).[7] Significantly, *my father* and *my brother-in-law*, both fellow executioners, each appear three times in a professional context. There is no mention at all of Schmidt's wife, seven children, or numerous associates—not entirely unsurprising, given the focus of the journal. But there is also no acknowledgment of kinship or affinity with any of the crime victims or perpetrators, many of whom he demonstrably knew personally, including his other brother-in-law, a notorious bandit.[8] He makes no explicit religious statements and in general uses moralizing language sparingly. How could such a studiously impersonal document provide any meaningful insight into the life and thoughts of its author? The ultimate reason that no one had yet made use of Meister Frantz's journal as a biographical resource, I decided, might just be that there simply wasn't enough of Meister Frantz in it.[9]

My project too would have been doomed at the outset were it not for two important breakthroughs. The first occurred a few years after my initial encounter with Meister Frantz when, while working on a different project, I discovered in the city library (Stadtbibliothek) of Nuremberg an older and more accurate manuscript copy of the journal itself than any previously used. Whereas the editors of the two previous published editions relied on late-seventeenth-century copies, both modified by baroque copyists for greater readability, this biographical portrait draws on a copy completed in 1634, the year of Schmidt's death.[10] Some of the variations introduced in the later versions are minor: different spelling of certain words, numbering of the entries for easier reference, slightly divergent dates in a few places, syntactical improvements, and the insertion of punctuation in the later versions. (There is no punctuation in the 1634 version, and it's probable that Schmidt, like most writers of his educational background, used none in the original journal.) Many discrepancies, however, are significant. Some versions omit entire sentences and add completely new lines of moralizing language, as well as various details culled from Nuremberg's city chronicles and criminal records. These later pastiche versions rendered the journal more appealing to the bourgeoisie of eighteenth-century Nuremberg, among whom these limited-edition manuscripts circulated privately. But at the same time they often robbed the journal of Meister Frantz's distinctive voice, and thus his perspective. In later editions, the final five years in particular diverge radically from the 1634 version, leaving out several entries altogether and omitting the names of most perpetrators, as well as details of their crimes. In all, at least a quarter of the older text varies to some degree from later versions.

The most interesting—and useful—difference appears at the very outset of the journal itself. In the 1801 and 1913 published editions, Frantz inscribes his *work begun for my father in Bamberg in the year 1573*. In the version used for this book, the young executioner instead writes *Anno Christi 1573rd Year* [sic]: *Here follows which persons I executed for my father, Heinrich Schmidt, in Bamberg*. The distinction, at first sight a subtle one, in fact sheds light on the most elusive question about the entire journal: Why was Frantz Schmidt writing it in the first place? The wording in the later copies suggests more of a paternal imperative than a dedication, with the elder Schmidt dictating that his journeyman son begin building the equivalent of a professional curriculum vitae for prospective employers. But the older version of the journal specifies that it was the first five years of executions, not the writing itself, that Frantz undertook for his executioner father (also mentioned here by name). In fact, as a later reference in this version makes clear, the journal itself was begun not in 1573 but in 1578, the year of Schmidt's appointment in Nuremberg. Looking back, twenty-four-year-old Frantz can only remember his previous five years of executions and omits virtually all his corporal punishments, since *I no longer know which persons I so punished in Bamberg*.

This discovery immediately prompted several new questions, most notably, if Frantz Schmidt did not start writing for his father in 1573, who was he in fact writing for and why? It's doubtful that he intended the journal for subsequent publication, particularly given the sketchiness of most entries for the first twenty years. Perhaps he imagined that

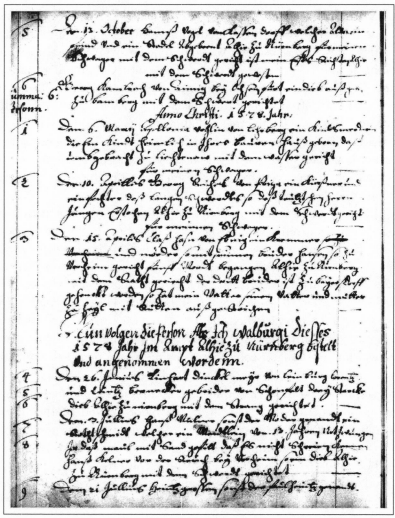

A page from the 1634 copy of Frantz Schmidt's journal, the oldest extant version, located in the Stadtbibliothek Nürnberg. The enumeration of executions in the left margin was likely added by the copyist.

eventually it might be circulated in manuscript copies—as was indeed the case—but again, the earlier years are far less detailed (or interesting) than the city's other competing chronicles and overall read more like a ledger than a genuine literary attempt. Possibly the journal was never meant for anyone but the author himself, but this raises the question of why he started it when he did, at the time of his appointment as Nuremberg's full-time executioner in 1578, as well as why he steadfastly avoided any mention of private matters.

The second key that unlocked the mystery of Frantz Schmidt's journal is a moving document from his later years, now preserved in the Austrian State Archives in Vienna. After spending his entire life in a profession that was widely despised and even officially designated as "dishonorable," the seventy-year-old retired executioner made a late appeal to the emperor Ferdinand II to restore his family's good name. The petition was clearly formulated and penned by a professional notary, but the sentiments expressed are highly personal, even surprisingly intimate at times. Most revealingly, the elderly Frantz recounts the story of how his family unjustly fell into their infamous profession as well as his lifelong determination to avoid the same fate for his own sons. The thirteen-page document includes the names of several prominent citizens healed by Schmidt, who maintained a sideline as a medical consultant and practitioner—a surprisingly common occupation among executioners—as well as an enthusiastic endorsement from the Nuremberg city council, his employer for four decades. His long service to the city and personal propriety, the councilors declared, had been "exemplary," and they urged the emperor to restore his honor.

Could it be that the council itself had been the journal's intended audience all along, with Schmidt's quest to have his honor restored the guiding motif? He might have been the first, but hardly the last German executioner to adopt this strategy.[11] Rereading Meister Frantz's journal entries with this foundational motive in mind, I began to see a thinking and feeling author step slowly from the shadows of what had initially seemed an impersonal account. Thematic and linguistic patterns emerged; discrepancies and shifts in style grew more significant; an evolving self-identity became ever more pronounced. Here was an author utterly uninterested in self-revelation, yet one who inadvertently exposed his thinking and passions in virtually every entry. The very subjectivity that later copyists had unintentionally expunged became a gateway, revealing the author's antipathies, fears, prejudices, and ideals. Well-defined notions of cruelty, justice, duty, honor, and personal responsibility emerged and, over the course of the journal, converged to provide the outline of a coherent worldview. The journal itself took on a moral significance, its very composition a testament to the author's unwavering lifelong campaign for respectability.

The complex individual who emerges from this reading, supplemented by extensive archival sources, is a far cry from the stereotypical emotionless brute of popular fiction. Instead we encounter a pious, abstemious family man who is nonetheless excluded from the respectable society he serves, forced to spend most of his time with convicted criminals and the thuggish guards who assist him.[12] Though effectively isolated, the longtime executioner paradoxically exhibits a high degree of social intelligence, a capacity that makes possible both his brilliant professional success and his gradual reversal of the popular stigma oppressing him. Thanks to the broad chronological scope of the journal, we witness the literary and philosophical evolution of a minimally educated autodidact, whose journal entries progress from laconic summaries of his criminal encounters to virtual short stories and in the process reveal ever more of their author's innate curiosity—particularly on medical matters—as well as his moral cosmos. Despite his repeated exposure to the entire gamut of human cruelty and his own regular administering of horrific violence, this apparently genuinely religious man seems never to waver in his belief in ultimate forgiveness and redemption for those who seek it. Above all, we vicariously experience a professional and private life dually animated by a man's bitter resentment of past and present injustices as well as by his unshakable hope for the future.

The book that has resulted from all of this digging contains two intertwining stories. The first is that of the man Frantz Schmidt. Starting with his birth into an executioner family in 1554, we follow him through a youthful apprenticeship at his father's side to his independent travels as a journeyman executioner. Moving back and forth between his own words (always in italics) and a re-creation of his historical world, we become familiar with the necessary skills of a professional executioner, his uneasy social status, and Frantz's early efforts at self-advancement. As he matures, we encounter the legal and social structures of early

modern Nuremberg, the middle-aged executioner's relentless attempts
to advance socially and professionally, and his concepts of justice, order,
and respectability. We also meet his new wife and growing family as
well as a motley assortment of criminals and law enforcement associates. Finally we witness the blossoming in later life of two increasingly
dominant identities—moralist and healer—and in the process catch a
glimpse of the inner life of this professional torturer and killer. The accomplishments of his final years are rendered bittersweet by disappointment and personal tragedy, but the steadfastness of his solitary quest
for honor remains in itself an object of wonder and even admiration.

At the heart of this book lies another narrative, a reflection about
human nature and social progress, if there are such things. Which
assumptions and sensibilities made the judicial violence that Meister
Frantz regularly administered—torture and public execution—acceptable
to him and his contemporaries yet repugnant to us in our own times?
How and why do such mental and social structures take hold, and how
do they change? Certainly early modern Europeans did not enjoy any

The only fully reliable portrait of Frantz Schmidt that has survived, drawn in the
margin of a legal volume of capital sentences by a Nuremberg court notary with
artistic aspirations. At the time of this event, the beheading of Hans Fröschel on
May 18, 1591, Meister Frantz was about thirty-seven years old.

monopoly on human violence or cruelty, nor on individual or collective retribution. Judged purely by homicide rates, the world of Frantz Schmidt was less violent than that of his medieval forebears but more violent than the modern United States (no mean feat).[13] On the other hand, measured by state violence, the higher rates of capital punishment and frequent military pillaging of all premodern societies pale in comparison to the total wars, political purges, and genocides of the twentieth century. The continuing worldwide practice of judicial torture and public executions alone underscores our ongoing affinity with "more primitive" past societies, as well as the tenuousness of the social transformation that allegedly separates us from them. Is capital punishment truly destined to become extinct everywhere, or is the human drive toward retribution too deeply rooted in the very fiber of our being?

What was Meister Frantz thinking? Whatever we find out, the godly executioner from Nuremberg will always remain a simultaneously alien and familiar figure. It's hard enough to understand ourselves and those most intimate to us, let alone a career killer from a distant time and place. As in all life stories, the revelations from his journal and other historical sources inevitably leave many unanswered—and probably unanswerable—questions. In the only contemporary drawing of Schmidt that can be deemed reliable, the steadfast executioner is—fittingly—turned away from us. Yet in making the effort to understand Frantz Schmidt and his world, we experience more self-recognition and empathy than we might have expected when engaging with this professional torturer and executioner. The story of Meister Frantz of Nuremberg is in many ways a captivating tale from a faraway era, but it is also a story for our time and our world.

Notes on Usage

Quotations from Frantz Schmidt

All direct quotations from Schmidt are set in italics and are my own translations, based on the 1634 copy of his journal and the 1624 petition for restitution of honor.

Names

Spelling was not yet standardized during the early modern period and Meister Frantz, like other writers, often spelled the same proper names differently, sometimes within the same passage. I have modernized the names of towns and other locations as well as most personal first names; family names have retained their early modern orthography, albeit in a standardized form for the sake of clarity. I have also kept female surnames in their early modern form, typified by an occasional vowel shift in the penultimate syllable and the invariable *-in* ending. For example, Georg Widmann's wife would be known as Margaretha Widmänin or Widmenin, while Hans Krieger's daughter becomes Magdalena Kriegerin or Kriegin, and so forth. Popular nicknames and aliases have been translated from contemporary street slang (known as *Rotwelsch*) to their closest modern U.S. equivalents, thus permitting some artistic license on my part.

Currency

There were many local, imperial, and foreign coins in circulation during the early modern era in German lands, and currency exchange values also naturally varied over time. For the purposes of scope and comparison, I have provided the approximate equivalent of each sum in florins (or gulden, abbreviated *fl.*), the largest denomination. A household servant or municipal guard during this period might earn ten to fifteen gulden per year, a schoolteacher fifty, and a municipal jurist three or four hundred. A loaf of bread cost four pence (0.03 fl.), a quart of wine about thirty pence (0.25 fl.), and a year's rent in a slum apartment about 6 fl. The approximate equivalencies are as follows:

1 gulden (fl.) = 0.85 thaler (th.) = 4 "old" pounds (lb.) = 15 batzen (Bz.) = 20 schilling (sch.) = 60 kreuzer (kr.) = 120 pence (d.) = 240 heller (H.).

Dates

The Gregorian calendar was introduced in German Catholic lands on December 21, 1582, but not adopted in most Protestant states until

March 1, 1700, or later. As a result, the intervening years saw a discrepancy of ten days (later eleven) between Protestant territories such as Nuremberg and Catholic states such as the prince-bishopric of Bamberg (e.g., June 13, 1634, in Nuremberg was June 23, 1634, in Bamberg. Contemporaries thus sometimes wrote June 13/23, 1634). Throughout the book I rely on Nuremberg's calendar, where (as in most places by this time) the year began on January 1.

THE FAITHFUL
EXECUTIONER

1

THE APPRENTICE

A father who does not arrange for his son to receive the best education at the earliest age is neither a man himself nor has any fellowship with human nature.   —Desiderius Erasmus, "On the Education of Children" (1529)[1]

A man's value and reputation depend on his heart and his resolution; there his true honor lies.   —Michel de Montaigne, "On Cannibals" (1580)[2]

Neighbors in Bamberg had become accustomed to the weekly ritual getting under way in the back courtyard of Meister Heinrich Schmidt's house and went about their business uninterested. Most of them were on cordial terms with Schmidt, the prince-bishop's new executioner, but remained wary of inviting him or any of his family members into their homes. His son, Frantz, the focus of his father's attention on this May day in 1573, appeared to be a polite and—if one could say this of the offspring of a hangman—well-bred youth of nineteen. Like many teenagers of the day, he planned to follow his father into the same craft, a path he began as early as the age of eleven or twelve. Frantz's childhood and adolescence had been spent in his native Hof, a small provincial town in the far northeast corner of modern-day Bavaria, ten miles from what is now the Czech border. Since the family's move to Bamberg eight months earlier, he had already accompanied Heinrich to several executions in the city and nearby villages, studying his father's techniques and assisting in minor ways. As he grew in size and maturity, his responsibilities and skills developed apace. Ultimately he intended to become, like his father, a master in the practice of "special interrogation" (i.e., torture) and in the art of efficiently dispatching a condemned soul in the manner prescribed by law, using methods that ranged from the common *execution with the rope*, to the less frequent death by fire or by drowning, to the infamous and exceptionally rare *drawing and quartering*.

Today Meister Heinrich was testing Frantz on the most difficult—and most honorable—of all forms of execution, *death by the sword*, or beheading. Only during the past year had father considered son capable and worthy of wielding his cherished "judgment sword," an engraved and elegantly crafted seven-pound weapon that spent most of its time hanging in an honored spot over their fireplace. They'd begun their practice months earlier with pumpkins and gourds before moving on to sinewy rhubarb stalks, which better simulated the consistency of the human neck. Frantz's first attempts were predictably clumsy and at times endangered himself and his father, who held *the poor sinner* firmly in place. Over the weeks, his gestures gradually became more fluid and his aim more accurate, at which point Meister Heinrich deemed his son ready to ascend to the next level, practicing on goats, pigs, and other "senseless" livestock.

Today, at Schmidt's request, the local "dog slayer," or knacker, had assembled a few stray canines and brought them in his ramshackle wooden cages to the executioner's residence in the heart of the city. Schmidt paid his subordinate a small tip for the favor and removed the animals to the enclosed courtyard behind the house, where his son was waiting. Though there was only an audience of one, Frantz was visibly anxious. Pumpkins, after all, did not move, and even pigs offered little resistance. Perhaps he felt a twinge of apprehension about killing "innocent" domestic animals, though this is likely an anachronistic projection.[3] Above all, Frantz knew that successful decapitation of the former pets before him, each requiring one steady stroke, would be the final step in his apprenticeship, a visible sign of his father's approval and of his own readiness to go out into the wider world as a journeyman executioner. Meister Heinrich again played the part of the assistant and held the first yapping dog fast while Frantz tightened his grip on the sword.[4]

A dangerous world

Fear and anxiety are woven into the very fabric of human existence. In that sense they link all of us across the centuries. The world of Heinrich Schmidt and his son, Frantz, however, was characterized by much more individual vulnerability than members of a modern, developed society might imagine bearable. Hostile natural and supernatural forces, mysterious and deadly epidemics, violent and malevolent fellow human beings, accidental or intentional fires—all haunted the imaginations and daily lives of early modern people. The resulting climate of insecurity may not account entirely for the frequent brutality of the era's judicial institutions, but it does offer a context for understanding how institutional enforcers like the Schmidts might simultaneously be viewed with gratitude and disgust by their contemporaries.[5]

The precariousness of life was evident from the very beginning. Having survived a combined miscarriage and stillborn rate that claimed at least one in three fetuses, Frantz Schmidt entered the world with only a fifty-fifty chance of reaching his twelfth birthday. (Childbirth also presented real risks for the mother, with one in twenty women dying within seven weeks of delivery—a significantly higher rate than in even the worst-off of modern developing nations.) The first two years of a child's life were the most dangerous, as frequent outbreaks of smallpox, typhus, and dysentery proved particularly fatal to younger victims. Most parents experienced firsthand the death of at least one child, and most children the death of a sibling and one or both parents.[6]

One of the most common causes of premature death was infection during one of the innumerable epidemics that swept through Europe's cities and countryside. Most people who reached the age of fifty would have survived at least half a dozen outbreaks of various deadly infections. Large cities like Nuremberg and Augsburg might lose as much as a third to a half of their entire population during the one-to-two-year course of an especially severe epidemic. The most feared disease, though not necessarily the deadliest by this point, was the plague. Outbreaks of the plague became especially frequent in central Europe during Frantz Schmidt's lifetime—occurring more often than at any other time or place in European history since the Black Death's first appearance in the mid-fourteenth century. They were also fearsomely capricious in their timing and their virulence.[7] Individuals' traumatic memories and experiences generated a shared cultural dread of all contagion, further underscoring the fragility of human life and the extent of individual vulnerability.

Floods, crop failures, and famines also struck at frequent—though rarely predictable—intervals. The Schmidts had the particular misfortune to live during the worst years of the period known to us as the Little Ice Age (c. 1400–1700), when a global drop in year-round temperatures resulted in longer, harsher winters, and cooler, wetter summers, particularly in northern Europe. During Frantz Schmidt's lifetime, his native Franconia saw much more snow and rain than in previous years, resulting in flooded fields and crops left rotting in place. In some years there were not enough warm months for grapes to ripen, thus yielding only sour wine. Harvests produced desperately little, and the resulting famine left humans and their livestock prey to disease and starvation. Even wildlife populations shrank dramatically, with starving wolf packs increasingly turning their attention to human prey. The scarcity of all foodstuffs sent inflation soaring and, faced with starvation, many formerly law-abiding citizens turned to poaching and other stealing to feed themselves and their families.[8]

Pummeled by natural forces beyond their control, the people of Frantz Schmidt's day also had to contend with the violence of other humans, particularly the seemingly ubiquitous bandits, soldiers, and assorted lawless men who roamed the land freely. Most territorial states, including the prince-bishopric of Bamberg and the imperial city of Nuremberg, mainly consisted of virgin forests and open meadows, dotted with tiny villages, a few towns of one to two thousand inhabitants, and one relatively large metropolis. Without the protection of city walls or concerned neighbors, an isolated farmhouse or mill lay at the mercy of just a few strong men with modest weapons. Well-traveled paths and country lanes often lay far from help as well. The roads and forests just outside a city, along with all border territories, were especially dangerous. There a traveler might fall prey to bandit gangs led by vicious outlaws such as Cunz Schott, who not only beat and robbed countless victims, but also made a point of collecting the hands of citizens from his self-declared enemy, Nuremberg.[9]

The largest German state of the day was in fact—as Voltaire later

An early-sixteenth-century drawing of Nuremberg omits the poor suburbs outside the city's walls but captures the fortress character of town living, which promised protection from the many menaces of surrounding forests (1516).

famously quipped—neither Holy, nor Roman, nor an Empire. Responsibility for law and order was instead divided among the empire's more than three hundred member states, which ranged in size from a baronial castle and its neighboring villages to vast territorial principalities, such as Electoral Saxony or the duchy of Bavaria. Seventy some imperial cities, such as Nuremberg and Augsburg, functioned as quasi-autonomous entities, while some abbots and bishops, including the prince-bishop of Bamberg, had long enjoyed secular as well as ecclesiastical jurisdiction. The emperor and his annual representative assembly (known as the Reichstag, or diet) provided a common focus of allegiance and held symbolic authority throughout German lands, but remained utterly powerless in preventing or resolving the feuds and wars that regularly broke out among member states.

Just two generations before Frantz Schmidt's birth, the reforming emperor Maximilian I more or less conceded the violent chaos that prevailed throughout his realm, proclaiming in his 1495 Perpetual Truce:

> No one, whatever his rank, estate, or position, shall conduct feud, make war on, rob, kidnap, or besiege another . . . nor shall he enter any castle town, market, fortress, villages, hamlets, or farms against another's will, or use force against them; illegally occupying them, threaten them with arson, or damage them in any other way.[10]

In those days, feuding nobles and their entourages proved the greatest cause of unrest, conducting frequent small-scale raids against one another—and in the process burning many rural inhabitants out of their homes and property. Worse still, some of these nobles freelanced as robber barons, running criminal rackets based on robbery, kidnapping, and extortion (commonly referred to as *Plackerei*), further terrorizing rural folk and travelers.

By the time of Frantz Schmidt, incessant feuding between noble families had largely ceased, thanks in equal measure to greater economic integration among the aristocracy and the rise of stronger princes.[11] However, having consolidated their power in large states such as the duchy of Württemberg and the electorate of Brandenburg (later Prussia), these powerful princes now set out to conquer still more territory, using much of their considerable wealth to raise large armies of soldiers for hire. This thirst for war coincided with a steady decline in the number of nonmilitary jobs available to commoners during an exceptionally long period of inflation and high unemployment that historians have dubbed the long sixteenth century (c. 1480–1620). The ranks of soldiers for pay accordingly ballooned twelvefold over the course of the sixteenth and seventeenth centuries, spawning a terrifying new threat to personal safety and property in German lands: the universally despised landsknechts, or mercenaries.

One contemporary characterized landsknechts as "a new order of soulless people [who] have no respect for honor or justice [and practice] whoring, adultery, rape, gluttony, drunkenness . . . stealing, robbing, and murder," and who live "entirely in the power of the devil, who pulls them about wherever he wants." Even the emperor Charles V, who relied heavily on such men, acknowledged the "inhuman tyranny" of the roving bands of landsknechts, which he considered "more blasphemous and crueler than the Turks."[12] While engaged, the mercenaries spent most of their time loitering in camps and sporadically pillaging the hinterlands of their contracted enemy—perpetrating countless acts of small-scale localized violence like that captured chillingly in an episode from Hans Jakob Christoffel Grimmelshausen's seventeenth-century novel *Simplicissimus*:

> A number of soldiers began to slaughter, to boil and roast things, while others, on the other hand, stormed through the house from top to bottom. Others still made a large pack out of linens, clothes, and all kinds of household goods. Everything they didn't want to take with them they destroyed. A number of them stuck their bayonets into the straw and hay, as if they didn't already have

A German landsknecht, or mercenary (c. 1550).

enough sheep and pigs to stick. Many of them shook out the feath-
ers from the bedcovers and filled them with ham. Others threw
meat and other utensils into them. Some knocked in the oven and
the windows, smashing copper utensils and dishes. Bedsteads,
tables, stools, and benches were burned. Pots and cutting boards
were all broken. One servant girl was so badly handled in the barn
that she couldn't move any longer. Our servant they tied up and
laid on the ground and rammed a funnel in his mouth and then
poured a ghastly brew full of piss down his throat. Then they
started to torture the peasants as if they wanted to burn a bunch
of witches.[13]

Things were not much better in times of peace. When unemployed
or simply unpaid (a frequent occurrence), some of these groups of
mostly young men roved about the countryside in search of food, drink,
and women (not necessarily in that order). Frequently joined by run-
away servants and apprentices (known in England as "ronnegates") as
well as by debt-laden wife deserters, banished criminals, and other vagrants, these "sturdy beggars" survived mainly by panhandling and
petty theft. Some became more aggressive, terrorizing farmers, villagers,
and travelers with the same *Plackerei* as robber knights and professional
bandits. The distinction between full-time and part-time extortionists
and robbers was of course irrelevant to their many victims, as in the
instance of two professional thieves flogged out of town by the adult
Frantz Schmidt, who along with their companions, some begging mercenaries, *forced the people at three mills to give them goods and tortured
[them], taking several hatchets and guns.*[14]

Among the many crimes associated with robber bands and other
roving ruffians, one struck special terror in the hearts of the rural popu-
lace: arson. In an era long before fire departments and home insurance,
the very word was incendiary. One carefully placed torch could bring a
farm or even an entire village to ruin, turning prosperous inhabitants
into homeless beggars in less than an hour. In fact, the mere threat of
burning down someone's house or barn—often used as a form of
extortion—was considered tantamount to the deed itself and thus subject to the same prescribed punishment: being burned alive at the
stake. Some gangs—known as murderer-burners—actually thrived on

the extortion money they extracted from farmers and villagers threatened with this terrifying crime.[15] Fear of professional arsonists was rampant in the German countryside, but most intentional house fires were the by-product of endemic private feuds and attempts at revenge, sometimes preceded by the warning figure of a red hen painted on a wall or a dreaded "burn letter" nailed to a front door. Fire prevention in most cities had advanced little since the Middle Ages, and rural dwell-

A lone peddler is ambushed by highwaymen; detail from a landscape painting by Lucas I. van Valkenborch (c. 1585).

ings and barns remained completely without protection. Only the wealthiest merchants could afford insurance, and even then it usually covered only goods in transit. Whether natural or man-made, house and barn fires spelled financial devastation to virtually all households.

Beset by all the dangers above, the people of Frantz Schmidt's day feared yet another unseen, lurking threat: the bewildering array of ghosts, fairies, werewolves, demons, and other supernatural attackers traditionally believed to inhabit field and forest, road and hearth. Clerical reformers of all religious denominations attempted in vain to quash such ancient beliefs, while at the same time generating even more widespread anxiety by trumpeting what they believed to be the greater supernatural threat of a genuine satanic conspiracy at work in their time. The specter of witchcraft hovered menacingly throughout Frantz Schmidt's lifetime, often leading to the tragic real-world consequences we know today as the European witch craze of 1550–1650, during which at least sixty thousand people were executed for the crime.

Where did one turn for protection and consolation in this vale of tears? Family and friends, the typical refuge from the world's cruelties, might help an individual cope with misfortune but could offer little preventive help. Popular healers ("cunning people"), barber-surgeons, apothecaries, and midwives could offer occasional relief from some pains and wounds, but they remained helpless against serious diseases or most of the dangers of childbirth. Physicians, the modern medical expert of choice, were rare, expensive, and just as constrained by the medical knowledge of the day. Astrologers and other fortune-tellers might provide some sense of control and even destiny to troubled souls, but, once more, they could offer no protection from the world's dangers themselves.

Religion continued to serve as one of the main intellectual resources of the age, offering explanations of misfortune and occasionally putative preventive measures. The teachings of Martin Luther and other Protestants from the 1520s on repudiated any reliance on "superstitious" protection rituals, but otherwise reinforced the common belief in a moral universe where nothing happened by chance. Natural disasters and epidemics were routinely interpreted as signs of God's displeasure and even anger, though the cause of that divine wrath was not always self-evident. Some theologians and chroniclers identified a particular unpunished atrocity—an act of incest or infanticide—as the catalyst. Other times, collective suffering was interpreted more generally, as a divine call to repentance. Luther, John Calvin, and many other early Protestants retained an apocalyptic expectation that they were living in the final days and that the tribulations of the world would soon be at an end. And of course the devil and his minions remained a key component of every explanation of disaster, ranging from claims that witches caused hailstorms to stories of demons endowing criminals with supernatural powers.

The most commonly used preventive measure against the various "angels of death" was simple prayer. For centuries, Christians had collectively intoned "Protect us, O Lord, from plague, famine, and war!"[16] Petitionary prayer to Christ, Mary, or a specific saint against a specific threat remained widespread throughout the later sixteenth century, even among Protestants, who formally rejected any supernatural intercession other than Christ's. For many believers, magical talismans—such as gems, crystals, and pieces of wood—provided supplementary protection against natural and supernatural dangers, as did a variety of quasi-religious items known as sacramentals among Catholics: holy water, pieces of a consecrated host, saints' medals, blessed candles or bells, and supposedly holy relics, such as an alleged bone fragment or other bodily part from a saint or member of the Holy Family. Other more explicitly magical spells, powders, or potions—some of them officially proscribed—promised recovery from illness or protection from enemies. If consolation and reassurance were the primary goals, we cannot so readily dismiss the efficacy of such measures. Belief in an afterlife, where the suffering and virtuous would be rewarded and the evil punished, may have offered additional solace, though even the strongest personal faith remained powerless to prevent or avoid catastrophe itself.

Assailed by dangers on all sides, Frantz Schmidt and his contemporaries were desperate for some sense of security and order. Secular authorities—from the emperor to territorial princes to the ruling magnates of city-states—all shared this longing and were determined to do something about it. Their paternalistic outlook was far from altruistic—entailing by definition an expansion of their own authority—but their concern for public safety and welfare was for the most part genuine. Their efforts to mitigate the effects of earthquakes, floods, famines, and epidemics may have offered some small aid to victims. But even the most ambitious improvements in public hygiene had a minimal impact before the modern era. The quarantines that many governments imposed during epidemics, for example, slowed the spread of contagion somewhat, as did better-regulated trash and waste disposal, but flight from urban areas during outbreaks remained the most effective measure among those who could afford it.

Law enforcement, on the other hand, offered an irresistible opportunity to demonstrate government's ability to curb violence and provide some measure of security for all inhabitants. It also ensured greater popular support and expanded power for secular leaders themselves. Frantz Schmidt and his contemporaries consequently shared a paradoxical attitude toward the violence that surrounded them. As we might expect, people resigned to regular assault by waves of unpreventable natural disaster and illness tended to regard the violence of their fellow humans with a similarly fatalist resolve. At the same time, the heightened aspirations of political leaders in reducing such violence—or at least extracting a heavy price for it—clearly raised popular expectations and hopes. When legal authorities urged aggrieved individuals to avoid private retribution and turn to their own courts and officials, they were scarcely prepared for the onslaught of petitions and accusations that flooded their chanceries. Requests for official intervention ranged from complaints about road repairs and trash collection to requests to curb the public nuisance of aggressive beggars and rambunctious street children to reports of unruly or criminal activities among neighbors. The greater dominance these ambitious leaders sought came at the high price of having to listen to their subjects and provide visible proof that the people's confidence in official promises was not misplaced.

The skilled executioner was in that sense the ruling authorities' most indispensable means of easing their subjects' fear of lawless attacks and providing some sense of justice in a society where everyone knew that the great majority of dangerous criminals would never be caught or punished. The ritualized violence that the executioner administered on the community's behalf at once (1) avenged victims; (2) ended the threat represented by dangerous criminals; (3) set a terrifying example; and (4) forestalled further violence at the hands of angry relatives or lynch mobs. Without the executioner's carefully orchestrated, highly visible, and often brutal assertion of civic authority, secular rulers knew that "the sword of justice" would remain an empty metaphor and that their self-proclaimed role as the guarantors of public safety would be regarded as meaningless. As their representative, the executioner undertook the precarious operation of achieving the desired semblance of orderly justice while in the process of physically assaulting or killing another human being. An aspiring master such as Frantz Schmidt would need to convince prospective employers not only of his technical abilities but also of his capacity to remain calm and dispassionate in even the most emotionally charged situation. This was a daunting goal for one so young, but one that Meister Heinrich and his apprentice son embraced with singular and unflinching resolve.

A father's shame

The relative social tolerance that Heinrich Schmidt and his family enjoyed in the spring of 1573 was itself a recent development, and one by no means guaranteed to endure. Since the Middle Ages, professional executioners had been universally reviled as cold-blooded killers for hire and accordingly excluded from respectable society at every turn. Most were forced to live outside the city walls or near an already unclean location within the city, typically the slaughteryard or a lazar house (for lepers). Their legal disenfranchisement was just as thorough: no executioner or family member could hold citizenship, be admitted to a guild, hold public office, serve as a legal guardian or trial witness, or even write a valid will. Until the late fifteenth century, these outcasts received no legal protection from mob violence in the event of a botched execution, and a few were actually stoned to death by angry spectators. In most towns, hangmen—as they were most commonly known—were forbidden to enter a church. And if an executioner wished to have his child baptized or desired last rites for a dying relative, he depended on the willingness of the sometimes less-than-compassionate local priest to set foot in an "unclean" residence. They were also banned from bathhouses, taverns, and other public buildings, and it was virtually unheard-of for an executioner to enter the home of any respectable person. People of Frantz Schmidt's era harbored such a pervasive fear of social contamination at the very touch of an executioner's hand that respectable individuals jeopardized their very livelihoods by even casual contact. Folklore abounded with tales of the disasters that befell those who broke this ancient taboo, and of beautiful condemned maidens who chose death over marriage to willing hangmen.[17]

The source of this deep anxiety seems obvious, given the distasteful nature of the hangman's trade. Even today, direct contact with dead bodies carries a polluting stigma in many traditional societies. In early modern Germany, the associated "infamous occupations" thus not only included executioners, but also gravediggers, tanners, and butchers.[18] Most people also considered hangmen a type of amoral mercenary and thus excluded from "decent" society in the same manner as vagrants, prostitutes, and thieves, as well as Gypsies and Jews. Contemporaries and even some modern scholars commonly supposed that any individual attracted to such an unsavory occupation must be a criminal himself— even though the evidence of such a correlation remains inconclusive. It was likewise presumed that socially marginalized figures had been born out of wedlock, with the distinction between illegitimate (*unehelich*) and dishonorable (*unhehrlich*) often elided, so that even official documents might casually refer to "the whoreson hangman."[19]

Not surprisingly, hangmen and other dishonorable individuals tended to bond together, both professionally and socially. Executioner dynasties sprang up across the empire, built on both mutual exclusion and strategic intermarriage. Some of these families bore ominous surnames— such as Leichnam (corpse)—while most gained fame principally among their fellows in the trade, such as the south German families of Brand, Fahner, Fuchs, and Schwartz.[20] Over the course of generations, these interconnected families developed many of the same ritual initiations and other forms of corporate identity common to "honorable" crafts such as goldsmiths and bakers. Like the honorable craftsmen who spurned them, executioners also developed professional networks, oversaw the training of new practitioners, and sought to secure gainful employment within the trade for their sons.

The full extent of Heinrich Schmidt's ambitions for his own son at this moment, however, was far greater than either of them dared admit to anyone outside their own household. Together they sought to undo the family curse that had condemned them and all their progeny to the gutter status of the executioner—an audacious dream of social ascent that was virtually unthinkable in their rigidly caste-conscious world. The secret reason for the family's descent into shame—a story passed down from father to son—would only be revealed to the wider world by Meister Frantz in his old age. But on this day, as the young Frantz raised his sword over the trembling body of an unlucky stray, that secret shame burned fresh in his mind.

Until the fall of 1553, Frantz's father, Heinrich Schmidt, had enjoyed a comfortable and respectable life as *a woodsman and fowler* in the town of Hof, situated in the margravate of Brandenburg-Kulmbach, the territory of a Franconian noble of middling rank. Schmidt and his family had survived and even prospered during several years of upheaval caused by the expansionist ambitions of their young lord, Albrecht II Alcibiades (b. 1522), popularly known as *Bellator* (warrior). Like his Athenian namesake, Albrecht Alcibiades frequently shifted allegiances during the religious conflicts of the 1540s and 1550s, ultimately alienating both Catholic and Protestant states with his savage raids of their territories. Most recently, the Warrior's aggression and duplicity had even succeeded in uniting against him troops from the Protestant states of Nuremberg, Bohemia, and Braunschweig, with those of the Catholic prince-bishoprics of Bamberg and Würzburg, in what would later be known as the Second Margrave War. Albrecht's act of unintentional ecumenism culminated in his enemies' joint invasion of his territory and their siege of many strongholds, including the city of Hof.

One of Albrecht's better-fortified towns, Hof was surrounded by stone walls twelve feet high and three feet thick. The margrave himself was not resident when the siege began on August 1, 1553, but the local militia of some six hundred men held their own against a surrounding army of more than thirteen thousand troops for over three weeks, until a letter from Albrecht arrived, announcing that reinforcements were on the way. The promised relief never came, however, and after four more weeks of daily bombardments, raiding parties, and mass starvation, the battered town capitulated. The subsequent occupation was mild. Nonetheless, the conquerors had to force Hof's angry citizens to formally

The universally reviled
Albrecht Alcibiades of
Brandenburg-Kulmbach,
author of the Schmidt
family's misfortune in Hof
(c. 1550).

welcome their own lord when he finally rode into town with an entou-
rage of sixty knights on October 12. Within a few weeks of his return to
Hof, Albrecht succeeded in not only further alienating his resentful
subjects but also reigniting hostilities with the victorious army still
camped outside the city walls. This foolhardy campaign ended in disaster, with the conquerors inflicting a much more severe occupation on
the city and the margrave himself forced to flee the city. Declared an
imperial outlaw, he spent four years as a wandering exile in France,
before dying in 1557 at the age of forty-five. By then, large parts of Albrecht's territory lay in ruins and his name was bitterly cursed among
his former subjects.

Heinrich Schmidt and his son had a still deeper and more enduring
grudge against the disgraced margrave than did other residents of Hof.
It originated on Monday, October 16, 1553, three days after Albrecht Alcibiades had returned to the devastated Hof with his retainers. Like
other German towns of its size, Hof could not afford to maintain a full-
time executioner. But when the widely despised Albrecht had three
local gunsmiths arrested in an alleged plot on his life, rather than send-

ing for a traveling professional to execute them—the usual course of action—the headstrong margrave invoked an ancient custom and commanded a bystander to carry out the deed on the spot. The man singled out for this terrible distinction was Heinrich Schmidt. Having lived as a respectable citizen of Hof, Schmidt vehemently protested to his ruler that this act would bring infamy upon him and his descendants—but to no avail. *Unless [my father] complied*, recounted the seventy-year-old Frantz, *[the margrave] threatened to string him up instead, as well the two men standing next to him.*

Why was the innocent woodsman singled out for this dreadful commission? The answer lies in another story that Frantz would not reveal until late in his life—a bizarre and improbable case of a dispute with a man about a dog. A few years before the fateful confrontation with Albrecht Alcibiades, Frantz's grandfather, the tailor Peter Schmidt, was approached by a weaver journeyman from Thüringen and asked for permission to wed his daughter. The young couple subsequently married and settled in a small farmstead near Hof. One day, as the weaver (named Günther Bergner, Frantz recalled eight decades later) was strolling the countryside, he was attacked by a large dog. In anger, Bergner picked up the animal and hurled it at its owner, a deer hunter, *to his misfortune and ours* (Frantz later recalled) *killing him.* Though not prosecuted, the weaver was thereafter considered dishonorable and barred from all crafts. *Since no one wanted to be around him, out of desperation and melancholy he became an executioner.* The stigma did not apparently carry over to his father-in-law Peter Schmidt, who continued to work as a tailor in Hof. A few years later, though, when the anxious margrave sought someone to dispatch his would-be assassins, the infamous occupation of Heinrich Schmidt's brother-in-law Bergner (who presumably was not himself available) sealed the choice of a new executioner.[21]

As Schmidt had predicted, from his moment of capitulation to Albrecht's order, he and his family were ruthlessly and definitively excluded from honorable society by their own neighbors and former friends, simultaneously tainted by their association with an odious trade and a reviled tyrant. The dishonored Heinrich Schmidt could have attempted to escape ignominy by starting anew with his family in a distant town. Instead, he chose to remain in his ancestral home and attempt to earn a living from the only craft now open to him. Thus was a new executioner dynasty born—though if the plan that Heinrich would later share with his son, Frantz, succeeded, it would be a short-lived one.

Frantz Schmidt entered the world within months of his father's dramatic fall from grace, sometime between late 1553 and mid-1554.[22] The Hof of his childhood and adolescence remained a closed society of at most one thousand people, its insularity and social rigidity exacerbated by its remote location. Later known as the Bavarian Siberia, the region surrounding the town on the Saale River was wrapped in dense, ancient forests and overshadowed by mountains up to one thousand meters high. Long, brutal winters and a native soil riddled with chalk and iron made farming difficult. Weaving and other cloth-related trades dominated economic life in the town, cattle- and sheepherding in the countryside. Mining had provided another source of wealth for centuries, in the days of Frantz Schmidt yielding finds of gold, silver, iron, copper, tin, granite, and crystal.[23]

Hof was also a frontier town in the cultural sense. To Thuringians and Saxons, it was the far south; to Franconians their own far north. Just west of the Bohemian border, the town was shaped by a unique mix of Slavic and German influences and in 1430 had actually been

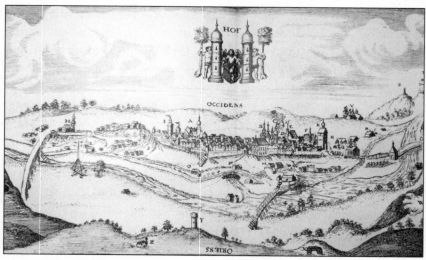

The town of Hof as seen from the east (c. 1550).

sacked by invading Hussites, radical followers of the martyred religious reformer Jan Hus. The regional identity most closely associated with Hof was that of the Vogtland. By the sixteenth century, the territory originally named for its imperial *Vögte* (lord protectors) had become more of a vague cultural construct than a political entity, distinguished most by its dialect, sausages, and exceptionally potent beer. Much later, among nationalists of the nineteenth century, the scenic and pristine Vogtland would represent an ur-Germanic wilderness, possessing an idealized but also savage beauty. For the ostracized Schmidt family, the geographical isolation of Hof merely deepened their own state of internal exile and despondency.

Heinrich Schmidt's reasons for staying put after his disgrace are unclear. At least the political aftermath of Albrecht Alcibiades's disastrous reign was more favorable to his imposed profession. Upon Albrecht's death in 1557, his cousin Georg Friedrich, margrave of neighboring Brandenburg-Ansbach, assumed control over Brandenburg-Kulmbach as well. Hof's new lord was as steady and circumspect as his kinsman had been rash. All the city's trees miraculously bloomed again that fall, reported the local chronicler Enoch Widman, as potent an omen as the earthquake that had presaged Albrecht's disastrous rampage.[24] From his residence in nearby Bayreuth, Margrave Georg Friedrich immediately set about rebuilding Hof and other damaged towns while repairing relations with neighboring states. He also initiated thorough financial and legal reforms, beginning with a series of new police ordinances and other criminal legislation. One immediate result was a sharp increase in the number and intensity of criminal prosecutions. In the twelve months leading up to May 1560, Heinrich Schmidt, the margrave's new executioner, was called on to perform an unprecedented eight executions in the district of Hof alone.[25]

Heinrich Schmidt's work for the margrave was consequently stable enough to provide him with a reliable income, which he was able to supplement with freelance execution work as well as the traditional executioner sideline of healing wounds. His chances of reversing the family's social misfortune while in Hof, however, were practically nil. He applied at least twice for executioner jobs elsewhere but not until 1572, when Frantz was eighteen, did he finally secure the position of executioner to the prince-bishop of Bamberg, a notable step up the career ladder.[26] After nearly two decades of being shunned by their former friends and neighbors, the Schmidts were finally free of provincial Hof, if still shackled to their painful memories and shameful legacy.

The diocese (later archdiocese) of Bamberg was one of the oldest and most prestigious sees in the empire. In 1572 its bishops had enjoyed four centuries of simultaneous secular and religious authority and, despite considerable losses to the Protestant Reformation during the previous four decades, still ruled over four thousand square miles of territory and approximately 150,000 subjects. The prince-bishopric's administration was relatively sophisticated and widely admired in the area of criminal law, particularly since the 1507 publication of its immensely influential code, the *Bambergensis*.[27] Bishop Veit II von Würtz-burg, Heinrich Schmidt's new lord, was better known among his subjects for his heavy taxes, but it was in any event his vice chancellor who supervised the new executioner and other judicial personnel. When Heinrich Schmidt reported to the cathedral city for duty in August 1572, he celebrated a significant personal as well as professional achievement.

The Schmidt family enjoyed a materially comfortable life in their new hometown, with a healthy income that averaged 50 fl. a year—as much as a pastor or schoolteacher—as well as other benefits Meister Heinrich accrued as a municipal employee.[28] Their spacious house, located on a peninsula in the northeastern corner of the city today known as Little Venice, came rent free for the duration of his work for the bishop. After the family's arrival in the late summer of 1572, the city undertook a thorough renovation and expansion of the house according to Heinrich's specifications.[29] Admittedly, the family was expected to share quarters with Hans Reinschmidt, the executioner's assistant (known in Bamberg as the *Peinlein*, or penalizer), but with Frantz the only child remaining at home, some degree of privacy was still possible.

Although still precarious, the family's social position became less oppressive than it had been in the smaller community of Hof. Bamberg was a relatively cosmopolitan town of about ten thousand, known principally (even today) for its magnificent thirteenth-century cathedral and the city's prolific production of a unique smoked beer. Locals proudly compared Bamberg's seven majestic hills, each crowned with its own distinctive church, to the seven hills of the Eternal City. At least in theory, the Schmidts' new home allowed them a much greater degree of anonymity in the streets and markets than provincial Hof, and perhaps even a degree of neighborly acceptance. Some churches in cities of this size had begun to permit executioners their own pews, and a few taverns even provided them with their own stool—sometimes three-legged, like a scaffold.[30] The Schmidts' Protestant faith undoubtedly created some additional barriers in the overwhelmingly Catholic city, but it apparently made no difference to Heinrich's Catholic employers, despite the bishopric's public embrace of the Counter-Reformation.[31]

The surest sign of the executioner's relatively enhanced (or rather, less degraded) status in this era was the increasing frequency of reactionary legislation that attempted to restore "traditional values" and the "natural" social order. Like the so-called sumptuary laws of the previous century, imperial police ordinances of 1530 and 1548 required executioners (as well as Jews and prostitutes) to wear "distinctive clothing by which they could be readily identified."[32] Many local decrees similarly decried the blurring of traditional boundaries and attempted to reverse the perceived trend toward tolerance of all "dishonorable" people, imposing hefty fines or even corporal punishment on those who transgressed.

Popular prejudice always dies slowly, especially among those individuals most anxious about their own deteriorating economic situation and unstable social status. The second half of the sixteenth century saw the emergence of an increasingly global marketplace, a shift with especially dire consequences for traditional craftsmen and their products. But rather than direct their anger at the new breed of extravagantly wealthy bankers or merchants, most "poor but honest" artisans instead attacked seemingly prosperous executioners such as Heinrich Schmidt and other individuals (notably Jews) whom they considered rightfully beneath them. Obsessed with preserving their self-defined "dove pure" honor, German craftsmen universally ignored the emperor's 1548 opening of guild membership to executioners' sons and continued to forbid their members any social contact whatsoever with them. Any artisan defying this sweeping ban—which also applied to butchers, cobblers, tanners, sack carriers, and a number of other "disreputable" occupations—risked social ostracism, loss of guild membership, or worse. One Basel artisan allegedly committed suicide because of his pollution by close contact with the local executioner; others so tainted felt compelled to leave town and start anew somewhere else. This rigid view of social status, based principally on birth, would continue to exercise enormous influence on how most people in Europe and in the German lands thought and acted for a long, long time—well into the modern era, in fact.[33]

Fortunately for the Schmidts, these heavy-handed legal attempts to single out marginal individuals and stymie their social advancement made no difference in day-to-day life and served little purpose other than to appease anxious artisans. Contrary to modern representations, for instance, Heinrich Schmidt and later his son, Frantz, were not compelled to wear any standard on- or off-duty uniform, and there is absolutely no evidence anywhere of the stereotypical black mask—likely an invention of nineteenth-century Romantics. A few cities required their executioners to don a bright red, yellow, or green cape, or wear a striped shirt, or perhaps a distinctive hat.[34] In illustrations from the second half of the sixteenth century on, though, they are invariably well dressed, sometimes to a dandified degree. In short, they dressed the same as any other middle-class burgher—and therein lay the problem for status-anxious craftsmen.

The toothlessness of such ordinances did not ease the uncertainty of the Schmidts' slightly improved social standing in urban Bamberg. Personal honor, based on both social rank and reputation, remained the most valuable—and fragile—commodity around. In Heinrich Schmidt's day, verbal insults to one's "name"—"rogue" or "thief" for a man, "whore" or "witch" for a woman—frequently led to physical assault or even homicide among individuals of every rank. "Whoreson of a hangman" remained a common curse (even appearing in Shakespeare's plays) and "it belongs to the gallows" was the most succinct way to condemn any frowned-upon practice. The Schmidts were likewise reminded of their lowly place with virtually every feast day, public procession, or other civic occasion, where both the reigning social hierarchy—and their own exclusion from it—were vividly reasserted. As in any racially or otherwise segregated society, law and custom still explicitly banned executioners and their families from many venues and severely constrained their opportunities for education, occupation, and housing, a condition that would persist for generations to come.

A Nuremberg chronicle's portrayal of Frantz Schmidt's execution of Anna Pei-
helsteinin on July 7, 1584, possibly drawn by an eyewitness. In the original, the
executioner wears the unusual—and visually striking—combination of pink
stockings, light blue hose with a pink codpiece, and a leather jerkin over a blue
doublet and white shirt collar, the jerkin offering some protection from blood-
stains (1616).

Perhaps the most insidious aspect of the stigma tied so deeply to
Heinrich Schmidt's profession was its unpredictable effect, which created a fragile and always socially tenuous atmosphere in any interaction
between family members and their Bamberg neighbors. Like other
elastic social concepts—the famed U.S. "middle class" comes to mind—
the definition of the executioner's dishonor might be interpreted variously
and selectively, and sometimes even spitefully, by different individuals
and communities. A visiting merchant from Lübeck might express
shock not only that the Augsburg "hangman" lived in the midst of town
but also that honorable people regularly ate and drank with him and
even entered his house. In another town, by contrast, there might be
regret but also little surprise when the wife of one executioner died in
childbirth because the midwife refused to set foot in their home.
Even a widely respected executioner might be reputed to have "a great
many friends in the village," and yet at his death have not a single soul
willing to serve as a pallbearer.[35]

Heinrich Schmidt knew well that neither his position as a well-paid government official nor his bourgeois standard of living nor his personal reputation for honesty guaranteed any kind of lasting acceptance or secure future for him or his family. Social humiliation in minor or major ways remained a routine experience, a continual reminder of his shame. His contemporaries considered his predicament an unalterable fact of life. But for Meister Heinrich and his equally determined son, the disgraceful occupation thrust upon them both would provide the very means of their family's attempted salvation.

A son's opportunity

Timing and luck are important to any personal success. Frantz Schmidt had the good fortune to come to maturity in what historians now call "the golden age of the executioner." This development was itself the culmination of a very gradual yet profound transformation of German criminal law that had been under way for at least two centuries. Since the days of the Roman Empire, Germanic peoples had treated most crimes as private conflicts to be resolved by some form of financial compensation (wergild) or by a customary punishment, such as loss of a limb or banishment. State officials, who remained few in number until the later Middle Ages, typically played the role of referee, ensuring orderly procedures but leaving instigation, trial, and judgment to elders or other local jurors. The main goal in this approach was modest—to prevent blood feud and ongoing violence—certainly not to punish all malefactors, which would have seemed a simultaneously alien and impractical objective. Usually a male relative of a murder victim was allowed to execute the perpetrator himself; other state-endorsed killings used freelance hangmen or court beadles (low-level enforcers), paid on an ad hoc basis, by the execution.[36]

The late medieval origins of a more active, even interventionist, governmental role in criminal justice lay in two intertwined but distinctive impulses. The first was a broader, more ambitious definition of sovereignty itself that first surfaced in prosperous city-states, such as Augsburg and Nuremberg. Eager to make their jurisdictions safe and attractive havens for trade and manufacturing, municipal guilds and ruling patrician families began to issue ordinances governing a wide variety of behavior previously left to the private sphere. Some of the new regulations appear odd, even quaint to modern eyes, particularly the many sumptuary ordinances ostensibly aimed at preserving the public peace by restricting clothing and dancing of various sorts. Only noblemen might wear swords or fur, for instance, while their wives and daughters might possess exclusive right to don jewelry and certain multicolored fabrics. More significant, by the beginning of the sixteenth century, more than two thousand cities and other jurisdictions in Germany had sought and been granted the monopoly of high justice, or the right to try capital crimes. Most of these local courts continued to rely on private settlements for lesser offenses but jealously guarded the privilege to perform their own executions. Lynch justice—whether by stoning, beating, or hanging—became almost as much a target as crime itself, since such spontaneous mob actions deeply undermined the authority that governmental officials sought for themselves.

Of course it is one thing to loudly proclaim new laws and state prerogatives and a different matter entirely to enforce them, particularly in a highly decentralized empire. At this point a new generation of reforming lawyers emerged, providing the second key element in the transformation of German criminal law and practice. These academically trained jurists convinced their more business-oriented magisterial colleagues that the increasing number and complexity of new laws and procedures rendered the old legal apparatus inadequate and instead required an ever-growing cadre of professional functionaries at all levels.

In a similar vein, the patrician magistrates of both Augsburg and Nuremberg became the first to conclude that in order to prosecute criminals more effectively, their cities needed to employ a full-time expert trained in the methods of judicial interrogation (including torture) and execution. Elevating the hangman to the position of a permanent civic employee helped legitimize his work, in theory associating him more with scribes and municipal inspectors than with mercenary soldiers and their "evil turbulent lust for spilling human blood."[37] Offering the city executioner a long-term contract also gave local authorities a greater sense of security and control over these presumably loyal implementers of their expanded legal ambitions. By the beginning of the sixteenth century, the trend throughout the empire toward permanent executioners appeared irreversible.

The full transformation of the part-time hangman into the full-time professional executioner, however, like the evolution of German criminal justice itself, required several generations and was still not complete by the time of Frantz Schmidt's birth in 1554. In some areas, officials continued to pay the hangman on a per-execution basis as late as the eighteenth century.[38] Many smaller jurisdictions simply could not justify the expense of a full-time executioner, while others selectively followed the medieval tradition of requiring a young male member of the community to carry out the odious task of judicial killing—a scenario intimately familiar to the Schmidt family. A few more isolated localities continued the still more ancient custom of bestowing the right of administering final justice to a male member of the victim's family. Even among the majority of German lands that employed a salaried executioner by the sixteenth century, prosecution and punishment of crime remained one part of a job description that also included a number of other distasteful tasks, ranging from oversight of the city's brothel to garbage disposal to burning the bodies of suicides.[39]

The mid-sixteenth century nonetheless inaugurated a new era of opportunities for the professional executioner. Even more fortuitously, Frantz's two future employers, the prince-bishop of Bamberg and the imperial city of Nuremberg, stood at the forefront of that very reform of German criminal justice. Jurists trained in civil (Roman) law were particularly influential in Franconia, leading to two exceptionally influential pieces of criminal legislation: the 1507 *Bambergensis*, officially titled the *Bambergische Halsgerichtsordnung* (literally, "neck-court-ordinance," because of its focus on capital punishment), and its 1532 successor, the imperial *Constitutio Criminalis Carolina* (or Criminal Constitution of [Emperor] Charles V), popularly known as the *Carolina*.[40] The older publication, compiled by the Franconian nobleman Johann Freiherr von Schwarzenberg, was intended as a manual for lay judges who, like Schwarzenberg himself, had not trained as jurists, and was thus written in a direct and unornamented German, accompanied by many illustrative woodcuts. Though the book lacked official endorsement, it became immensely popular, going through several editions within the first ten years.

The full-fledged, imperially sponsored offspring of the *Bambergensis*, the *Carolina*, incorporated much of the parent text's directness but was more ambitious in its political goals. By the early sixteenth century, territorial rulers and the emperor himself had come to appreciate the value of standardized legal procedures in governing their own realms, but they faced considerable opposition from many quarters on the use of Roman law in their attempted codifications. The *Carolina* hit upon a workable compromise between innovative jurists attracted by the substance and consistency of Roman law and conservative secular authorities suspicious of "foreign laws and customs" and jealous of their own prerogatives.[41] While "we would in no way detract from the old, lawful, and just customs of electors, princes, and estates," the authors of the *Carolina* sought to establish fair and consistent standards and procedures among the empire's diverse jurisdictions, involving trained legal professionals as much as possible. Rather than just proscribing a variety of crimes, the new code meticulously defined the scope and nature of the offenses, provided standards for arrest and establishing evidence, and issued formulas for judicial proceedings themselves. Clarity and regularity in practice were the goals. With the notable exceptions of magic and infanticide (newly promoted to capital crimes), the *Carolina* did not alter customary definitions of serious criminal offenses. Virtually all medieval forms of execution—including live burial, live burning, drowning, and quartering—likewise remained untouched in substance.

Most important for young Frantz Schmidt, the *Carolina* endorsed the *Bambergensis*'s detailed guidelines for the performance of each judicial functionary, including the individual formerly known as the hangman, now consistently referred to as the executioner (*Nachrichter*, literally, "after-judge") or the "sharp (i.e., sword) judge" (*Scharfrichter*).[42] The document strongly recommended regular salaries for "reputable individuals," to be supplemented by a sliding scale of compensation for different types of executions (with drawing and quartering earning the most). The *Carolina* also formally guaranteed a professional executioner immunity from all popular or legal retribution for his work and required that courts publicly reaffirm this status at each judgment. Cruel, corrupt, or otherwise unprofessional executioners were to be dismissed immediately and punished appropriately. Finally, to prevent the capricious or otherwise unjustified use of physical coercion, the new imperial ordinances set out copious instructions on what evidence might be

considered sufficient to initiate torture (e.g., the testimony of two impartial witnesses), which crimes qualified for such "special interrogation" (most notably witchcraft and highway robbery), and how such
duress was to be applied (listing the standard implements of torture
on an ascending scale of severity, beginning with thumbscrews for
women).[43]

The *Carolina*'s higher professional standards for executioners typically translated into better pay, but the law code's broader social impact
enhanced Frantz Schmidt's position beyond anything its framers could
have imagined. Within one generation of the *Carolina*'s proclamation,
criminal arrests, interrogations, and punishments all spiked dramatically throughout the empire. The execution rate likewise skyrocketed,
in some places by more than 100 percent over the previous half
century—and many times that if witch panics are included in the
statistics—creating a huge demand for trained executioners. In fact,
Nuremberg's average execution rate of nine per year during Meister
Frantz's lifetime (in a city of forty thousand) was the highest per capita
of any city in the empire. But many larger jurisdictions saw similar levels of activity. Heinrich Schmidt himself averaged nearly ten executions
a year during his service in the more populous prince-bishopric of
Bamberg, and the yearly total for the still larger nearby margravate of
Brandenburg-Ansbach totaled nearly twice that during the same
period.[44]

What accounts for this apparent surge in crime and punishment?
Rising unemployment and inflation—which led to more theft and
violence—naturally played a role in the perceived crime wave of Frantz
Schmidt's day. But the most powerful reason for the increase in prosecutions was, paradoxically, the *Carolina* itself. The new imperial law
code achieved much that was good. But like many well-intentioned
reforms, the *Carolina* also yielded unintended consequences that exacerbated the situation in several unprecedented ways. First, the new
codes inadvertently opened local authorities up to greater popular
manipulation, most infamously in the case of the witch craze, when
mobs or even a single individual could demand the prosecution of a
suspected witch, who if convicted now faced the death penalty. Second, the *Carolina*'s attempt to eliminate arbitrariness and "unneces-
sary" cruelty in criminal prosecution produced exactly the opposite

effect in the use of torture, the so-called last resort of the interrogator. Some jurisdictions, Nuremberg for example, adhered more closely to the *Carolina*'s prerequisites for administering torture. But elsewhere local authorities paradoxically perceived the imperial code's multiple guidelines and restrictions on the appropriate use of "special interrogation" to be a learned endorsement of physical coercion during questioning.

At the same time, another section of the *Carolina*, which was intended to prevent recidivism, unintentionally forced the execution of many repeat offenders—often for mere property crimes such as theft that, in an earlier time, would not have sent them to the gallows. How did this happen? To discourage criminals from returning to crime, the *Carolina* prescribed an ascending scale of punishment: public flogging for a first offense, banishment for a second offense, and in the event that an exiled offender returned and was convicted of a third offense, execution. This frustratingly narrow set of punishment options forced the hand of local governments with tragic consequences. Crimes against property, for instance, had previously resulted in less than a third of the executions in German lands, but during Frantz Schmidt's lifetime they accounted for nearly seven in ten executions.[45]

This seemingly inexplicable harshness was less the product of new cruelty than of deep frustration over the ineffectiveness of existing punishments. Most of the thieves that Meister Frantz hanged during his career had lengthy criminal records, comprising numerous imprisonments, various corporal punishments, and banishments. Occasionally flogging, both painful and humiliating, followed by banishment from the territory—the typical punishment for first- and second-time offenders—produced the desired effect. After the adult Meister Frantz publicly whipped two teenage brothers, who *stole here and there at the markets*, they disappeared from Nuremberg's criminal records.[46] More often, however, the publicly humiliated and exiled offenders—now permanently cut off from whatever kin and social network they had enjoyed—simply returned to the only life they knew and resumed stealing in another location, often nearby, or even in the city itself.

The obvious ineffectiveness of local banishment for nonviolent crimes led some European states to adopt a more permanent kind of exile for thieves and other undesirables, known as transportation. But sending deviants across the ocean was not a ready option among landlocked German states such as Nuremberg and the prince-bishopric of Bamberg, which possessed neither fleets nor foreign colonies. The duke of Bavaria did persuade the city of Nuremberg to experiment briefly with leasing its convicted thieves out to Genoese galleys. But after five years its frugal leaders concluded that the venture was too unreliable. Forced enlistment in the emperor's Hungarian army was another frequently suggested solution but apparently also remained small-scale and short-lived.[47]

The modern-day solution to this problem—internal exile, or extended incarceration—entailed a much greater conceptual leap and was thus even slower to gain acceptance. Most governmental authorities considered long-term imprisonment—except in the case of the dangerously insane—too costly and too cruel. The popular precursor to modern prisons, the workhouse, would gain many adherents during the seventeenth century, largely because it was touted to be financially self-supporting. But Frantz Schmidt's Nuremberg superiors accurately determined early on that such an institution would in fact be a money pit, and thus resisted the new fad for another century.[48] Instead they embraced the allegedly more efficient punishment of chain gangs for begging and thieving youths and young men, a practice until then limited principally to France. Known as *Springbuben* or *Schellbuben* ("knaves" wearing foot irons and belled hats respectively), these prisoners typically faced several weeks of street cleaning and repairs, including the collection and disposal of human and animal waste and other garbage. Like banishment, the chain gang deterred some but not all young thieves from continuing in their criminal ways, as Meister Frantz would later note when many of them ended up before him on the gallows.[49] Perceiving themselves as out of options for dealing with recidivist thieves and other "unreformable" nonviolent offenders, governmental authorities during the second half of the sixteenth century thus turned increasingly to the "last resort" of hanging.

The subsequent rise in demand and salaries for trained executioners was obviously good news for a budding young professional of Frantz Schmidt's background and aspirations. The *Carolina*'s elevation of his craft to the indispensable servant of justice further strengthened his hand. Protestant Frantz was probably most grateful for a blessing from the father of the Reformation himself. "If there were no criminals, there

Condemned Nuremberg prisoners on their way to serve galley sentences of two to ten years. This form of banishment was much more common in Mediterranean lands (1616).

would also be no executioners," Martin Luther preached, adding, "The hand that wields the sword and strangles is thus no longer man's hand but God's hand, and not the man but God hangs, breaks on the wheel, beheads, strangles, and makes war." Lest the implications for the reviled hangman be lost, Luther concluded,

> Thus is Meister Hans [the stereotypical executioner] a very useful and even merciful man, since he puts a stop to the villain so that he can do no more and warns others so that they do not do [the same]. The one has his head chopped off by him; the others behind him he admonishes that they should fear the sword and keep the peace. That is a great mercy.

While John Calvin remained content to acknowledge the executioner as "God's instrument," the ever-ebullient Luther went so far as to provide a celebrity endorsement for the profession: "If you see that there is a lack of hangmen, constables, judges, lords, or princes, and you find that you are qualified, you should offer your services and seek the position so that the essential governmental authority may not be despised or become enfeebled."[50]

The clerical elevation of the Schmidts' profession, while a welcome development for executioners, was slow to spread outside of learned circles. Luther's pleading tones still resonated in one famed jurist's 1565 defense that "although the name of executioner is still hated by many [and] it is perceived as an inhuman, bloody, and tyrannical office, he does not sin before God or the world if he acts on orders, not of his own will but out of justice, as God's servant." Like the judge, jurors, and witnesses in the trial, the executioner was himself blameless unless he acted "out of greed, jealousy, hate, vengeance, or lust"; otherwise, he was as indispensable to law and order as the princes themselves. Another legal scholar compared the disgust directed at the executioner's task to the shame associated with excretion—both distasteful but necessary parts of God's plan. The source of continuing popular opprobrium, all agreed, lay less in the office itself than in the job's tendency to attract "godless and rash people, [among them] sorcerers, robbers, murderers, thieves, adulterers, whoremongers, blasphemers, gamblers, and others burdened with coarse sins, scandals and troubles," when what effective courts needed were "pious, debt-free, kind, merciful, fearless men, well-experienced in such work and executions, who carry out their office more for the love of GOD and the Law than out of preexisting hate and scorn for poor sinners."[51]

Frantz Schmidt thus entered the profession of executioner at a time of significantly greater remuneration and social acceptance than his predecessors, but also of higher personal standards and expectations. A generation or two earlier, secular authorities necessarily tolerated the unsavory background of many recruits to the office and still saw some executioners who eventually ended up on the wrong side of the scaffold or pyre. By Frantz's day, professionals' reputations as "very orderly and law-abiding" had become a prominent part of their public profile, with any kind of criminal transgression resulting in swift dismissal and punishment. In return, the previously ironic designation of every practitioner as Meister took on a new dignity, with a few executioners even permitted to practice other arts or even granted their own coat of arms.[52]

Centuries of accumulated superstition, disgust, and fear were not easily erased, of course, and the relatively greater opportunities Frantz enjoyed must be weighed against the still heavy social cost. Whatever magistrates and ministers said, most of Frantz's contemporaries still considered executioners to be suspicious, if not sinister figures. In a society obsessed with the ritualistic display of rank and honor, pious and honest hangmen were a welcome development, but the perception that these people would pollute others by their mere touch persisted.

Many doors would remain closed to the son of Heinrich Schmidt throughout his life. But the growing demand for a new kind of executioner provided young Frantz with an opening, one that he would gladly exploit to achieve the dream that eluded his father and die an honorable man.

The art of the executioner

We know nothing directly of Frantz Schmidt's childhood and youth in Hof. A surprising number of his experiences would have been similar to those of any middle-class boy in sixteenth-century Germany, despite his father's infamous occupation. His first six or seven years were spent mostly in the company of adult women as well as other children. Frantz's mother died sometime before his sixth birthday, possibly during or shortly after his birth—an all-too-common occurrence at the time—at which point an aunt or grandmother most likely stepped into the maternal role. In 1560 he acquired a stepmother, also a common experience for the day, when his widower father married Anna Blechschmidt, likely from an executioner family herself, in nearby Bayreuth.[53] Despite the bad press of the Brothers Grimm, many early modern stepmothers enjoyed positive, even loving relationships with their stepchildren. We can only hope that this was the case for young Frantz.

If the family's social isolation in Hof was as severe as Frantz later suggested, his childhood must have been a solitary one. Toddlers and young children of the day were fairly unsupervised—at least by modern Western standards—and were free to explore open wells, cooking fires, and a multitude of other dangerous places that routinely claimed many young lives. Perhaps this liberty provided Frantz with some playmates, undaunted by the prejudices of their parents. We know that he had at least one older sister, Kunigunda, who reached adulthood; it's possible, even likely, that he had other siblings who were victims of the dreadful 50 percent mortality rate for all children under the age of twelve.

About the time that Heinrich Schmidt remarried, Frantz probably acquired more household chores and began to learn the basics of reading, writing, and arithmetic. In some locations, executioners' children were permitted to attend a local Latin school or German grammar school, always on a fee basis. Frantz's Nuremberg kinsman Lienhardt Lippert later complained bitterly that other parents refused to let their children sit next to his own son in school, but city officials refused to intervene, suggesting instead that the boy be taught at home.[54] Hof maintained both a parochial (German) school and a Latin school (founded by a student of Philipp Melanchthon), but the matriculation records have not survived, so we can't be sure whether Frantz learned to read and write at school, from a private tutor, or from one of his parents. His adult writing, as well as his elegant signature, suggest rudimentary training in German and perhaps some Latin. But he writes completely without punctuation and employs idiosyncratic syntax and spelling, displaying no apparent awareness of literary or even plain notarial style. Like many "semieducated" artisans of the day, Frantz Schmidt wrote as he spoke, without artifice. He was a practical chronicler who valued fact and expediency, sometimes even at the expense of clarity.

Frantz likely received his religious training at home, although a local pastor—if one would consent to enter the Schmidt household—may have instructed the boy in the rigors of the catechism. It was the Evangelical, or Lutheran, faith that informed the boy's earliest religious sensibilities. The city of Hof had broken with the Catholic Church and allied itself with the new Lutheran faith during the early, strife-ridden days of the Reformation in the 1520s. By the time of Frantz's birth a

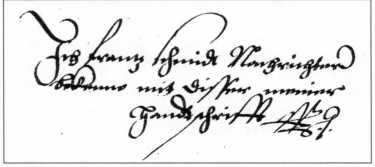

Frantz's signature on his 1584 employment contract. The form is exceptionally neat for the era but clearly distinctive from the notarial hand that drew up the document itself, thus likely a genuine autograph.

generation later, Hof had become a bastion of Lutheranism, with virtually every citizen adhering to its Protestant creed. The adult Meister Frantz held strong religious convictions, and it's likely that he learned to take his faith seriously from his parents or other members of the immediate household who did so as well. Many children of the era studied religion at home. In fact, church leaders preached that every *Hausvater* (literally, "house father") had a divine responsibility to ensure that children received proper instruction. As in most households, young Frantz and his sister, Kunigunda, would thus study the Lutheran perspective on the central doctrines of Christianity at an early age, learning of both original sin and divine forgiveness, of the centrality of faith in the human experience, and of the imperative to persevere in godly living.

Frantz's apprenticeship in the executioner craft probably began around the age of twelve. Whatever Heinrich Schmidt's presence in his son's life had been until this point, he now became the boy's most important personal and professional role model. Honorable trades—such as tailoring or carpentry—typically required a formal apprenticeship contract of two to four years with an acknowledged master, who received a sizable annual fee from the young man's family. Some executioners' sons did leave to work for a kinsman or other master executioner on such terms. But such masters were relatively few, so most sons stayed at home and learned the craft "from youth on" under their own fathers' tutelage.[55] An executioner's son like Frantz was of course forbidden to train in another, respectable craft, nor could he pursue a university education or even seek to enter the ministry—all deeply entrenched prohibitions that were still widely in force two centuries later. Such realities could not prevent him, of course, from imagining a different life for himself or for his children.

What did the teenage Frantz learn from his father? Above all, he formed his fundamental notion of what it meant to be a man. Early modern masculinity was particularly focused on the notion of honor, both personal and collective. As Heinrich impressed upon Frantz from an early age, the hated margrave had robbed them of everything they held precious: an honorable profession, the right to citizenship, the company of friends, and their very name. The details that the seventy-year-old Meister Frantz would include in his own much later recounting—the full names of his late grandfather and uncle (in an era when most people never knew their own grandparents), the fatal en-counter with the deer hunter and his dog, the exact words of the mar-grave to his father, the number of the would-be assassins, and so on—all bear the hallmark of a much-told family tale. Most early modern men were preoccupied with attacks on their honor; the Schmidts were—understandably—morbidly obsessed with the subject, not least because of the daily reminders of their ignominy. Frantz's own understanding of personal honor evolved over his lifetime, but, like his father, he held fast to a burning anger over the fundamental injustice of his family's pre-dicament. One wonders, in fact—was it mere coincidence that Hein-rich and Frantz went on to serve the cities of Bamberg and Nuremberg, once the bitterest enemies of the hated Albrecht Alcibiades?

The only other knowledge we can be sure that Heinrich Schmidt imparted to his son concerned the practical side of masculinity—a craft. "The art of the executioner" in fact comprised several discrete skills. The sine qua non was technical competence: how to effectively administer torture and a range of corporal punishments, ranging from eye-gouging and finger-chopping to flogging with birch rods to several forms of execution. First, however, Frantz performed the menial tasks delegated to any apprentice: cleaning and maintaining his father's sword and torture equipment, gathering and preparing supplies for public ex-ecutions (shackles, rope, wood), fetching food and drink for his father and his assistants, and perhaps even helping to dispose of the bodies (and heads) of decapitated felons.

As he grew older and stronger, Frantz advanced to helping restrain prisoners during interrogation or execution, and he began to accompany his father on trips to various execution sites throughout the Franconian countryside. By observing and listening to the experienced Meister Heinrich, Frantz learned where to place the double ladder at a hanging and how to manage both rope and chains with a resistant victim. He helped construct the temporary wooden platforms used for drowning in rivers and observed how to expedite this inevitably difficult and often prolonged ordeal. Most crucially, Heinrich Schmidt taught his son how to apply the various instruments of torture at his disposal during "pain-ful interrogation," and how to judge a subject's capabilities of endur-ance, so as to avoid a premature death.

One area of expertise for the typical executioner often comes as a shock to modern observers: the frequent sideline as a popular healer. Some professionals exploited the magical aura of their craft to attract clients, but it was their familiarity with human anatomy—and particularly with various wounds—that ensured the reputations of the hangman healer. Thus Meister Heinrich also passed on to Frantz his own knowledge (likely learned from other executioners) of which healing herbs and salves to apply to the wounds of a torture victim and how to mend the broken bones of a prisoner in preparation for a public execution. Having mastered such skills, the adult Frantz Schmidt earned a significant supplementary income as a healer and medical consultant throughout his life—and finally went on to establish for himself an alternate professional identity after his retirement.

Finally, a successful executioner, especially in this era of heightened expectations, also needed what we would call people skills and a certain degree of psychological insight. Abilities of this nature were of course more difficult to teach, but Heinrich Schmidt at least provided an example of how to deal with both status-conscious patrician superiors and less-than-reliable lower-class subordinates, as well as agitated poor sinners in the torture chamber and at the gallows. For Heinrich's Bamberg employers, the key attributes of a successful executioner were obedience, honesty, and discretion—all explicit in his oath of office:

> I shall and will protect my gracious Lord of Bamberg and His Grace's diocese from all harm, conduct myself piously, serve faithfully in my office, judicially interrogate and punish as I am commanded each time by His Grace's secular authority; also not take more than the appropriate fee, all in accordance with this ordinance; also whatever I hear during criminal interrogation or am otherwise commanded to keep secret, the same I will not further disclose to anyone; nor will I travel anywhere without the explicit permission of my gracious Lords Chamberlain, Marshall, or House Steward and I will be obedient and compliant in all affairs and commands of the same, faithful and without trouble in all things. So help me God and the saints![56]

Frantz witnessed firsthand the transactional character of each capital case that came before his father, the difficult balancing of diverse interests and objectives, as well as the business dimension of criminal justice in practice. Whether Heinrich provided a positive or negative model in each of these areas we cannot know, but the teenage Frantz quickly realized that technical proficiency would in fact be less crucial to his professional success than would his ability to instill confidence in his employers, fear in subjects under interrogation, and respect among his neighbors. The performative aspect of his job, in other words, was not limited to those dramatic (and still important) minutes on the scaffold. The position of executioner would be an all-encompassing lifelong role, demanding unrelenting self-awareness and vigilance.

People skills also came into play in an executioner's relationships with his fellow professionals. Like all specialists, Meister Heinrich and his counterparts in other cities employed an insider lingo, often based on the street cant of the day, known as *Rotwelsch* or *Gaunersprache*. Among fellow practitioners, hanging was known as "lacing up" and beheading as "slicing." An especially skilled colleague might be admired for "making a fine knot," "playing well with the wheel," or "carving nicely."[57] Executioners also had their own word for a botched beheading (*putzen*), as well as their own nicknames for their craft, such as Punch, Killer, Crusher, Slicer, Freeman, and Cruncher. Though hardly flattering, these self-designations were at least less condescending (and colorful) than the dozens of more popular appellations, such as "shortener," "bogeyman," "blood-judge," "bad man," "thief hanger," Hans, "heads-off," "chopper," "little hammer," Master Hammerling (also a nickname for the devil), "racker," Snip Johnny, "tie maker," "holy angel," Master Ouch, Master Fix, and, most simply, "butcher."[58]

As in other guilds and brotherhoods, early modern executioners called one another "cousin" and enjoyed common social gatherings, coming together informally at weddings and festivals or in larger numbers at occasional organized assemblies. The most famous German executioner conference, known as the Kohlenberg Court, began in fourteenth-century Basel and recurred irregularly there until the beginning of the seventeenth century. The gathering played out as a typical late medieval "court of equals," combining dispute resolution with comical rituals and copious eating, drinking, and swapping of tales. In this instance the membership comprised not only executioners but also many of the other dishonorable "traveling folk" who had no guild or justice of their own. By the sixteenth century, the assembly was dominated by executioners and sack carriers, but other marginalized men and women continued to participate. According to a 1559 account, the court convened in the square outside the executioner's residence on the Kohlenberg, "beneath a large lime tree [the German tree of justice] and another tall tree here that is called the Vinegar Tree." The presiding judge, elected by the assembly, sat "with his bare feet in a tub of water, summer or winter," and heard cases of defamation and other disputes among his fellow executioners. Upon polling the seven jurors, the judge then pronounced his decision and emptied the tub, and the festivities for the day began. One disgruntled husband, summoned to appear before the court by his wife's executioner paramour, contemptuously described the gathering as "full of foreign ceremonies" and disregarded by all locals except those up to mischief (including, apparently, his own wife).[59]

Frantz Schmidt's journal does not mention attending the Kohlenberg Court—or any other social occasion, for that matter. Perhaps Heinrich compelled him to come along once to Basel or another assembly. It's more likely that father and son considered such boisterous and indiscriminate mixing with prostitutes and beggars as unseemly, an unwelcome reminder of their craft's lingering shameful associations. The carnivalesque and irregular character of the court also belonged to an earlier time, before the introduction of more sophisticated legal machinery and professionalization of the executioner craft. Frantz already knew many of his fellow professionals via his father and certainly corresponded with some of them. Celebrating their corporate identity and trade secrets, however, was something that his generation of executioners mostly preferred to do in private, and certainly away from the skinners, tanners, and other disreputable individuals from whom they had worked so hard to distinguish themselves.

The culmination of Frantz Schmidt's apprenticeship returns us to his training with the judgment sword. Unlike axes, which on the Continent were commonly associated with mercenaries and woodsmen, swords in premodern Europe embodied honor and justice. Emperors, princes, and other rulers spoke of their own God-given legal authority in terms of the sword, and the weapon itself played a prominent part in coronation and other formal ceremonies. The right to carry a sword long remained a jealously guarded privilege of nobles alone, an immediately visible display of their high status. Beheading by the sword, consequently, had since Roman times been the privilege of citizens and aristocrats and the universally preferred form of execution, as much for its connotation of honor as for its swiftness.

The executioner's sword itself had become an object of particular symbolic and monetary value. It was large—on average measuring more than forty inches long and weighing about seven pounds—and often impressively ornamented. By the mid-sixteenth century, the typical battlefield sword used by medieval executioners had been mostly replaced by a specially designed weapon, with a flat rather than pointed tip and a more carefully balanced distribution of weight, adapted to the exclusive purpose of beheading. Many such swords have survived to the present and bear witness to the extraordinary craftsmanship and deliberation that went into their creation. Typically, each sword carried a unique inscription, such as "Through justice will the land prosper and thrive; in lawlessness it will not survive," or "Guard thyself from evil deeds, else thy path to the gallows leads," or, more succinctly, "The lords prosecute, I execute."[60] Several swords also bore engraved images of the scales of justice, Christ, or the Madonna and Child, or of the gallows, wheel, or a disembodied head. Some executioner dynasties inscribed the names and dates of each owner, and one family even notched on their sword the number of people it had executed.

Meister Heinrich's judgment sword was thus more than a sign of his technical prowess; it represented his ostracized family's last tenuous link with honor. For his apprentice son, it also stood as a symbol of the new, professional, even respectable executioner, a stark contrast to the mercenary butcher who still lived on in many people's imaginations. As an adult, Frantz wielded a sword designed to his own specifications, proudly borne throughout the entire execution ritual in its own wood and leather sheath and removed only at the ultimate moment of the public drama. In his journal, he would carefully note the exact dates of his *first execution with the sword, first execution with the sword in Nuremberg,* and *first execution with the sword [and the victim] standing.*[61]

In the spring of 1573, two hurdles remained on Frantz Schmidt's path to master executioner status. Like all craftsmen, he needed to spend several years as a journeyman, traveling the countryside, working on a fee basis, and gaining valuable experience along the way. But before he could begin his professional wanderings, he had to pass a master test. By the eighteenth century, Prussia actually required aspiring executioners to pass an extensive written and practical examination, judging whether the applicant could apply torture without breaking bones, burn a corpse completely to ashes, and show proficiency with all the interrogation and execution equipment.[62] The procedure in sixteenth-century Bamberg was much less thorough or formalized, but it remained essential for an apprentice to attain the ritualistic approval of his craft's masters if he hoped to secure a good position in the future.

Frantz's own day of reckoning came on June 5, 1573, when he was nineteen. Five years later, when he began his journal, it was the only exact date he could recall from this period, underscoring its momentous place in his life. With his father at his side, he made the two-day journey to the village of Steinach, forty miles northwest of Bamberg. The condemned was one Lienhardt Russ of Zeyern, whose full description in Frantz's journal is *a thief.* It's possible that some of Heinrich's colleagues or associates came to witness the execution, an otherwise routine hanging, given its momentous nature in the lives of father and son. The form of execution ranked as the least prestigious for a professional, but it was also the least likely to go wrong. What was young Frantz thinking as he led Russ to the gallows, bound his wrists and ankles in the prescribed manner, and moved him up the ladder toward the waiting noose? Did his voice falter as he called for the condemned to speak his final words? Did the assembled crowd of villagers remark on the youth of the executioner or question his skill? About these things we can only speculate. What we do know is this: Frantz completed his task without any apparent misstep. As the body of the condemned man swung lifeless from the gallows, Meister Heinrich or another master strode forward to where young Frantz stood. With ritual aplomb he administered three face-slaps, "according to ancient custom," and then loudly proclaimed to all assembled at the execution that the young man had "executed adroitly, without any mistakes," and should henceforth be acknowledged as a master. Frantz would later receive a notarized certificate (*Meisterbrief*) to show to prospective employers, proclaiming that the new master had performed his task "with all bravery to absolute satisfaction"[63] and was eligible to be hired—and paid—as a master.

As in other crafts, a successful master executioner test often gave way to a festive gathering of family members and friends, all eager to enjoy the hospitality of the proud father. If such a celebration was planned for Frantz, it would most likely have taken place later, in Bamberg.

Half a century after this day, a melancholic bitterness still permeates the recollections of the elderly former executioner as he describes the *great misfortune [that] forced the office of executioner on my innocent father as well as on myself, since as much as I would have liked, I couldn't escape it.*[64] But his account also evinces an unmistakable sense of accomplishment in having spent a lifetime restoring *peace, calm, and unity* to the land. At the age of nineteen, still fresh from *my first execution,* the future Meister Frantz had just begun to experience this complex mix of revulsion and pride regarding his ordained profession. It was a duality of feeling that would propel him up the career ladder in the years following that milestone day, but it would also pit the young executioner against himself and render elusive the genuine personal and professional satisfaction he sought.

2

THE JOURNEYMAN

Mixing with the world has a marvelously clarifying effect on a man's judgment.   —Michel de Montaigne, "On the Education of Children" (1580)[1]

> I must be cruel, only to be kind.
> Thus bad begins and worse remains behind.
> —William Shakespeare, *Hamlet*, act 3, scene 4, 177–78 (1600)

Formally initiated into the brotherhood of executioners, the nineteen-year-old Frantz Schmidt could now begin building the professional résumé that might one day secure him a permanent position. Shortly after his professional debut in Steinach in June 1573, the young journeyman was called to the town of Kronach, halfway between Bamberg and Hof, to administer his first *execution with the wheel*. His recording of the occasion is terse, as was his habit during these journeyman years. We learn only that the robber in question, one Barthel Dochendte, was guilty of at least three murders with his unnamed companions, and that his painful final ordeal was preceded by the uneventful hanging of a thief—a double execution and thus another first for the novice executioner. The young Schmidt does not in any way commemorate these novel professional experiences, at least not in writing.

Assisted by his father, Frantz secured an impressive total of seven commissions during his first twelve months on the job. Most of these involved the execution of thieves *with the rope*, all described by Frantz in succinct and emotionless terms. Hanging was a relatively simple, albeit grisly operation: the young executioner mounted a double ladder with the poor sinner, then simply pushed his victim off. Some jurisdictions used stepstools or chairs, but the platform with the trapdoor did not make its appearance anywhere in Europe before the late eighteenth century. Thus there was no sharp drop to break the neck, but rather prolonged choking, which might be accelerated by the executioner or his assistant pulling on the legs of the convulsing victim, typically wearing special gloves made of dog leather. Once the desperate struggle for survival came to an end, Frantz removed the ladder and left the executed corpse hanging on the gallows until it decayed and dropped into the pit of bones below the gallows.

Three of Frantz's assignments during his first year involved *execution with the wheel*, an extended procedure requiring a much greater degree of physical and emotional stamina on his part. It was also the most explicitly violent, even gruesome act the young executioner would be required to carry out as a professional. Typically reserved for notorious bandits and other murderers, this method of final dispatch essentially consisted of public torture, akin to the more infamous—and also much rarer—drawing and quartering. But whereas the much more common interrogatory torture of the prison chamber ostensibly sought information leading to conviction or vindication, the very public breaking with the wheel aspired to no more than providing a ritualized outlet for the community's rage and a terrifying warning to any spectators with murderous inclinations.

All three men Frantz executed with the wheel during his first year were multiple murderers, but only Klaus Renckhart from Veilsdorf, the young executioner's seventh victim, merited more than a line or two in his journal. Sometime during the second half of 1574, Meister Heinrich arranged for his son to travel to the village of Greiz, about forty miles northeast of their native Hof. Upon the completion of his four-day journey from Bamberg, Frantz came face-to-face with Renckhart himself, convicted of three murders and numerous robberies. Their initial contact was likely brief, but during the last hour of the condemned man's life, the journeyman executioner and his victim would be constant companions.

Immediately following the local court's pronouncement of the death sentence, Frantz shepherded the shackled Renckhart to a waiting horse-drawn cart. During their slow procession to the execution site, Frantz administered the court-prescribed number of "nips" with red-hot tongs, ripping flesh from the condemned man's arm or the torso. Frantz rarely comments in his journal on this aspect of the ordeal, but it could not have been more than four nips, which was commonly considered fatal. Upon their arrival at the execution scaffold, Frantz then forced the weakened and bloody Renckhart to strip down to undergarments, then lie down while the executioner staked his victim to the ground, meticulously inserting slats of wood under each of the joints to facilitate the breaking of bones. The number of blows with a heavy wagon wheel or specially crafted iron bar was also preordained by the court, as

Frantz Schmidt's 1585 execution of the patricide Frantz Seuboldt, from a popular broadsheet. The upper left portrays Seuboldt's "inhuman" ambush and murder of his own father while the latter was setting bird traps. In the forefront, Meister Frantz administers the nips with glowing tongs during the procession to the execution grounds. Upon their arrival at the Raven Stone, Seuboldt is staked out and executed with the wheel, his corpse then hoisted atop the wheel and displayed next to the gallows (in background, with heads on stakes nearby).

was the direction of the procedure. If the judge and jurors had wished to be merciful, Frantz proceeded "from the top down," delivering an initial "blow of mercy" (coup de grâce) to Renckhart's neck or heart before proceeding to shatter the limbs of his corpse. If the judges had deemed the crime especially heinous, the procedure went "from the bottom up," prolonging the agony as long as possible, with Frantz hefting the wagon wheel to deliver thirty or more blows before the condemned murderer expired. Again, Frantz does not remark whether a mercy blow preceded this particular ordeal but it seems unlikely, given the alleged atrocities involved. Finally, the young executioner untied Renckhart's mangled body and placed it atop a wheel on a pole, which he then hoisted to an upright position so that it might serve as a feast for carrion birds and as a graphic admonition to all new arrivals of the authorities' deadly seriousness about law enforcement.

How did Frantz feel about his role in these macabre blood rituals? His journal entries provide little insight, except perhaps in their very brevity. Was his performance during these journeyman years as tentative as his subsequent recording of it? After all, witnessing such gruesome spectacles was quite another thing from perpetrating them with his own hands. Just as important as attaining the appropriate level of technical expertise, he had to develop the psychological fortitude to look into the eyes of condemned criminals like Renckhart before terminating their earthly existence. Did the young journeyman's ambition override his innate distaste for his unsavory work, or did he find other ways to make the job more palatable? Above all, how would he keep the near daily violence he administered from consuming him?

The short paragraph that Frantz writes about Renckhart in his journal provides a partial answer. Rather than describe the execution ritual itself, as he often does later in life, the journeyman executioner focuses on Renckhart's crimes, giving most attention to a recent atrocity that clearly chilled the journeyman executioner to the bone. After briefly mentioning the robber's other murders, Frantz recounts how one night Renckhart and a companion attacked an isolated rural home known as the Fox Mill. Upon their break-in, Renckhart *shot the miller dead [and] forced the miller's wife and maid to his will and raped them. He then made them fry an egg in fat and lay it on the dead miller's body [and] forced the miller's wife to join him in eating. Also kicked the miller's body and said, "Miller, how do you like this morsel?"* The robber's shocking violations of all human decency in Frantz's eyes provided all the justification he required in his subsequent administering of *death by the wheel*. This stratagem of recalling and recording the heinous offenses that had made necessary the very punishments he carried out was a useful discovery that provided continual reassurance to Frantz throughout his long career.

On the road

From the age of nineteen to twenty-four, Frantz continued to use his parents' home in Bamberg as a base while he traveled the Franconian countryside from one temporary assignment to another. In this respect, his life differed little from the lives of most journeymen his age, all of whom sought to build a reputation and secure a permanent position as a master. Meister Heinrich's name and professional contacts served him well during this period, providing him entrée into several villages in need of an ad hoc executioner for interrogation or punishment. None of these small communities offered Frantz any hope of a permanent position, but collectively they allowed him to earn his keep while gaining invaluable experience.

His journal entries during these years record twenty-nine executions in thirteen towns, most frequently Hollfeld and Forchheim, each less than a two-day journey from his new home (see map on page ix). He also performed three executions in his father's stead in Bamberg, one in 1574, the other two in 1577.[2] In later years, Frantz would sometimes write long, reflective journal entries in which he speculated on such questions as the motives of the people he executed. But in these early years, only the Renckhart execution runs to more than a terse one or two lines. Instead, professional advancement dominated the young journeyman's thoughts and writings, and so he concentrates on documenting the number of executions he performed and the variety of killing methods in his repertoire. Even the briefest hint of introspection would have to wait until he was established and secure.

Like many ambitious young men, Frantz evidently knew—perhaps thanks in part to his father's counsel—that technical proficiency alone would not earn him a coveted permanent position. In the increasingly lucrative, and thus competitive, world of professional executioners, a man also had to cultivate a social network and build a respectable name. Heinrich Schmidt could help his son get in the door, but ultimate success depended on Frantz's own ability to impress influential legal authorities with both his professional skills and his personal integrity. To that end, building a reputation for honesty, reliability, discretion, and even piety went hand in glove with gaining experience at the gallows. In later years, Frantz would improve his reputation by drawing nearer and nearer to respectable society. At the onset of his career, though, his more urgent need was to push away—to the extent possible—his association with disreputable society. This precocious act of self-fashioning made his journeyman years more difficult and lonely—but it also allowed him to establish many of the habits and character traits for which the later Meister Frantz was known and revered.

In his journeys as a "wander bird," Frantz encountered individuals from virtually every social rank. We tend to think of premodern Europe as fairly static, but there was in fact considerable geographical mobility. The young executioner was able to identify most travelers immediately by their attire and means of transportation. Fur-bedecked nobles and patricians in silk traveling cloaks were—as they intended—the most conspicuous, journeying by horse or carriage, usually accompanied by at least a few armed retainers. Merchants, bankers, physicians, and lawyers also typically traveled by horse and dressed in crisp woolen mantles. Frantz himself might have had use of his father's riding horse, but more likely he journeyed as did most other honest folk of modest means, by foot. Along the dirt paths and muddy roads of the Franconian countryside, he would frequently be overtaken and passed by galloping couriers and even plodding transport carts filled with manufactured goods, wine, or foodstuffs. Pilgrims traveling to a religious shrine wrapped themselves in penitential white or sackcloth and moved at a slower gait, while families traveling to a wedding feast or farmers on the way to market hastened along amid boisterous chatter. A young journeyman wearing a modest hat and traveling cloak, perhaps with a walking staff in hand, was one of the most common sights of all.

Rural travel, as Frantz well knew, posed many dangers. Whatever personal encounters he had with highwaymen or other ruffians while under way are lost to history. We do however know of a more insidious threat the young executioner regularly faced and likewise struggled to evade—association with the dishonorable "traveling folk" who also filled the roads.[3] The least marginalized of these were the numerous migrant agricultural workers and traveling tradespeople: peddlers, hawkers, tinkers, pewterers, knife grinders, and ragmen. Executioners themselves, like butchers and tanners, were still widely considered part of this group, as were entertainers of all sorts—acrobats, pipers, puppeteers, actors, and bear baiters. If he mingled in public with any of these individuals during his travels, Frantz risked bringing down on his head the very social stigma he sought to escape.

His deep personal familiarity with the criminal underworld, the so-called thieves' society, put Frantz in an even more uncomfortable spot. Many of his father's assistants came from unsavory backgrounds, as did of course most of his victims. Like all executioners, Heinrich and Frantz Schmidt were both fluent in *Rotwelsch*, the colorful street slang of vagrants and criminals that combined elements of Yiddish, Gypsy, and assorted German dialects. A denizen of the underworld, for instance, who had "bought the monkey" (was drunk) might be wary of running into a "lover" (police official), especially if he had recently been "fencing" (begging), "bargaining" (swindling), or "burning" (blackmailing).[4] Frantz also knew the signs and symbols that such vagabonds carved or chalked for one another on hospitable houses and inns.[5] The extensive personal contact that young Schmidt had with hardened professionals, albeit not in a social context, meant that in most ways he was more a part of their "wised-up" (*kocheme*) society than the general public's "witless" (*wittische*) world. His familiarity with the denizens of both worlds admittedly gave him an advantage in recognizing and steering clear of shady characters, but his years of assisting his father had also taught him that the line between honest and dishonest was neither fixed nor always obvious.

In that respect, the greatest challenge for a young man of the day seeking to establish an upright name came from other young men. Everywhere that Frantz went, he encountered the dominant culture of unmarried males—whether honest journeymen like himself or those engaged in shadowy enterprises—a social world based primarily on drink, women, and sport. Alcohol in particular constituted a key component of male friendship in early modern Germany and held special significance in the rites of passage among young men. Accompanied by raunchy songs and poems, the prolific quaffing of beer or wine could establish the ephemeral bonds of drinking buddies or be part of formal initiation into a local youth group, a military cohort, an occupational association, or even some form of blood brotherhood. Taverns with now quaint names such as the Blue Key or the Golden Hatchet were usually the first stop for all male travelers upon arrival in a village or town, and buying a round of drinks was a particularly effective way for a newcomer to command respect and make new friends, at least at a superficial level.

Like today, young male friendships of the era thrived on competition of all sorts. Card playing and gambling were givens. Wrestling or archery matches provided both a test of physical skill and yet another opportunity for betting. German men indulged to a legendary degree in prolonged drinking bouts and "duels" of wine and beer that occasionally resulted in serious internal injuries or, in rare cases, death. The drunken camaraderie of the taverns often led to much bragging—and exaggeration—about sexual prowess. And of course the dangerous combination of alcohol and testosterone inevitably sparked violence, not just brawls and knife fights among the young men themselves but also attacks on others, especially sexual assaults against women.[6]

Participation in this rambunctious world was not an option for an ambitious young executioner. His efforts to avoid such company, as well as association with any dishonorable individuals, needed to be relentless and total. The subsequent self-isolation must have been emotionally difficult for Frantz, especially since he had not yet gained the acceptance of honorable society either. Respectable innkeepers remained wary about housing a man of his background, regardless of his commission from the prince-bishop or how finely attired or well-mannered he appeared. On the road, Schmidt could attempt to conceal his profession, even lie about it, or seek lodging elsewhere, in the house or barn of a hospitable stranger. Upon his arrival in the village of execution, though, it became impossible to hide his identity from anyone, so he was effectively shut out of all social gatherings. The only young males willing to share Frantz's table (and his bar tab) were the very individuals he was trying to avoid—beggars, mercenaries, and probable criminals. His options for female companionship were just as limited: honorable artisans' daughters wanted nothing to do with him, and consorting with prostitutes or other loose women would undermine the very reputation he was seeking to establish.

Thus Frantz did not make any great social sacrifice when he came to what was a remarkable decision for a man of his era: never to drink wine, beer, or alcohol of any kind. It was a vow he apparently kept for the rest of his life and for which he eventually became widely known and admired. Frantz's religious beliefs may have played a role in this choice, but complete abstention from alcohol was rare in the sixteenth century, even among the most godly men and women. Our modern inclination might be to speculate that he had suffered from the embarrassing behavior or drunken violence of someone close to him—perhaps

Early modern taverns provided young men like Frantz with the opportunity to drink as well as gamble, fight, and pursue sexual exploits. Some moralists considered the taverns "schools of crime," where thefts and other schemes were often planned, while innkeepers acted as fences and prostitutes known as "thief-whores" picked the pockets of unsuspecting and inebriated customers (c. 1530).

even his own father. But whatever his religious or emotional reasons, Schmidt's vow not to drink was also a carefully calculated career decision. Early modern Europeans considered it a given that the executioner would drink to excess—a stereotype with a great deal of truth behind it. Compelled to kill and torture their fellow human beings again and again, many in Frantz's profession sought preexecution courage in a tankard or two of beer or oblivion after the fact in a large quantity of wine. By publicly refuting the legendary fondness of his fellow executioners for the bottle, Frantz found an extraordinary means of underscoring the sobriety, both literal and figurative, of the way he had chosen to live. This jujitsu maneuver cleverly took the disadvantage of his de facto social isolation and turned it into a virtue that distinguished him in the eyes of future employers, and perhaps even society at large. The quiet journeyman who sat without companions—or drink—in a far corner of the tavern may have been lonely, but he knew exactly what he was doing.[7]

Violence in the pursuit of truth

To obtain a permanent position, Frantz needed, of course, to prove his proficiency in two particular aspects of law enforcement: interrogation and punishment. Both involved a much greater degree of physical violence than most modern legal authorities would consider permissible (at least on the record). It's reassuring to believe that this contrast is grounded in our own time's greater sensitivity to human suffering and higher respect for human dignity—but the daily headlines regularly mock any smug sense of superiority on this score. The same unstable alchemy of compassion and retribution that fuels modern debates on criminal justice animated the response to crime in Frantz Schmidt's time. Why then was early modern criminal justice itself so much more visibly brutal? And why was a compliant instrument of that state violence like Frantz Schmidt so much in demand?

Again, legal authorities of the day, particularly in "progressive" states such as Nuremberg, struggled in vain to span the chasm between their ambition to practice a new, more effective system of criminal prosecution and their continuing reliance on traditional and largely insufficient means to that end. Despite the imperial codifications of the *Bambergensis* and *Carolina*, most local authorities' procedures, personnel, and overall mentality remained grounded in the private accusatorial model of centuries past. In some instances, newly energized criminal courts became tragically susceptible to popular prejudices and personal rivalries, as in the case of the notorious witch panics of the era. More often, secular authorities simply struggled to conceal their profound inability to prevent crime in the first place or to apprehend criminals after the fact. Frantz's journal is filled with accounts of notorious outlaws who easily evaded authorities, sometimes living *out in the open in a foreign jurisdiction*, until they were at last brought to court by a victim, a victim's family member, or a private posse (*posse comitatus*).[8]

A cool and reliable executioner typically played the pivotal role in making the most of the few opportunities when a suspected culprit actually landed in official custody. He was the one who began the process by obtaining information from recalcitrant suspects, and he was the one who brought it to a close by orchestrating the ritualized public spectacle of punishment. If at least two impartial witnesses aged twelve or older provided testimony, a suspect usually confessed, and Frantz's skills in the torture chamber were not required. Material proof—such as stolen items or a bloody murder weapon—could also make the prosecution's task much easier. Unfortunately, the courts frequently found neither witness nor physical evidence, and the investigation stalled because of the paltry capabilities of pre-nineteenth-century forensic science. Absent any other compelling evidence, conviction of the average suspect thus depended almost exclusively on the accused person's self-incrimination. At that point, a professional executioner would be summoned. In Bamberg Frantz played the part of the assistant to his father; in those locations he visited on his own, he was in charge.

Like professional interrogators today, Frantz Schmidt and his superiors knew the effectiveness of intimidation and other forms of emotional pressure. One nonviolent but nonetheless psychologically intense method of obtaining a murder confession was the so-called bier test. This ancient Germanic custom, familiar to readers of the *Niebelungenlied* and other medieval sagas, remained a powerful tool in the professional interrogator's arsenal. Assembling a room full of witnesses, the executioner and his assistant would force the accused—or even a group

The ancient bier test as practiced by a late medieval court. By the sixteenth century, this last remnant of trial by divine ordeal had lost all official backing, but many people continued to believe that a murder victim's corpse would bleed or move at the touch of its killer's hand (1513).

of suspects—to approach the victim's corpse on its stretcher and touch it. If the body bled or gave any other sign of guilt (such as apparent movement), the killer would supposedly be compelled to confess.[9]

No jurist considered such an event sufficient or even necessarily credible evidence, but the trauma did often succeed in exposing a guilty conscience. Frantz only writes of one application of the bier test during his career, and it happened long after his journeyman days. The accused Dorothea Hoffmennin vehemently denied strangling her own newborn daughter, but *when the dead child was brought before her, laying its hand on her skin—which she did with a terrified heart—it received a red bruise on the same spot.* Since the young maid kept calm and refused to confess, she was merely *whipped out of town with rods.* The very fear of undergoing such an ordeal nevertheless provided a vulnerability that the experienced executioner might exploit. Years later, Frantz wrote how another suspected murderer incriminated herself by loudly forbidding her accomplice to reenter the house of the patrician spinster they had just killed in her sleep, fearing that the corpse would "sweat blood" if he approached.[10]

If initial interviews were unsatisfactory and the consulting jurists found sufficient "indices" to begin torture, Frantz's superiors ordered him to "strictly bind and threaten" the suspect, the first of five increasingly severe grades of torture.[11] The journeyman Schmidt left no record of his interrogation method during these years, but it was likely similar to the well-defined routine he later used in Nuremberg. First he and his assistant would escort the accused from his or her cell to a sealed room with the instruments of torture prominently displayed. In Nuremberg this took place in the "Hole," or dungeon, in a specially designed torture chamber, which was nicknamed "the chapel" because of its arched ceiling (and perhaps to provide a hint of macabre irony). The small, windowless room of approximately six by fifteen feet stood directly beneath a meeting room in the town hall. In the room above sat two patrician jurors, shielded from the gruesome spectacle below, who consulted their case notes and questioned the suspect through a specially designed air duct linked to the chamber.

Even at this point, the executioner relied more on emotional vulnerability and psychological pressure than on sheer physical coercion. In the "chapel," Meister Frantz and his assistant would tightly bind the subject—occasionally on the rack, but usually in a chair bolted to the floor—and then painstakingly describe the function of the torture implements on display. One veteran jurist advised inexperienced executioners such as the young Frantz not to be gentle or humble at this point, "but to employ rumor and speculation . . . saying amazing things [*Wunder-Dinge*]: that he was a great man who had done great deeds . . . learned and practiced in his arts, that no person was capable of concealing the truth from his ruses or movements . . . as he had already happily proven to all the world with the most obstinate villains."[12] Perhaps Frantz even learned from his father a version of "good executioner, bad executioner," with the two men alternately threatening and consoling a terrified suspect. Most subjects yielded some kind of confession under such conditions, seeking to avoid both the pain and subsequent social stigma of torture.[13]

For those few other individuals who still resisted, typically hardened robbers, the executioner and his assistant would then begin to apply whatever method of physical coercion their superiors had approved. In Bamberg and Nuremberg the approved options included thumbscrews (usually reserved for female subjects), "Spanish boots" (leg screws), "fire" (candles or torches applied to the subjects' armpits), "water" (today known as waterboarding), "the ladder" (aka the rack; the subject was strapped to a ladder and either stretched or rolled back and forth on a spiked drum), and "the wreath" (aka "the crown": a metal and leather band was placed on the forehead and slowly tightened). The most commonly applied torture in Bamberg and Nuremberg was "the stone," more commonly known as the strappado, in which the subject's hands were bound behind the back and slowly drawn upwards on a pulley, with stones of varying weight pulling down on the feet. Human ingenuity and sadism inevitably produced countless other stylized forms of inflicting pain—the Pomeranian Cap, the Polish Ram, the English Shirt—as well as crude but effective means of degradation, such as forcing victims to eat worms or feces, or sliding pieces of wood under their fingernails.[14] Frantz Schmidt undoubtedly knew of most, if not all, of these methods. But did he or his father— perhaps out of frustration with a particularly recalcitrant suspect—ever resort to such nonsanctioned techniques? Predictably, both his journal and the official records are mute on this point.

The interrogation technique known as the strappado, showing a suspect before one of the stones is attached to his feet (1513).

On rare occasions, Frantz's instructions prescribed the length of time that duress might be employed, for instance, no more than fifteen minutes for recently delivered mothers. Generally, responsibility for judging the subject's "torturability" (*Foltertauglichkeit*) rested entirely with the executioner. Surgeons and physicians did not attend torture sessions until the practice itself was on the verge of being abolished, two centuries later.[15] In theory, Frantz's nonacademic training in human anatomy enabled him to apply sufficient pain without causing serious injury or death. Once he was himself a master, he would be able to call off, postpone, or mitigate torture, though his judgments might occasionally be subject to being overruled. One thieving mercenary who "was already seriously wounded not only on the head but also on both hands and legs" was judged by an older Frantz unlikely to survive a session with the strappado. When the same culprit's testimony under thumbscrews failed to satisfy the executioner's superiors, however, Schmidt was ordered to apply more strenuous means, ultimately two torture sessions with fire and four with the wreath. The accused robber's even more resistant brother-in-law was forced to endure the ladder six times, including frequent torture with wax candles under his left armpit. Not surprisingly, both ultimately confessed and were *executed with the sword out of mercy.*[16]

The executioner also bore primary responsibility for keeping all suspects in relatively good health, both before and after interrogation. Frantz knew well the harsh effects of imprisonment, especially on women, and bemoans in his journal when any suspect was forced to endure "the squalor of incarceration" for many weeks in a tiny cell intended for brief holding before interrogation and sentencing.[17] He personally tended to the broken bones and open wounds of prisoners and brought in nurses for recently delivered child murderers and other ailing women. This paternal concern for the well-being of imprisoned suspects strikes modern sensibilities as contradictory and even cruel, particularly when the individual was purposely given time to heal so that he or she could be effectively tortured or executed. The irony of the situation was not lost on Frantz and his colleagues. One prison chaplain recounted how a barber-surgeon brought in to assist the executioner "remarked to me during the [condemned's] treatment that it troubled him he spent so long healing what Meister Frantz would again ruin."[18]

Delivering a convicted offender in satisfactory condition for public punishment was never a simple matter, even after Frantz had gained years of experience. A farmer arrested and tortured in 1586 on suspicion of having murdered his stepchild had no sooner confessed to the crime when "God immediately provided a visible sign [of his guilt]" and the suspect fell dead, presumably of a heart attack.[19] Torture could also lead to psychological damage, which posed an equal or greater threat of jeopardizing a smooth and effective public execution. After one "hard, stubborn thief" was tortured three times with fire in a single session—and continued to swear to God his innocence—he began to behave "very strangely and unruly" in his cell, alternately weeping uncontrollably and lashing out violently, as well as trying to bite the prison keeper. Until then he had "prayed diligently," but now he refused to do so or to speak to any person, instead squatting in a corner of the cell and chanting to himself "Dum diddy lump, dear devil come!"[20]

Young male thieves and robbers, entering the torture chamber with an ample supply of street smarts and bravado, predictably displayed the greatest obstinacy and resilience. Since neither the journal nor the interrogation protocols ever mention comments by the executioner, it's unclear whether Frantz grew more frustrated during especially long torture sessions with stubborn suspects or with his unrelenting patrician superiors. The truculent sixteen-year-old Hensa Kreuzmayer, accused of arson and attempted murder, was tortured repeatedly over the course of a single day—with the strappado, the wreath, and fire—but in the end, the most he would acknowledge was "uttering a sacramental curse out of anger" at various unfriendly villagers.[21] Jörg Mayr, an astonishingly prolific thief of the same age, fought off several similar charges over the course of six weeks before he finally succumbed to despair and literally threw himself on the mercy of the interrogating jurors.[22] Older and more seasoned veterans generally recognized the futility of resistance and broke sooner. After one extended but unsuccessful torture session with a veteran highwayman, Frantz's magisterial superior calmly reassured the suspect that "we will again do with [you] what we want and even have [you] torn to pieces if [you] are not able to confess to having committed a murder," whereupon the suspect recognized the hopelessness of his situation and confessed in full.[23]

How did Frantz himself feel about his role as a professional torturer? As the person with the least seniority, the young journeyman was charged with the most brutal parts of the entire ordeal—pulling the rope of the strappado, turning the screws, burning a screaming subject. Most master executioners supervised the procedure but left the actual dirty work to their more dishonorable assistants. Whether Frantz readily passed on these tasks when he himself became a master is unknown—mainly because in nearly half a century of writing, he seldom explicitly acknowledged his own role in the administration of torture. There is no list of torture sessions alongside his tally of executions and corporal punishments, even though private interrogation was a more frequent and longer-lasting activity for him than both of those public performances combined.[24] If not for the surviving interrogation transcripts, his participation in these monthly, sometimes weekly, procedures would be completely hidden from view.

Was Frantz ashamed of his unsavory work in the torture chamber or merely reticent about drawing attention to it? The task was in itself no more dishonorable than the public floggings, hangings, or wheel executions that he continued to administer personally until retirement many decades later. Nor, apparently, did he consider such measured violence unjustified. The few times that he writes about torture, Frantz sounds confident that virtually all individuals who made it to this stage, especially the already notorious robbers and thieves, had some degree of culpability. The sole occasion when Frantz expressed regret about the practice came when the mass murderer Bastian Grübel falsely denounced a companion *out of enmity and [caused] the man [to be] brought into this town and examined by torture in his presence. [He] did him wrong in this for the murders were not true but lies, thinking that by doing the farmer this injustice the murders would not be discovered and that he would himself be released.*[25] The executioner's indignant tone conveys his usual sympathy for all victims as well as an implicit reassurance to himself that unjustified torture remained an anomaly. Otherwise the subject of torture was much more likely to come up in the older Frantz Schmidt's descriptions of the atrocities committed by marauding robbers during their savage home invasions—an interesting evasion on the executioner's part.[26]

Did Frantz really believe the legal axiom of the day that "pain releases truth?" It's hard to say. He nearly always tried to prompt a confession by using psychological pressure and other nonviolent methods before he resorted to inflicting physical pain. This suggests that he saw torture as a sometimes necessary evil but hardly considered it an indispensable part of the truth-finding process. His repeated expressions of empathy for a suspect's suffering also make it clear that Frantz Schmidt was no sadist.

Frantz's assessment of the reliability of physical coercion is harder to gauge. He remarks once in passing that an accused child murderer *revealed the truth* under torture but this remains an isolated example.[27] Throughout the journal he displays an apparent credulity about details produced under torture that would have been virtually impossible for a suspect to remember, but even these, he might have countered, did not affect the ultimate question of guilt.

Did Frantz ever worry that a confession obtained under torture might lead to the execution of an innocent person? It's impossible to know for sure. Always sensitive to his place in the social hierarchy and the importance of career advancement, an eager young journeyman could console himself that the responsibility for ordering torture lay with his superiors, whom he was bound by oath (and self-interest) to obey and to please. A more experienced and financially secure executioner might find an even greater number of rationalizations to quiet a nagging conscience: if the accused was not guilty of this crime, he was probably guilty of others; speaking up for a possibly innocent suspect wasn't worth jeopardizing both job and family security; his job was to carry out orders, not decide innocence or guilt.

Above all, Frantz did not consider himself the immovable opponent of a tortured subject, fixated on procuring a damning confession at all costs. His official prerogative to halt or forgo torture gave him considerable discretionary powers in cases where he had doubts about culpability, sometimes resulting in complete dismissal of charges. On at least two occasions later in life, for instance, he successfully recommended the release of older women suspected of witchcraft, on the grounds that they could not withstand the physical strain of even the mildest torture.[28] Frantz could also comfort himself with the knowledge that only a tiny minority of the many suspects brought before the council were subjected to torture, that those who were had typically been accused of quite violent crimes, and that even among those who were tortured, only a few suffered more than one session. Finally, he knew that the majority of those tortured would ultimately escape the death penalty, and perhaps one in three would be released with no subsequent punishment whatsoever.[29] This crucial semblance of moderation and due process is particularly helpful in understanding how an otherwise empathetic, intelligent, and pious individual might make peace with his role in routinely perpetrating the abominable personal violation that is torture.

Violence in the pursuit of justice

Frantz's success in carrying out the public spectacle of judicial violence was the sine qua non of his professional reputation. Many premodern criminal punishments appear alternately barbarous or quaint to modern eyes. There seems to be a childlike literalness at work in the way the crime was matched to the punishment, what Jacob Grimm called "a poetry in the law."[30] Some of the essential components—especially collective and public retribution—remained rooted in distant Germanic times, while other ancient influences, notably the *lex talionis*, or Mosaic law ("an eye for an eye"), gained new life thanks to the evangelical reforms of the previous two generations. The religiously charged atmosphere of the day also added a particular urgency to the legal process, since it was believed that unpunished offenses might bring down divine wrath on an entire community (*Landstraffe*), in the form of flood, famine, or pestilence. Throughout Frantz Schmidt's life (and well into the eighteenth century), God the Father's keen interest in effective criminal law enforcement remained a frequent catalyst to new law-and-order campaigns and even influenced some legal decisions.

Frantz's ability to effectively administer corporal punishment was a prominent part of his job description. Here the medieval fondness for colorful and "appropriate" public humiliations comes readily to mind: quarreling housewives adorned with "house dragon" masks or "violins" (elongated wooden shackles around the neck and wrists), fornicating young women forced to carry the "stone of shame" (weighing at least thirty pounds), and of course the stocks, where a variety of exposed malefactors endured verbal abuse, spittle, and occasionally thrown objects.

Among more established members of the community, by contrast, privately negotiated financial settlements remained the norm.

More violent punishments—such as chopping off the two oath fingers (index and middle) of perjurers and tearing out the tongue for blasphemy—had been relatively common before the sixteenth century. But by Frantz's time most German authorities deemed such traditions ineffective and potentially disruptive, because they came across as alternately ludicrous or gratuitously cruel. One Nuremberg jurist considered the brutal practice of eye-gouging (for attempted murder) "a harsher punishment than beheading," and in most parts of the empire it was discontinued by 1600.[31] Similarly gruesome mutilations, such as castration and hand-chopping, were also virtually unheard-of by this time.

Despite these trends, Frantz Schmidt was not spared from administering disfiguring corporal punishments. Bamberg and Nuremberg both maintained the punishment of cutting off perjurers' and recidivists' fingers and casting them in the river, long after other jurisdictions had abandoned the ancient custom. Over the course of his long career, Frantz would stand on Nuremberg's Fleisch (Flesh) Bridge to chop off

By the late sixteenth century, the traditional punishment of eye-gouging had become rare in German lands (c. 1540).

the fingers of nine offenders, including prostitutes and procuresses, false gamblers, poachers, and false witnesses. He would also brand a large N (for Nuremberg) on the cheeks of four pimps and con men, clip the ears off four *thief-whores*, and snip the tongue-tip off one blaspheming glazier.[32]

Between the mid-sixteenth-century decline of legal mutilations and the seventeenth-century rise of workhouses and prisons—in other words, Meister Frantz's lifetime—the most common corporal punishment in German lands was banishment, often preceded by flogging with rods. Given the dearth of options for addressing lesser crimes, especially minor theft and sexual offenses, Frantz's superiors in Bamberg and later Nuremberg simply adapted this medieval custom to their needs. Banishment became lifelong (instead of one to ten years), now covered "all the towns and fields" of their respective jurisdictions (instead of just the city proper), and was increasingly underscored by a painful public whipping, or at least time in the stocks. In large German towns, flogging out of town became a regular, at times weekly, event. Between the fall of 1572 and the spring of 1578, Frantz assisted or observed his father's scourging of twelve to fifteen people a year.[33] During his subsequent solo career in Nuremberg, he would himself flog at least 367 individuals, an average of about nine annually, twice that during his peak period of 1579 to 1588. Internal references in the journal indicate that there were still other occasions that Frantz did not include in his tally and many more whippings administered by his assistant.[34] Corporal punishment of all kinds was so frequent in Nuremberg that on one occasion all six of the city's stocks were occupied and Meister Frantz had to bind a recidivist false gambler *in the Calvinist Preacher's chair on the stone bridge* (today's Maxbrücke) and chop off his two oath fingers there, before whipping him out of town once again.[35]

The ritualistic expulsion of undesirable individuals from a city's borders had all the essential components that sixteenth-century magistrates loved: strong assertion of their own authority in the beadle's loud proclamation of the sentence and the churches' ringing of the "poor sinner's bells," the executioner's humiliating stripping of the culprit to the waist (occasionally women were permitted a cloth for modesty), and the culprit's painful whipping at the stocks or during the procession to the city's gate to instill the lesson, as well as an alleged opportunity for

A Nuremberg chronicle portrays Meister Frantz simultaneously whipping four offenders out of town. Note that although the men's backs are completely exposed, they retain their hats, as does Meister Frantz, who also dons a red cape for the occasion (1616).

the offender to reform, or at the very least to avoid further offenses within their jurisdiction. As in public executions, the danger of mob violence always loomed. In one flogging of "three pretty young women" in Nuremberg, "an enormous crowd ran [after the procession], so that some were crushed under the Ladies' Gate."[36] Despite the risks, paternalistic rulers found themselves unable to resist the seemingly harmonious blend of retribution and deterrence in these ritualized expulsions—particularly given the absence of viable alternatives.

The flogging itself was typically administered by the executioner's assistant or a journeyman executioner, such as young Frantz Schmidt. In Bamberg Heinrich Schmidt chose to perform the task himself, most likely because he was still paid on a fee basis for his work. Out of deference to his father or based on his own work ethic, Frantz would continue to personally perform (and dutifully record) the floggings he administered long after he began earning an annual salary and could have delegated the unpleasant task. He also chose to employ birch rods, which were reputedly more painful than other instruments of flogging and capable of causing permanent injury, or in rare cases death.[37] Even so, the executioner himself acknowledged the frequent ineffectiveness of these rituals of pain and humiliation, commenting in his journal on the many culprits he confronts who have already been *banished with rods*. His jurist colleagues in Nuremberg similarly advised their Augsburg counterparts to use the punishment sparingly with less hardened culprits such as sturdy beggars and other vagrants, else they risked turning them into professional criminals.[38]

Of course the officially sanctioned violence for which the early modern executioner was most known, and where Frantz's proficiency needed to be the greatest, was in the public execution itself. One early-twentieth-century German historian considered the criminal justice of this period to be typified by "the cruelest and most thoughtless punishments imaginable," but in fact a great amount of thought—specifically about the appropriate level of cruelty or ritualized violence—went into every form and instance of punishment.[39] As in their modification of traditional corporal punishments, secular authorities in the late sixteenth century also sought an unprecedented and delicate balance of severity and mercy in public executions, all aimed at furthering the rule of law and their own authority in enforcing it. Proceedings that gave off the slightest whiff of mob rule or vigilantism—such as the mass executions of Jews or witches—could no longer be tolerated in "advanced" jurisdictions such as Nuremberg. Medieval traditions that opened the magistracy up to ridicule also needed to be eliminated. These included public trials for criminal corpses as well as for murderous and "abominable" animals (which continued in less enlightened areas well into the eighteenth century).[40] A technically proficient and reliable executioner was himself the very embodiment of the sword of justice in action—swift, unwavering, deadly, but never appearing susceptible to arbitrary or gratuitous cruelty.

The new standards that the ambitious Frantz Schmidt had to meet were evident in the transformation of virtually every form of execution in his repertoire. The criminal punishment of women provides an especially vivid example of new adaptations of "simultaneously mild and gruesome" Germanic customs.[41] During the Middle Ages and into Frantz Schmidt's day, most female culprits were punished either by some combination of public humiliation and physical pain or by a financial penalty. Temporary banishment was also a popular option for a variety of offenses. In those few cases where a woman was sentenced to death, by contrast, the punishment could be quite horrendous. Since hanging was considered indecent for women (it allowed spectators to see under their skirts) and beheading was typically reserved for honorable men, the most common form of female execution before the sixteenth century was live burial under the gallows. Long before Frantz Schmidt's birth, Nuremberg's leaders declared this punishment "cruel" as well as embarrassingly out of date: "such a death penalty is [still] practiced in few locations within the Holy Empire." Their decision was also influenced by the messiness of live burial, even if expedited by a stake through the heart. One condemned young woman "struggled so that she ripped off large pieces of skin on her arms, hands and feet," ultimately leading Nuremberg's executioner to pardon her and ask magistrates to abolish this form of execution, which they officially did in 1515. Surprisingly, the 1532 *Carolina* retained the punishment of live burial for infanticide—"to thereby prevent such desperate acts"—but the stipulation was rarely enforced.[42]

The form of execution most German authorities substituted for condemned women does not appear much of an improvement to modern eyes. Drowning in a hemp sack was also an ancient Germanic punishment, mentioned as early as Tacitus (A.D. 56–117). Many sixteenth-century authorities found the unseen death struggle in the water an appealing alternative to the visible thrashing about in live burial, which often generated a level of sympathy they wished to avoid. Professional executioners such as Frantz Schmidt, however, found the spectacle of forced drowning just as difficult to manage and in some instances even more prolonged. One condemned woman in 1500 survived long enough underwater to free herself from the sack and swim back to the execution platform from which she had been pushed. Her spirited explanation— "[Because] I drank four [liters] of wine ahead of time . . . the water couldn't come into me"—failed to impress the attending magistrates, who promptly ordered her buried alive. Shortly before Frantz's arrival in Nuremberg, his predecessor's assistant used a long pole to keep the struggling poor sinner from bringing her sack back to the surface, "but the staff broke and an arm came up [out of the water], with much screaming, so that she survived under the water for almost three-quarters of an hour."[43]

Frantz himself does not comment on the relative smoothness of his first drowning execution, a young maid from Lehrberg convicted of in-

Even in medieval times, live burial of women was considered a horrendous spectacle, often cut short by a stake through the heart of the struggling victim, as in this illustration of the last such execution in Nuremberg in 1522 (1616).

fanticide in 1578.[44] He is unusually forthcoming and even boastful two years later, though, when he and the prison chaplains bring about the abolishment of this form of execution in Nuremberg—a legal precedent gradually imitated throughout the empire. Schmidt's initial appeal to his superiors was shrewdly practical: the Pegnitz River was simply not deep enough in most spots and, in any event, at the moment (mid-January) "completely frozen over." Many councilors resisted any change, countering that women should naturally "sink to the bottom out of meekness" and that the young executioner just needed to do a better job of accelerating the process. When Frantz later proposed that three women convicted of infanticide be beheaded, a punishment unprecedented for women, some councilors called the plan too generous and not enough of a deterrent to this "shocking and too frequent crime"—especially given the large crowd likely to attend the imminent joint execution. Fortunately, Frantz's clerical allies furnished the additional argument that water actually gave power to "the evil spirit," inadvertently prolonging the ordeal. His jurist backers delivered the coup de grâce, acknowledging that drowning was "a hard death" and undoubtedly deserved, but countered that beheading provided a more effectively shocking deterrent, "since in drowning, one can't see how the [condemned] person behaves at the end," while beheading in the open provided a more visible and thus effective "example" to all present. *The bridges, which I had had consecrated, were already prepared for all three to be drowned,* Frantz writes in his journal, when the magistrates finally relented—with the notable condition that afterward the executioner was to *nail all three heads above the great scaffold.*[45]

This compromise solution for the execution of women provided a template for the rest of Frantz's career, effectively balancing magisterial demands for both "shocking" public examples and smooth, orderly demonstrations of their authority. Nailing heads or limbs of executed

In some jurisdictions, as here in Zurich, the poor sinner was drowned from a boat. In Nuremberg the executioner constructed a temporary scaffolding for this purpose (1586).

culprits to the gallows fulfilled the atavistic bloodlust for retribution and humiliation, while eliminating the public torture aspects of many traditional forms of execution lent the entire procedure a greater legal and even sacred aura. All but two of the poor sinners condemned to be burned at the stake later in Meister Frantz's career were burned only after beheading or were spared the fire altogether.[46] (Burning for witch-craft remained of course pandemic elsewhere in Germany, rarely with strangulation beforehand.) Only one woman was ever again drowned by Frantz—a member of an especially cruel and notorious robber band—and none was ever again buried alive or impaled in Bamberg or Nurem-berg (although both practices survived in some Swiss and Bohemian localities for at least another century).[47] Instead, the heads of female murderers were often posted on the gallows or poles nearby, as were all four limbs of one traitor, sentenced to be drawn and quartered but *executed with the sword here out of mercy.*[48]

There remained only one traditional form of public execution that regularly placed torture at center stage: breaking on the wheel. As in infanticide cases, the deep fears and subsequent outrage unleashed by the crimes of brutal robbers and mercenaries often outweighed the risks to a consistent appearance of governmental calm and moderation. Crowds roared in approval as the vicious robber Niklaus Stüller (aka the Black Banger) *was pulled along on a sled at Bamberg, his body torn thrice with red-hot tongs* by the journeyman executioner. Together with his companions, the brothers Phila and Görgla von Sunberg, he had murdered eight people, among them two pregnant women from whom they cut out live babies. According to Stüller, *when Görgla said they had committed a great sin [and] he wanted to take the infants to a priest to be baptized, [his brother] Phila said he would himself be priest and baptize them, took them by the legs and slammed them to the ground.* Stüller's subsequent *death by the wheel* at Frantz's hands seems mild in compari-son to the punishment of his companions, *later drawn and quartered in Coburg* by another executioner.

The ripping of the condemned's flesh with red-hot tongs and metic-ulous breaking on the wheel were the most explicitly violent acts Frantz was required to carry out as a professional. Although the number of nips with burning tongs and the number of blows at the wheel were both carefully prescribed in the death sentence, the executioner appears to have enjoyed some leeway, particularly in severity of the blows. At one point later in his career, Frantz's superiors in Nuremberg actually ordered him "not to go easy on the condemned persons, but rather earnestly seize them with the tongs, so that they experience pain."[49] Yet even in these instances of shocking deeds—such as Hans Dopffer, *who murdered his wife, who was very pregnant*—the presiding judge and jurors often capitulated to requests for a more merciful and honorable beheading, as long as the bodies were later broken and left to rot on a nearby wheel.[50]

As with his torture work, Frantz remained mostly silent about the details of his executions with the wheel—seven during his journeyman years and thirty over the course of his entire career. He only once mentions the number of blows administered and otherwise spends the bulk of each entry recounting the multiple grave crimes of the individual in question.[51] We know from various accounts, however, that the gruesome ordeal could be quite prolonged and that it evoked genuine terror in captured robbers. Meister Frantz himself describes one traumatized condemned man who *had a knife with him [in his cell], stabbed himself twice in the stomach and then threw himself on the knife, but it did not pierce him; also tore his shirt and tried to strangle himself with it, but could not bring it off.* Magister Hagendorn, the chaplain, writes in his journal of another murderous bandit who similarly attempted suicide to avoid his fate by "giving himself three cuts in the body with an instrument he had concealed." Each survived, was nursed back to health by Meister Frantz, and in his time received his prescribed punishment on the Raven Stone.[52]

Although less violent than the wheel, death by hanging was universally considered just as shameful, in some ways even more so. The indignity of publicly choking to death at the end of a rope or chain was bad enough; the subsequent exposure to ravens and other animals was even more shameful. Many master executioners also delegated this distasteful task to subordinates, but until his retirement four decades later, Frantz Schmidt insisted on carrying out with his own hands the most odious parts of an already disreputable profession. Beginning with his very first execution at the age of nineteen, the journal records his hanging of fourteen men from 1573 to 1578 and 172 individuals over the course of his entire career, mostly adult male thieves, but also two

The rare hanging of a nobleman, the finance minister of Augsburg, at the same time as what appears to be a youth. The executioner remains on the double ladder until the victims are dead, while the chaplains celebrate below (1579).

young women and nearly two dozen youths aged eighteen or younger. Frantz was himself taken aback when ordered to hang the two women in 1584—*it had never before happened* that a woman was hanged in Nuremberg. He appeared even more uncomfortable about the hanging of "unreformable" teenage thieves, but in each instance the diligent professional performed his duty with no reported mishaps.[53]

Meister Frantz, like most in his profession, would also have disdained hanging as not much of a technical challenge. The executioner's job at a hanging amounted to not much more than placing a noose around the condemned man's neck and pushing him off a ladder. In towns without permanent gallows, Frantz was sometimes asked to inspect a temporary structure, but the construction itself was carried out by trained craftsman. As in all executions, it was up to the executioner to keep the condemned person under control during the entire procedure, wherein the greatest difficulty was usually getting the accused to mount the ladder to the noose. Nuremberg chronicles show Meister Frantz and his assistant employing a double ladder for this purpose, sometimes aided by a pulley, a procedure that culminated in the executioner simply shoving the poor sinner off the other ladder "so that the sun shines through between the body and the earth."[54] Some executioners sought to make death especially painful or humiliating for the condemned, hanging them upside down from a chain after strangulation. Nuremberg's gallows actually maintained a special Jews' point at one corner for this purpose, but it was never used by Meister Frantz, who instead garroted one Jew in a chair in front of the gallows (*as a special favor*) and hanged another "in the Christian way."[55]

In Frantz's first three years as a journeyman, all but one of his eleven execution jobs involved the two most dishonorable forms of dispatch, hanging and the wheel. These lowly assignments were an inevitable part of paying his professional dues and building up his credentials in the region. As a result, during the three subsequent years, he was called on to execute nearly as many individuals with the sword (ten) as with the rope (eleven)—a clear indicator of his rising status. Over the course of his long career, in both Bamberg and Nuremberg, these two forms of capital punishment—hanging and beheading—would constitute over 90 percent of his 394 executions.[56]

The growing preference for decapitation was in fact part of a general trend in German lands over the course of Frantz's professional life, rooted in both the gradual decline of executions for theft (and thus hangings) and a concurrent rise in mitigation of more extreme forms of final dispatch. During the first half of Schmidt's career, hanging was nearly twice as common as beheading; by the early seventeenth century, the proportions had reversed.[57] Popular recognition of the skill and professional status of the trained executioner rose accordingly.

Frantz's skill with the sword provided the bedrock of his own professional identity, certainly not his inglorious work as a hangman, a derisive term that he scrupulously avoided. In his own writing, he is always an *executioner*, a title that emphasizes his close association to the law and courts as opposed to his unsavory work in the torture chamber or with the wheel or rope. The two hangings Frantz decides to date during his journeyman years are singled out only because they were *my first execution* (1573) and *my first execution at Nuremberg* (1577). *My first execution with the sword* (1573), on the other hand, is celebrated as a moment of personal achievement, unparalleled by specific commemoration of any other firsts during his career.[58]

The sentence the Romans called *poena capitas*—and professionals like Frantz knew more simply as "capping"—also put the spotlight more fully on the executioner than did hanging.[59] Frantz decided first of all whether the poor sinner would kneel, sit, or stand. Standing subjects, who tended to shift around, posed the greatest challenge to the sword-wielding executioner, and Frantz makes careful note of his five successes with this method, all before he reached the age of thirty.[60] Once his finesse and reputation were established enough to secure a lifelong employment contract, he reverted to the much more common practice of decapitating a subject who knelt or sat. Sitting bound in a judgment chair became more common over the course of Schmidt's career, and was especially preferred for women, who supposedly moved around more at the crucial moment. Following a final prayer from the chaplain, the executioner carefully positioned his feet—not unlike a golfer preparing for a perfectly calibrated swing—and trained his eyes on the middle of the subject's neck. He then raised his blade and struck one graceful blow, typically from behind on the right side, cutting through two cervical vertebrae and completely severing the head from the body. In the words of a common legal formula, "he should chop off his head and with one blow make two pieces of him, so that a wagon wheel might freely pass between head and torso."[61] Following a clean blow, the poor sinner's head plopped serenely at his or her own feet, while the seated torso continued to splatter the executioner and his assistant with blood from the severed neck. Frantz never mentions any especially prodigious feats with the sword—such as lopping off two heads with one swing, as one of his successors did—but he does ruefully note the few occasions when an additional stroke was required to sever the head completely, a dangerous breech in the dramatic narrative, to which we now turn.

Producing a good death

Public executions, like corporal punishments, were meant to accomplish two goals: first, to shock spectators and, second, to reaffirm divine and temporal authority. A steady and reliable executioner played the pivotal role in achieving this delicate balance through his ritualized and regulated application of violence on the state's behalf. The court condemnation, the death procession, and the execution itself constituted three acts in a carefully choreographed morality play, what historian Richard van Dülmen called "the theater of horror."[62] Each participant—especially the directing executioner—played an integral role in ensuring the production's ultimate success. The "good death" Frantz and his colleagues sought was essentially a drama of religious redemption, in which the poor sinner acknowledged and atoned for his or her crimes, voluntarily served as an admonitory example, and in return was granted a swift death and the promise of salvation. It was, in that sense, the last transaction a condemned prisoner would make in this world.

Let us take the example of Hans Vogel from Rasdorf, *who burned to death an enemy in a stable [and] was my first execution with the sword in Nuremberg* (while still a journeyman) on August 13, 1577. As in all public performances, the preparation behind the scenes was crucially important. Three days before the day of execution, Vogel was moved to a slightly larger death row cell. Had he been seriously wounded or otherwise ill, Frantz and perhaps another medical consultant would have tended to him and perhaps requested delays in the execution date until Vogel regained the stamina required for the final hour. For the most part, though, the executioner focused his attention during this period on ensuring the condition of the Raven Stone or other site, procuring all the necessary supplies, and finalizing the logistics of the trial and procession to execution.

While awaiting judgment day, Vogel might receive family members and other visitors in the prison or—if he was literate—seek consolation by reading a book or writing farewell letters. He might even reconcile with some of his victims and their relatives, as did a murderer who accepted some oranges and gingerbread from his victim's widow "as a sign that she had forgiven him from the depths of her heart."[63] The most frequent visitors to Vogel's cell during this period would be the prison chaplains. In Nuremberg the two chaplains worked in concert and sometimes in competition, attempting to "soften his heart" with appeals combining elements of fear, sorrow, and hope. If Vogel couldn't read, the clerics would have shown him an illustrated Bible and attempted to teach him the Lord's Prayer as well as the basics of the Lutheran catechism; if he was better schooled, they might engage him in discussions about grace and salvation. Above all, the chaplains—sometimes joined by the jailer or members of his family—would offer consolation to the poor sinner, singing hymns together and speaking reassuring words, while repeatedly admonishing the stubborn and hardhearted.

Obviously, a submissive prisoner made for a smoother execution, but the visiting clerics had nobler motives. Dying "in the faith" was of special concern to Frantz's Nuremberg colleague Magister Hagendorn, and in addition to preparing a prisoner to go to the execution site with calm resignation, he hoped to instill in the condemned some degree of piety and understanding. His own journal entries reveal a particular tenderness toward young women convicted of infanticide. He is initially troubled that Margaretha Lindtnerin, condemned in 1615, has learned so little of her catechism, despite over seven weeks of confinement. In the end, however, she obligingly displays all the hallmarks of a good death:

She was very perseverant in her Cross, prayed fervently, and every time that her baby or parents were mentioned, she began to weep bitter tears; had quite resigned herself to her imminent death, strolled out very calmly, enthusiastically blessed those known to her while under way (since she had served here eight whole years at different places and was fairly well-known) and fervently prayed with us. When we came with her to the execution site, she started and said, "Oh God, stand by me and help me get through it." Afterward she repeated it to me, blessed the crowd and asked their forgiveness, [then] she stood there, as if stunned and could not talk until I spoke to her twice or thrice, then she began to talk, again blessed the crowd and asked their forgiveness, [then] commended her soul to the hands of the Almighty, sat down in the chair, and properly presented her neck to the executioner. Since she persevered in the right and true faith until her end, she will also [attain] the end of her faith, which [according to] 1 Peter chapter 1 is the salvation and blessing of souls.[64]

Whatever their success in effecting an internal conversion, the clerics were at minimum expected to sufficiently calm the condemned Vogel for the final component of his preparatory period, the famed "hangman's meal." Ironically, Frantz was not directly involved in this ancient custom (possibly because of its disreputable name), and allowed the prison warden and his wife to oversee its implementation in a special cell with table, chairs, and windows, known in Nuremberg as "the poor sinner's parlor." As in those modern countries that still maintain capital punishment, Vogel could request whatever he wanted for his last meal, including copious quantities of wine. The chaplain Hagendorn attended some of these repasts and was frequently appalled by the boorish and ungodly behavior he witnessed. One surly robber spat out the warden's wine and demanded warm beer, while another large thief "thought more of the food for his belly than his soul . . . devouring in one hour a large loaf, and in addition two smaller ones, besides other food," in the end consuming so much that his body allegedly "burst asunder in the middle," as it swung from the gallows.[65] Some poor sinners, by contrast (especially distraught young killers of newborns), were unable to eat anything whatsoever.

Once Vogel was adequately satiated (and inebriated), the executioner's assistants helped him put on the white linen execution gown and summoned Frantz, who from this point on oversaw the public spectacle about to unfold. His arrival at the cell was announced by the warden with the customary words, "The executioner is at hand," whereupon Frantz knocked on the door and entered the parlor in his finest attire. After asking the prisoner for forgiveness, he then sipped the traditional Saint John's drink of peace with Vogel, and engaged in a brief conversation to determine whether he was ready to proceed to the waiting judge and jury.

A few poor sinners were at this point actually jubilant and even giddy about their imminent release from the mortal world, whether out of religious conviction, exasperation, or sheer intoxication. Sometimes Frantz decided that a small concession might be enough to ensure compliance, such as allowing one condemned woman to wear her favorite straw hat to the gallows, or a poacher to wear the wreath sent to him in prison by his sister. He might also ask an assistant to provide more alcohol, sometimes mixed with a sedative he prepared, although this tactic could backfire, leading some women to pass out and making some of the younger men still more aggressive. The highwayman Thomas Ullmann almost beat Frantz's Nuremberg successor to death at this juncture until subdued by the jailer and several guards. Once confident that Vogel was sufficiently calmed, Frantz and his assistants bound the prisoner's hands with rope (or taffeta cords for women) and proceeded to the first act of the execution drama.[66]

The "blood court," presided over by a patrician judge and jury, was a forum for sentencing, not for deciding guilt or punishment. Vogel's own confession, in this case obtained without torture, had already determined his fate. During the Middle Ages, this judicial pronouncement had been the central moment of the condemnation process, usually taking place in the town square. By the sixteenth century, the subsequent execution now enjoyed this elevated status, with the "court day" itself taking place in a special chamber in the town hall, closed to the public. As in the subsequent procession and execution, the overarching goal of this preliminary stage was to underscore the legitimacy of the proceeding, but in this instance the audience being reassured comprised the executing authorities themselves.

The brisk procedure was accordingly ritualistic, hierarchical, and formal. At the end of Nuremberg's chamber, the judge sat on a raised cushion, holding a white rod in his right hand and in his left a short sword with two gauntlets hanging from the hilt. Six patrician jurors in ornately carved chairs flanked him on either side, like him wearing the customary red and black robes of the blood court. While the executioner and his assistants held the prisoner steady, the scribe read the final confession and its tally of offenses, concluding with the formulaic condemnation "Which being against the laws of the Holy Roman Empire, my Lords have decreed and given sentence that he shall be condemned from life to death by [rope/sword/fire/water/the wheel]." Starting with the youngest juror, the judge then serially polled all twelve of his colleagues for their consent, to which each gave the standard reply, "What is legal and just pleases me."

Before confirming the sentence, the judge addressed Vogel directly for the first time, inviting a statement to the court. The submissive poor sinner was not expected to present any sort of defense, but rather to thank the jurors and judge for their just decision and absolve them of any guilt in the violent death they had just endorsed. Those relieved souls whose punishments had been commuted to beheading were often effusive in their gratitude. A few reckless rogues were so bold as to curse the assembled court. Many more terrified prisoners simply stood speechless. Turning to Frantz, the judge then gave the servant of the court his commission: "Executioner, I command you in the name of the Holy Roman Empire, that you carry [the poor sinner] to the place of execution and carry out the aforesaid punishment," whereupon he ceremoniously snapped his white staff of judgment in two and returned the prisoner to the executioner's custody.[67]

The second act of the unfolding drama, the procession to the site of execution, brought the assembled crowd of hundreds or thousands of spectators into the mix. Typically, the execution itself had been publicized by broadsheets and other official proclamations, including the hanging of a bloodred cloth from the town hall parapet. Vogel, his hands still bound in front of him, was expected to walk the mile or so to the gallows. Sometimes, if the condemned suffered from physical exhaustion or an infirmity, Frantz's assistants transported the poor sinner on an elevated chair. This was often the case with the elderly and disabled women such as the swindler Elisabeth Aurholtin, who *had only one leg*.[68] Violent male criminals and those sentenced to torture with hot tongs were bound more firmly and placed in a waiting tumbrel or sled, pulled by a workhorse used by local sanitation workers, known in Nuremberg as a Pappenheimer. Led by two mounted archers and the ornately robed judge, also usually on horseback, Frantz and his assistants worked hard to keep up a steady forward pace while several guards held back the teeming crowd. One or both chaplains walked the entire way one on either side of the condemned, reading from scripture and praying aloud. The religious aura of the entire procession was more than a veneer, and in Frantz's career only the unconverted Mosche Judt was "led to the gallows without any priests to accompany or console him."[69]

During this phase, the executioner's customary obligation to respect the last wishes of the condemned as well as to avoid alienating the

An execution procession in the inner city of Nuremberg. Here two guards on horseback lead the poor sinner on foot, with a chaplain on either side of him (c. 1630).

crowd often required considerable restraint on Frantz's part. Hans Vogel apparently offered little resistance, but the thief and gambling cheat Hans Meller (aka Cavalier Johnny) *said to the jurors as he left the court, "God guard you; for in dealing thus with me you will have to see a black devil one day,"* and as he was led out to the execution displayed all kinds of arrogance. Still, the executioner waited patiently while Meller sang not one but two popular death songs at the gallows: "When My Hour Is at Hand" and "Let What God Wills Always Happen." The thieves Utz Mayer (aka the Tricky Tanner) and Georg Sümler (aka Gabby) were similarly *fresh and insolent when being led out, howling,* but also permitted to sing "A Cherry Tree Acorn" before the nooses were put around their necks.[70]

Satisfying his superiors' expectations of a dignified and orderly ceremony put even more pressure on the "theater of horror's" director. In addition to fending off derisive shouts and thrown objects, the executioner needed to maintain the somber mood of the proceedings. Frantz was understandably frustrated and embarrassed when one incestuous old couple turned their death procession into a ludicrous race, each attempting to outrun the other: "He was in front at the Ladies' Gate, but from here on she frequently outpaced him."[71] Frantz often laments when a prisoner *behaved very wildly and gave trouble*, but his patience appears to have been especially tried by the arsonist Lienhard Deürlein, *an audacious knave* who continued to drink hard from the bottle during the entire procession. Deürlein bestowed curses—rather than the customary blessings—on those he passed, and upon his arrival at the gallows handed the wine bottle to the chaplain while he urinated in the open. *When his sentence was read to him, he said he was willing to die but asked as a favor that he should be allowed to fence and fight with four of the guards. His request*, Meister Frantz drily notes, *was refused*. According to the scandalized chaplain, Deürlein then seized the bottle again "and this drink lasted so long that at last the executioner struck off his head while the bottle was still at his lips, without his being able to say the words 'Lord, into thy hands I commend my spirit.'"[72]

Outward signs of contrition carried particular significance for Frantz, especially during this third act, at the execution site. He writes with approval when one remorseful murderer *wept all the way until he knelt down* or when a penitent thief *took leave of the world as a Christian*. In stark contrast to his clerical colleagues, he clearly valued such visible evidence of a changed heart more than mastery of the specifics of evangelical doctrine. It's easy to imagine his quiet annoyance when a subdued and contrite Paulus Kraus proclaimed at the gallows ladder that he was about to atone for his sins, only to be loudly corrected by Magister Hagendorn, who pedantically admonished Kraus that "the Lord Christ had already atoned and paid for them [and] he should instead commend his soul to God, His heavenly father."[73]

Last communion represented an especially visible form of submission and Frantz fretted when poor sinners displayed last-minute obstinacy on this score. Vogel readily embraced the sacrament, but on another occasion Hans Schrenker (aka Crawler) consistently refused to receive the Lutheran communion, *because he was a Catholic*. The executioner was relieved, by contrast, that Cunz Rhünagel (aka Rough) *at first refused to receive the sacrament and used very abusive words, but afterward consented*. Even the robber Georg Prückner, whom Schmidt summed up as *a very bad character [who] had been several times impris-*

oned in the tower but was released on promise of doing good, in the end repented [and] behaved in a very Christian manner, receiving communion on the Raven Stone and loudly proclaiming his remorse to the assembled throng.[74]

The single worst death described by Frantz Schmidt later in life was the prolonged ordeal of the notorious highwayman Hans Kolb (aka the Long Brickmaker, aka Brother Standfast):

Because he could not escape from prison [here], he bit his left arm, cutting through the veins. When he was healed of this and led out on the last day, he again bit out a piece of his right arm as large as a batzen piece [coin] and an inch deep, thinking he would thus bleed to death . . . [instead,] as a murderer, robber, highwayman, and thief, who stole much many times, executed with the wheel, the four limbs first broken, and lastly as a counterfeiter the body was burnt. He pretended he could not walk so that he had to be carried. Did not pray at all and bade the priest to be silent, saying he knew it all beforehand and did not want to hear it, and that it made his head ache. God knows how he died.[75]

Virtually all Frantz's acknowledgments of difficult deaths came much later in his career, when he was professionally secure. Even then, he was not always completely forthcoming, especially with those fiascos that might reflect poorly on his own mastery of the situation. Of the prolific thief Georg Mertz (aka the Mallet), for instance, the executioner writes only that the condemned man *behaved strangely as he was led out: shook his head and only laughed, would not pray, only said to the pastors, "My faith has helped me."* The prison chaplain and court notary, by contrast, expanded considerably on the disastrous spectacle. According to Magister Hagendorn, the twenty-two-year-old Mertz insisted on being carried out and executed in his black cap and woolen shirt, promising to go peacefully if he was permitted this last wish.

But as soon as he left the prison he began to yell and play the fool: "Mine is the day, be comforted dear people," he cried out, with much else, and three times I had to return and help to drive him along. When we reached the town hall, he repeated the same words with loud cries, so that I had to restrain him and admonish him to be more moderate. Before the court he exhibited himself, grinning crazily, turning first to the right, then to the left, baring his teeth, and twisting his mouth so that I had twice to correct and admonish him . . . When he was sentenced he bowed himself, as if to show reverence to the council, and almost fell in a heap. When we came down with him from the town hall we could scarcely control him. He leapt in the air, raged, and fumed, as if he were raving mad . . . Then he gave orders that they should bring the chair, and when he had seated himself, and was bound, he began to stamp with his feet like a horse, raising and dropping his head, exulting and crying out: "I am comforted: my faith has saved me." He called the people angels, and many times requested that his hat might be removed so that he could see the angels.

During the procession, according to the court notary, Mertz not only forced Frantz's assistants to carry him but also

on the way he kicked the jailers so cruelly with his feet that they cried out, and frequently let him fall. At the same time he made funny faces, bared his teeth to the people, and thrust his tongue far out of his mouth . . . When he reached the accustomed execution place, and the executioner or hangman told him to climb the ladder, he replied, "Why are you in such a hurry with me? All times are good for hanging—morning or afternoon, late or early. It helps to pass a dull hour." And when he was on the ladder and Magister Hagendorn spoke to him, asking him to whom he was going to commend his poor soul, he gave a mighty leap and burst into laughter, crying, "Priest, what is all this talk? Who else but to my drinking companions, the rope, and the chains?"

Frantz hastened to end this embarrassing display, but the two chaplains continued to exhort the condemned Mertz to repent, only prompting his final words, "I would like to work my jaws much more, but I cannot do so. You can see that I have swallowed a lot of hemp and am likely to be suffocated with it so that I cannot go on talking."[76] Having thoroughly shattered the intended dignity and redemptive message of his own demise, Mertz allegedly died with a smirk on his face.

The greatest terror for any executioner—particularly a young journeyman—was that his own errors might effectively ruin the carefully managed drama of sin and redemption and endanger his own job or worse. The large crowd of spectators—always including many loud drunks among its number—put immense performance pressure on the sword-wielding executioner. Long farewell speeches or songs with multiple verses helped build suspense for the crowd, but also tried the patience and nerves of the waiting professional. One chronicler detected Meister Frantz's eagerness for resolution in the beheading of the murderer Margaretha Böckin, still standing after enduring *her body nipped thrice with red-hot tongs*, but so weak that she could barely talk. "He indicated that he would speak to the people for her [but] had barely said three words when he properly chopped off [her head] and executed her."[77] Elisabeth Mechtlin started out well on the path to a good death, weeping incessantly and informing Magister Hagendorn "that she was glad to leave this vile and wicked world, and would go to her death not otherwise than as to a dance [but] . . . the nearer she approached to death, the more sorrowful and faint-hearted she became." By the time of her execution procession, Mechtlin was screaming and yelling uncontrollably all the way to the gallows. Her continued flailing while in the judgment chair even apparently unnerved a by then very experienced Frantz Schmidt, untypically leading him to require three strokes to dispatch the hysterical woman.[78]

Fortunately, Hans Vogel's execution passed without any incident worthy of note. Bungled beheadings, though, appeared often in early modern chronicles, in Nuremberg several times before and after Frantz Schmidt's tenure. During his own forty-five-year career and 187 recorded *executions with the sword*, Meister Frantz required a second stroke only four times (an impressive success rate of 98 percent), yet he dutifully acknowledges each mistake in his journal with the simple annotation *botched*.[79] He also refused to fall back on the usual excuses proffered for a bungled beheading: that the devil put three heads in front of him (in which case he was advised to aim for the middle one) or that a poor sinner bewitched him in some other way. Some professionals carried with them a splinter from the judge's broken staff of justice to protect them against just such magical influences, or covered the victim's head with a black cloth to forestall the evil eye. Frantz's well-known temperance had fortunately immunized him from the more mundane explanation favored by contemporaries, namely the execu-

A botched beheading in the Swiss canton of Chur leads to the crowd's stoning of the bungling executioner. Spectators always reacted violently to miscarried executions, but executioner fatalities remained rare (1575).

tioner "finding heart" for the big moment in the bottle or an alleged "magical drink."[80] Most crucially, his slips did not occur during these journeyman years or even his early career in Nuremberg, but rather long after he had become a locally established and respected figure, his reputation and personal safety both secure.

Another young Nuremberg executioner not long after Meister Frantz's retirement was less fortunate. In 1641 the newcomer Valentin Deuser was to behead child murderer Margaretha Voglin, "an extremely beautiful person of nineteen years." According to one chronicle,

> this poor child was very ill and weak, so that she had to be carried and brought to the gallows, or Raven Stone, and when she sat down on the chair, Meister Valentin circled around her, like a calf around a manger, and with the sword struck a span of wood and a piece of skin as big as a thaler [coin] from her head, knocking her under the chair, and since he hadn't hurt her body and she fell so bravely, [the crowd] asked that she be released.

The inexperienced Deuser refused to pardon her, though, and from underneath the chair she then cried out:

> "Oh, help me for God's sake," which she said often and repeated. Then [the executioner's assistant] grabbed her and set her back on the chair, whereupon the executioner delivered a second blow and [this time] hacked in the neck behind her head, at which she however fell from the chair, still alive, again shouting, "Aiee, God have mercy!" After this the hangman hacked and cut at her head on the ground, for which cruel butchery and shameful execution [he] was surrounded by people who would have stoned him to death had not the archers present come to his aid and protected him from the people, and then stopped his bleeding, which already flowed freely from his head and down both front and back.

This disgraceful performance and the riot it triggered resulted in the young executioner's arrest and subsequent dismissal, despite his claim to have been "blinded or bewitched" by the condemned.[81]

Mishaps leading to mob violence and lynch justice jeopardized the core message of religious redemption and state authority. In some German towns an executioner was permitted three strikes (really) before being grabbed by the crowd and forced to die in place of the poor sinner. Frantz recognized the constant *danger to my life* in every execution, but whether by skill or luck, he himself only faced one such total breakdown in public order—a flogging that turned into a riot and fatal stoning—and that came long after his journeyman years.[82] Every beheading, by contrast, ended like his dispatch of the arsonist Vogel, with Frantz turning to the judge or his representative and asking the question that would complete the legal ritual: "Lord Judge, have I executed well?" "You have executed as judgment and law have required" came the formulaic response, to which the executioner replied, "For that I thank God and my master who has taught me such art."[83] Still at center stage (literally), Frantz then directed the anticlimactic mopping up of blood and appropriate disposal of the dead man's body and head—always fully aware of the hundreds of eyes still upon him. As Heinrich Schmidt had taught his son, the public performance of the executioner never ended.

The opportunity of a lifetime

The breakthrough moment in Frantz's early career came on January 15, 1577, when he was nearly twenty-three years old. Though some luck was involved, his father's skillful maneuvering played the larger part. Heinrich Schmidt had early on identified the job of Nuremberg's executioner as a plum position, perhaps the most prestigious in the empire and thus the most promising for restoration of their family's honor. In 1563, after filling in briefly for the frequently absent Conrad Vischer, Heinrich himself applied for the post, only to be brusquely turned away by Nuremberg's councilors.[84] Six months later, when the post again became vacant, Schmidt was again rejected, this time in favor of Vischer, who had returned. Perhaps Heinrich applied once more, upon Vischer's death in June 1565, or a year later when his successor, Gilg Schmidt, passed away. In any event, it was Lienhardt Lippert of Ansbach who eventually secured the coveted position in 1566 and would hold on to it for many years thereafter.

Undeterred, father and son managed to turn this disappointment to their advantage. Within a year of his appointment as Nuremberg's new executioner, Lienhardt Lippert asked the council for permission to marry his housekeeper, who happened to be Frantz's sister, Kunigunda. Exactly when and how this strategic placement occurred is not recorded, but such a fortuitous development was surely not unanticipated by the Schmidts. At first the council sternly refused Lippert's petition, "since he already has a wife" (presumably still in Ansbach), but exhausted by the relentless turnover of the preceding decade, the executioner's superiors allowed him to continue employing "this frivolous wench," as long as there was no public scandal. At some point within the next year and a half, Lippert and Kunigunda Schmidin were privately wed, and in October 1568 the bride gave birth to the first of seven children. Since both divorce and bigamy were unlikely to have been tolerated by Lippert's employers, we must assume a timely end for his estranged spouse during the interim.[85]

Frantz now enjoyed the great benefit of having a relative placed in the very job his father coveted (now on the son's behalf). The eager young journeyman was even luckier in the contrast that he presented to his incorrigible brother-in-law. Determined to avoid more instability in the position, Nuremberg's councilors long tolerated both Lippert's personal and professional shortcomings. Even his third disastrous beheading in a row on December 3, 1569—this one requiring three strokes—was met with only a mild reprimand, as well as reassurance that the council would always protect Lippert from any mob retribution. In November 1575, however, the executioner suffered a serious fall. Four months later, he claimed that he was too ill to mount the gallows ladder and suggested that his brother-in-law, young Frantz Schmidt, be allowed to act in his place. Instead, the council commuted the punishment to decapitation and ordered Lippert to earn his salary and carry out his duty. Subsequent complaints that he was too weak to torture were similarly batted away, with his assistant ordered to fill in for him indefinitely.[86]

Whether or not Lippert's infirmity was genuine, his sudden (and unapproved) two-week trip to "his father-in-law in Bamberg" in January 1577 required the council to hire "his kinsman, the foreign executioner," for the hanging of the thief Hans Weber.[87] Was this opportunity also engineered by Heinrich Schmidt? In any event, the result was, Frantz later wrote in his journal, *my first execution here*. Over the following sixteen months, the "new, young executioner" dispatched seven more poor sinners on behalf of the city of Nuremberg, all without incident— "very well," according to the court notary—but still on an ad hoc fee basis.[88] Finally presented with an attractive alternative to the trouble-some Lippert, the city's magistrates grew less tenuous in their admon-ishments of the older executioner, warning him that "if he didn't amend his laziness and disorderly life, he would be replaced with another master." Thus, on April 25, 1578, when Lippert informed his superiors that he was too ill to go on, they immediately accepted his resignation, spurned his requests for a pension or housing assistance, and uncere-moniously washed their hands of the twelve-year veteran—who died less than a month later. That same day, they appointed a new master executioner, Frantz Schmidt of Hof.[89]

Two weeks after his appointment, Frantz obtained permission from his new superiors to travel to Bamberg "for four or five days."[90] His cel-ebratory homecoming was a powerful moment for father and son. Frantz had secured the very job that had long eluded his father and taken a momentous step forward in their shared dream of restoring the family's stolen honor. What mixture of pride, envy, and relief did Heinrich expe-rience at learning the news? It was at this point, possibly at his father's urging, that Frantz decided to keep a journal. After enumerating his previous executions for his father (and claiming that he *can't remember* the corporal punishments), the young executioner came to the present moment. As usual, Frantz affected an emotionless style, but his joy in this victory shines through the bold letters of his proud pronounce-ment: **Here follow the persons [punished] after I was officially appointed and taken on here in Nuremberg on St. Walburga's Day [May 1] in 1578.**

3

THE MASTER

The conduct of our lives is the true reflection of our thoughts.
—Michel de Montaigne, "On the Education of Children" (1580)[1]

Do, but also seem. Things do not pass for what they are, but for what they seem. To excel and to know how to show it is to excel twice.
—Baltasar Gracián, *The Art of Worldly Wisdom* (1647)[2]

O n October 11, 1593, the notorious forger and con artist Gabriel Wolff met his end at the hands of Meister Frantz. Schmidt marked the occasion with one of the longest entries in his entire journal. Over the course of three decades, Wolff, the well-educated scion of a local citizen family, had perpetrated a series of audacious frauds throughout the noble courts of Europe under multiple aliases—*also known as Glazier; called himself Georg Windholz, secretary to the elector at Berlin; also Jakob Führer, Ernst Haller, and Joachim Fürnberger.* Among Wolff's many swindles, one figures most prominently in the executioner's account: this wellborn son of Nuremberg had *borrowed 1,500 ducats from the [city's] Honorable Council by means of a forged letter in the elector's name and under the seal of the Margrave Johann Georg in Berlin.* Other victims of his schemes included *a councilor at Danzig, the count of Öttingen, his lord at Constance, two merchants at Danzig, a [Dutch] master,* and assorted dignitaries in Lisbon, Malta, Venice, Crete, Lübeck, Hamburg, Messina, Vienna, Kraków, Copenhagen, and London. Wolff stole fourteen hundred krona from the duke of Parma and absconded to Constantinople, where he assumed the identity of the recently deceased Jakob Führer, *[taking] the latter's signet ring, books, and clothes, as well as a few thaler.* His roguish journey continued to Italy, where *he slept with and tried to abduct an abbess, but failed; he took, however, from her sister a silver gilt striking clock. On another occasion he took a silver clock from a knight of St. John called Master Georg, as well as a horse, and rode away. In Prague, where he was the emperor's personal attendant, being charged with pawning a lady's silver goblets and girdle for 12 fl., he stole [them] and sold them for 40 fl.* Eventually exhausted by his litany of Wolff's crimes and victims, Meister Frantz cuts short his account with the summation: *also practiced many other frauds over twenty-four years, causing false seals of gentlemen to be cut [and] wrote many forged documents*—but not before making two more telling comments. First, he notes that Wolff was *fluent in seven languages.* Second, that he was *out of mercy executed with the sword here at Nuremberg, [the body] afterward burnt. Should have had his right hand cut off first as decided and ordered, but he was subsequently spared this.*[3]

Why did this incorrigible and shameless trickster hold such fascination for his executioner? Certainly Wolff's picaresque adventures rivaled those of any of his literary brethren and undoubtedly supplied the many spectators at his beheading with entertaining stories for years to come. The scale of his thefts was likewise impressive, totaling several thousand gulden (hundreds of times the average artisan's annual earnings), all spent on long years of luxurious living among the rich and powerful of Europe. No doubt many in the crowd who came to witness Wolff's execution felt a frisson of guilty pride that this cunning son of Nuremberg had so magnificently duped the cosmopolitan elite of the day.

Whatever voyeuristic pleasure Meister Frantz may have taken in this celebrated case, there was for him a more serious—and personally significant—moral issue at stake. Born into a rigidly hierarchical society with both innate intelligence and multiple familial advantages, Wolff had chosen to cast aside his privileged position and betray virtually everyone he encountered: his family, his city's leaders, his noble employers, bankers, merchants, abbesses, and so on. More broadly, his treacheries undermined the very tenuous trust that allowed commerce and government to function across the patchwork of kingdoms, principalities, and city-states that constituted Europe at the time. More to the point, Wolff's crimes shook to the core the people's confidence in the ability of their legal officials (and their executioners) to detect and punish such abuses. For this reason, fraud, particularly of such magnitude, posed a much graver threat to the authority of Frantz Schmidt and his employers than it would for their modern counterparts—hence the prescribed punishment of being burned at the stake. Yet in the end, Wolff's citizenship and family connections—and quite likely his confidence man's way with words—came to his rescue. He was spared the humiliating and painful punishment of *having his right hand chopped off*, and he died not in the agony and ignominy of fire, but by the quick and honorable sword stroke of Meister Frantz. In the words of one chronicler, "he spoke well."[4]

Frantz Schmidt's consternation over the crime and punishment of Gabriel Wolff, a case that arose fourteen years after his own appointment in Nuremberg, underscores how little the young executioner's newfound job security and prosperity did to ease his incessant anxiety over social rank. Frantz's disquiet was far from unique. As the historian Stuart Carroll reminds us, honor "is not simply a moral code regulating conduct; like magic or Christianity, it is a world view."[5] As a subscriber to that worldview, Frantz experienced a deep inner conflict over the Wolff case. On the one hand, he felt revulsion for the wellborn Wolff, who squandered all the social advantages that an executioner's son never enjoyed and behaved in a thoroughly scandalous and immoral manner *for over twenty-four years*. The scoundrel's decapitation at Frantz's own hands provided the executioner with welcome reassurance that justice had finally been served and his own faith in the social order rewarded. Yet when Wolff was shown mercy—because of his privileged social status—and spared the court-ordered punishment of having his hand chopped off, Schmidt directs his anger not at the hypocritical double standard that made special allowances for him but at one specific instance of unjustified mercy. A lifetime of journal entries reveals the same consistent deference to the hierarchical status quo itself, Meister Frantz always making special note when a noble or patrician is the victim or perpetrator of a crime—hence the lengthy passage on Wolff—even employing full honorific titles in his private record. Still shunned by respectable people himself, the ambitious executioner did not rage against what he saw as an unalterable social reality, but rather sought to continually improve his own place within it. As ever, his progress in achieving that dream would turn on the unlikely prospect of making his own disreputable work the means to that end rather than its chief obstacle.

A man of responsibilities

Frantz's relocation from provincial Hof to urban Bamberg provided but a mild foretaste of the culture shock he faced upon his 1578 arrival in the celebrated imperial city of Nuremberg. With a population of over forty thousand souls inside the city walls and an additional sixty thousand in its surrounding territory of five hundred square miles, the city on the Pegnitz River was one of the largest cosmopolitan centers in the empire, surpassed only by Augsburg, Cologne, and Vienna. The French jurist Jean Bodin called it "the greatest, most famous, and best-ordered of the imperial cities" and the local son Johannes Cochlaeus patriotically declared it "the center of Europe as well as Germany."[6] Other citizens boastingly referred to their beloved home as the Athens of the North, the Venice of the North, or the Florence of the North—not least because of the fame it enjoyed thanks to the celebrated Albrecht Dürer (1471–1528) and a host of other prominent artists and humanists, including Willibald Pirckheimer (1470–1530) and Conrad Celtis (1459–1508).

Even more measured observers acknowledged that Nuremberg was one of the most politically and economically powerful states of the era. Despite officially embracing the Lutheran faith since 1525, the city fathers successfully maintained an advantageous relationship with the Catholic emperors Charles V and Maximilian II, emerging from the Augsburg religious peace of 1555 with the city's political influence unscathed. Nuremberg's banks and mercantile firms competed on a global scale with the Medicis of Florence and the Fuggers of Augsburg, and its printing industry was internationally renowned for its reliable maps and innovative "earth-apples," or globes, based on the latest reports from the New World. The city's craftsmen enjoyed comparable fame for a variety of high-quality manufactured goods and precision instruments,

Nuremberg as viewed from the southeast, with the Kaiserburg looming in the background and the gallows and Raven Stone drawn prominently just outside the city walls (1533).

including clocks, weapons, and navigational tools, as well as gingerbread and toys (two products for which the city continues to be known today). "What's good comes from Nuremberg" had become a popular adage throughout the empire and abroad, giving the city a level of brand prestige that would be the envy of any modern chamber of commerce.[7]

Frantz Schmidt's lifetime corresponded almost exactly with Nuremberg's zenith of wealth, power, and prestige. As he journeyed there from Bamberg, the newly appointed executioner emerged from the imperial forest a few miles north of the city and caught sight of the familiar but still stunning skyline. Most prominent, high on a hill within the city's walls, stood the majestic Kaiserburg, a towering castle over two hundred feet tall and six hundred feet long—about the size of the Roman Colosseum—that served as the emperor's residence during his visits to the city and was home to the imperial crown jewels until the late eighteenth century. Coming closer, Frantz glimpsed a patchwork of slate roofs descending the flanks of the castle hill—just a few of the hundreds of houses and shops that crowded the city streets below. And in the distance rose the spires of the city's main parish churches—Saint Sebaldus on the northern side of the Pegnitz, and Saint Lorenz, which would become his own congregation, just south of the river. A few miles farther along, young Schmidt passed through the poor outskirts of the city, a district of scattered houses and farms punctuated by patches of forest that might conceal robbers and other rough types. Finally, he arrived at the edge of a moat one hundred feet wide and about as deep. On the far side loomed a massive sandstone wall nearly fifty feet high, ten feet thick, and some seventeen thousand feet long that completely encircled the city and castle. Along this intimidating fortification stood eighty-three soaring towers, spaced approximately 150 feet apart and bristling with armed watchmen. The image of an island fortress was not far from the way Nuremberg's leaders imagined their home, and they would have been pleased at the sense of awe and admiration the city inspired in their new employee.

After arriving at the moat, Frantz paused for inspection at a small guardhouse and then proceeded across the narrow wooden bridge that spanned the water. Next came a larger guardhouse and a more thorough inspection, after which he was allowed to enter whichever of the city's eight massive gates he had selected—probably the northern Vestnertor. Passing through the well-fortified arch, he entered a long, narrow tunnel that took him through the ramparts and finally emerged within the inner city itself. Before him stood a maze of more than five hundred streets and alleys, mostly narrow and crooked, crammed with thousands of structures: stately public buildings, stunningly ornamented patrician houses, modest half-timber artisan residences, and numerous storage barns, stables, makeshift shelters, and commercial stands. The streets, all paved with cobblestones, bustled with vendors, traveling artisans and merchants, maids on errands, loitering youths, playing children, beggars, prostitutes, pickpockets, and rural folk with their livestock—as well as countless horses, dogs, cats, pigs, and rats. Despite the dense concentration of people and animals, Nuremberg's streets were remarkably clean for the era—a stark contrast to the festering ruts of Frantz's boyhood Hof—all thanks to a well-developed water and sewage system (including 118 public wells) and a battery of disposal workers, who dumped waste outside the city walls and sometimes, illegally, into the Pegnitz River. Magistrates still frequently complained about unsightly accumulations of garbage, but by early modern standards, the city appeared quite verdant and lovely, with a number of public parks, gardens, fountains, and decorated squares.

As Frantz knew from previous stays, Nuremberg's governing city council was dominated by a closed circle of forty-two ruling patrician families, and its "senators" highly cherished their homeland's hard-earned reputation as a bastion of law and order. Each of the city's eight districts maintained two district heads, assisted by forty or so municipal guards, known locally as archers, and twenty-four night watchmen.[8] Together with several voluntary street captains, these officials kept stores of weapons, ammunitions, horses, lanterns, ladders, and other supplies, and mobilized able-bodied men in their neighborhood in the event of fire, enemy attack, or other emergencies. The city government also employed teams of health inspectors and kept a close eye on craft production and prices, with all masters accountable to the city council rather than to independent guilds, as was the custom in most cities of the day.

Most relevant to Frantz Schmidt, Nuremberg maintained an especially active police network, including several paid informers, and boasted the highest capital punishment rate of any city in the empire. Anyone caught wandering the city's streets or alleys after sunset could be imprisoned for suspected burglary, and even minor infractions like public urination were subject—at least in theory—to a weighty twenty-thaler (17 fl.) fine—twice the annual salary of most domestic servants. According to one admiring (if hyperbolic) English resident, "So trew and Just are they that if you lose a purse with money in the street, Ring, bracelet or such Lyke, you shal be sure to have it again. I would it were so in London."[9] Of course, if all Nuremberg's denizens had truly been this honest, the city would hardly have needed its new executioner's services.

Frantz's immediate superiors were the fourteen city councilors known as the criminal jurors (*Schöffen*). As in all Nuremberg's administrative bodies, the precise composition of this group fluctuated somewhat annually, but all its members were invariably drawn from the same small pool of local patricians and trained jurists. The criminal bureau was managed on a daily basis by a standing judge, typically appointed for life. The patrician Christoph Scheurl, son of the city's most famous jurist, had been serving in this capacity for three years when he appointed "the young executioner from Hof" to his new position. Scheurl would continue in this role for the next fifteen years,

until he was succeeded by Alexander Stokamer, who himself served
for the following seventeen years. As in his other work relationships,
Frantz enjoyed the good fortune of continuity and stability in his superiors.

The financial package that the new executioner had secured in his
initial five-year contract was spectacular by the standards of the day. In
addition to a weekly salary of 2½ gulden (130 fl. annually), Frantz received a free and spacious lodging (with his own heated bath), a regular
supply of wine and firewood, reimbursement for travel and all other
job-related expenses, and lifelong tax-free status. He was also to be paid
1 thaler (0.85 fl.) per interrogation session and was permitted to earn
supplemental income as both a visiting executioner (with the council's
approval) and a medical consultant—the latter generating considerable
revenue. His base salary alone put him in the top 5 percent of earners
in Nuremberg and was 60 percent higher than the salary of his Munich

Nuremberg's magnificent town hall, as seen from the west. Convicted felons
waited in the Hole (dungeon) below until their final "trial" in the courtroom on
the first floor. The main marketplace is just to the right (south) in this picture
(c. 1650).

counterpart, making him probably the best-paid executioner in the empire and—at least financially—on par with some medical and legal professionals. On a more personal note, he would earn at least three times as much annually as his own father.[10]

How did a twenty-four-year-old journeyman—albeit one with sterling credentials for his age—achieve such a coup? Once more, timing, character, and contacts were crucial. Nuremberg's leaders were obviously impressed by Frantz's professional experience and expertise, as well as Lienhardt Lippert's recommendation, but it was his reputation for sobriety and reliability, combined with his youth, that likely clinched the offer. Sixteenth-century executioners were not known for their longevity in office, usually owing to a violent disposition or some physical infirmity. Among Frantz's predecessors in Nuremberg, one was executed for treason by his own assistant, another was dismissed after killing his assistant in a dispute over wages, a third was killed in an ambush, a fourth was removed after nearly stabbing a knacker's wife to death, and two others—including Lippert himself—were forced to retire because of old age or serious illnesses.[11] As a young yet accomplished and apparently pious professional, Schmidt promised the stability and seriousness that the office of executioner had hitherto been lacking. His family connections obviously got him a foot in the door, but Frantz made the most of his temporary assignments in Nuremberg, impressing observers with his skill and poise while ingratiating himself with law enforcement superiors during his brief encounters with them.

Masters in any craft were rarely single, and Frantz immediately set out to correct this social deficiency. At some point during the year and a half following his first visit to Nuremberg, the young executioner became acquainted with a woman, nine years his senior, named Maria Beckin. Maria was the daughter of the late Jorg Beck, a longtime warehouse worker, who upon his death in 1561 had left behind a widow and seven children under the age of sixteen.[12] The circumstances of Maria's subsequent courtship by the young man from Hof nearly two decades later are shrouded in mystery. Few respectable women, even of low birth, would have considered marrying an executioner, but a thirty-four-year-old spinster with no dowry and three other eligible sisters at home had few—if any—alternatives. Genuine attraction between the two should not be ruled out, but the match was clearly to their mutual benefit in practical terms, particularly given Frantz's large salary and house. On November 15, 1579, eighteen months after Frantz began his tenure as Nuremberg's permanent executioner, his engagement to Maria Beckin was publicly announced to the congregation of Saint Sebaldus Church. Three weeks later, the city council approved Meister Frantz's request to marry in his new residence—a church ceremony was still out of the question—and on December 7 he and Maria were formally wed.[13]

The municipally owned house that became the newlyweds' home was (and still is) known locally as the Hangman's House (*Henkerhaus*). Most German cities did not allow the executioner to live within the city walls. So even though his house stood in a district filled with other sites of infamy—including a slaughterhouse, the pig market, and a munici-pal prison—Frantz and his bride would have considered themselves lucky. The original house, built in the fourteenth century, was actually a small three-story tower (accordingly known as the Hangman's Tower) perched on a small island in the southern outflow of the Pegnitz. In 1457 the city erected a large wooden pedestrian bridge (henceforth known as the Hangman's Bridge) and incorporated the tower into it. Then builders added on to the tower, constructing a long half-timbered house with its foundation set right on the bridge. The expanded resi-dence had provided an exceptionally large space for a young single man, comprising six rooms and an indoor privy: a total of more than sixteen hundred square feet, in an era when the typical family of four managed with a third as much room. Fittingly, the house was at once centrally located and isolated, standing as it did in the middle of the Pegnitz, with the disreputable prison district on one bank and a proper bour-geois neighborhood on the other. True, Frantz would have to walk past the reeking stalls of the pig market each day to get to the town hall, but he could also gaze without obstruction through his own glazed win-dows at the opulent structures of the city center.[14]

Perhaps the young executioner initially continued to share the space with his recently widowed sister and her five surviving children. But such an arrangement would probably not have continued after his marriage to Maria—and certainly not after the birth of their first child, a son named Vitus, on March 14, 1581. Unlike most executioners' children, Vitus was immediately baptized in a church—Saint Sebaldus—as were all of Schmidt's subsequent progeny. Was it significant that Frantz decided not to name his oldest son, or any of Vitus's brothers, after their grandfather Heinrich, a common honorific in the era? Was he perhaps angling for future favors from his father's employer, Bishop Veit of Bamberg, whose name was the German form of Vitus? Or was Schmidt swayed, despite his Protestant faith, by the reputation of Saint Vitus as the patron of healing, the executioner's alternate career? Once more, Frantz's thinking remains hidden from us. His reasons for naming his two subsequent children, by contrast, presents less of a mystery, given that Margaretha (baptized on August 25, 1582) and Jorg (christened on June 2, 1584) ranked among the most popular girl and boy names of the era.

As a new *Hausvater* and a well-paid craft master, Frantz Schmidt finally possessed the social foundation he needed in his quest for respectability. The greater dignity that both he and his superiors sought to bestow on the office of executioner for his public persona, however, would not have been possible without the gradual redefinition of the Nuremberg executioner's job during the generation before him. Some of the executioner's most distasteful and dishonorable responsibilities, such as oversight of the municipal brothel (closed at the insistence of Protestant reformers in 1543), had long ago become obsolete. Other tasks had simply been outsourced to even more disreputable individuals, most notably the job of street cleaning and garbage disposal, now overseen by two highly compensated "dung-masters" (also called "night masters").[15]

The executioner's principal assistant, known in Nuremberg as "the Lion" (*Löwe*; a corruption of *lêvjan*, the Gothic word for a bailiff), would play an especially crucial role in helping Frantz pursue his ambition of a respectable life. In exchange for the supplemental income he earned for his various services, the Lion willingly assumed the bulk of the social stigma that earlier executioners had been forced to carry alone. Originally charged only with handing over prisoners condemned by the court, the Lion had, by the time of Frantz's arrival in Nuremberg, assumed oversight of the burning of suicides, the removal of dead animals, and the disposal of spoiled food, oil, and wine (which he usually threw into the Pegnitz). He also continued to serve subpoenas and assisted the executioner in all tortures, floggings, and executions, occasionally acting as his proxy.[16] Most crucially, the Lion acted as a buffer between Meister Frantz and the many dishonorable individuals connected to his work: knackers, skinners, gravediggers, jailers, and particularly the municipal archers, infamous for their brutality and corruption in serving as the city's de facto police patrolmen.

Frantz apparently enjoyed a good working relationship with his Lions, remarkably experiencing only one turnover in his forty years of service to Nuremberg. The veteran Augustin Amman already had thirteen years of experience when he began to assist the new young executioner, and Amman continued to fill that role until his retirement (or death) in 1590. His successor, Claus Kohler, worked at Meister Frantz's side for the remainder of Schmidt's career and even continued with the subsequent executioner for three more years, until his own death in 1621.[17] Schmidt no doubt developed a strong professional bond with his Lions. After all, he spent hours each day working with this assistant by his side, more time than he spent with anyone else except perhaps his family members. Moreover, the physical rigor, social sensitivity, and public nature of their job meant that executioner and Lion had to work in a profoundly coordinated, interdependent manner if they were to succeed in their duties. At one point in his journal, Frantz even refers to Nuremberg's *executioners* in the plural, suggesting that he considered his Lion as a partner rather than an underling.[18] Without a reliable and trustworthy Lion, the new executioner knew that his quest for respectability would be doomed from the beginning.

Close working ties did not necessarily translate into close social ties, however. In Bamberg Meister Heinrich's assistant had actually lived with the family, but in Nuremberg the Lion maintained separate quarters in a nearby municipal building. Whatever socializing Frantz's Lions did with the Schmidts, it was discreet and mostly behind closed doors. Two years after Frantz took his first oath of office in Nuremberg's town hall, several new citizens complained about having to take their own oaths next to the dishonorable Lion. The executioner was unable (or unwilling) to protect his faithful colleague from being henceforth banished to a separate annual swearing-in with the hated municipal archers.[19]

Nuremberg also spared its executioner the onus of overseeing its prison system, another time-consuming and odious task standard for many of Frantz's counterparts elsewhere in the empire. The majority of the city's prisons, including the Hole, were intended as holding cells for suspects awaiting judgment, with half of all suspects released within a week, and nine out of ten within a month.[20] Cells in the Luginsland Tower of the imperial castle and within the town hall itself were reserved for the use of patrician prisoners. Six self-standing barracks (designated A to F) were constructed during Frantz's tenure in Nuremberg to house unruly youths and other lesser delinquents. Debtors awaiting financial assistance from their friends and relatives were locked in a specially designated male or female prison. The remaining city towers handled prisoners-of-war and other spillover from the Hole, while a few, like the Frog Tower and Water Tower, simultaneously functioned as long-term insane asylums.[21] (See map on page xi.)

Each prison or tower had its own warden—like Frantz, who reported directly to the criminal bureau—as well as its own attachment of guards (known as "iron masters"). Though not officially dishonorable, prison employees were generally lowborn, poorly paid, and widely disdained. Their reputation for corruption and incompetence was fueled by the preservation of a medieval funding structure whereby prisoners were expected to pay for their own upkeep, thereby determining the level of "comfort" available. The exorbitant minimum rate of 36 pfennig per day (more than 2 fl. per week) merely assured an inmate of morning soup, a "good piece" of white bread, and a liter of wine. More food and other privileges—an extra blanket or a pillow, access to drinking water, more frequent changing of the excrement pail—each carried additional charges. Of course, destitute prisoners could not even afford the basic fee, and at the end of their incarceration—regardless of innocence or guilt—their charges were assumed by the city alms bureau or another charity.[22]

For the first twenty years of Frantz Schmidt's work in Nuremberg, he and his Lion worked more often with the longtime warden of the Hole, Hans Öhler, than with any of the other prison heads. Required by law to be both married and resident in the prison, Öhler shared a tiny apartment with two successive wives as well as his daughter, son, and two maids. Other than the marriage stipulation, the expectations for any individual willing to undertake such an unattractive position were understandably low. The criminal bureau's sole efforts at better enforcement appear to have been limited to an annual reminder to the warden and his wife that they should carefully explain the required duties to each new staff member.[23] The bureau also frequently admonished—but never dismissed—Öhler for the multiple shortcomings of that same staff, many of whom came from the same disreputable pool as the inmates themselves.

Frantz did not have to wait long to encounter the incompetence (or corruption) of his new associates at the prison. During the night of June 20, 1578, the thief who was to be the new executioner's first victim made a daring escape from the Hole. According to a contemporary account, Hans Reintein got the elderly guard watching him drunk and then fled through a secret underground passage to the imperial castle that he as a mason had helped construct. He used an iron bar to break through any locked doors and to bash a hole in the ceiling of a corridor under Saint Sebaldus Church, through which he ultimately crawled out to freedom.[24] In typical fashion, the guard received a tongue-lashing but kept his job. Two years later, another audacious escape—this one accomplished by an inmate who duped the warden himself out of an iron bar and used it to break into the subterranean passage—merely resulted in another "stern admonishment."[25] Such bold escapes continued to occur throughout Meister Frantz's career, as did frequent inmate suicides and occasional fatal brawls among inmates. The city council invariably responded to such disruptions in muted fashion, merely instructing the warden and his guards to search new prisoners more thoroughly to determine "whether they have a knife, nail, or anything else that they could use to harm themselves or to escape."[26]

Frantz Schmidt was understandably loath to be associated with such disreputable individuals and locations, yet his responsibility for prisoners' physical welfare required him to make frequent visits to the Hole and occasionally to some of the towers. In addition, all the interrogations he performed, whether with torture or without, took place in the Hole, beneath the town hall—a cramped, dirty, dark, and genuinely frightening place that generally conformed to our worst stereotypes of the medieval dungeon. The thirteen holding cells—each about thirty-six square feet, with one narrow wooden bench, a straw bed, and a pail—could barely accommodate the two prisoners required to share them, let alone a visiting interrogation team of two to five men, who instead stood outside in the corridor to ask their follow-up questions under the dim flicker of a small oil lamp. Primitive coal heating scarcely alleviated the harsh winter cold, nor did the few narrow ventilation shafts to the outside improve the putrid and dank air below. Only those inmates condemned to death enjoyed the slightly larger accommodations of the poor sinners' cells, or during their final three days the relative luxury of the so-called hangman's parlor, the only room in the prison with windows to the outside. Wending his way through the labyrinthine corridors on a near daily basis—whether to torture a recalcitrant suspect or to heal him—Frantz's greatest consolation was that his visits to this cesspool of sin and misery at least remained hidden from public view.

One disagreeable task that Meister Frantz could not avoid or conceal was the maintenance of the execution site itself, comprising both the gallows and the Raven Stone, a raised platform used for beheadings and for breaking on the wheel. Since 1441, both gallows and stone had been located just outside the portal in the city walls known as the Ladies' Gate, where they remained until the city became part of the duchy of Bavaria nearly four centuries later. By Schmidt's time, the once modest three-legged gallows and adjacent small mound had been transformed into two stately brick edifices, one a solidly built four-beamed scaffold, the other an elevated stage, covered with turf. Law and custom dictated that the execution site remain a horror to behold, adorned as it was by the rotting corpses of one or more thieves that twisted in the breeze for weeks until they dropped off unceremoniously into the pit of bones beneath. Nearby stood a series of sharpened stakes, decorated with decapitated heads and other body parts, accompanied sometimes by the mangled body of a poor sinner broken on the wheel raised high on the instrument of its demise. Popular superstitions abounded over every aspect of the cursed execution ground, its eerie silence broken only by the cawing of hungry ravens and the often noted whistling of the wind through the ramparts.

The week after his first public performance as Nuremberg's executioner—a triple hanging—Meister Frantz initiated a complete renovation of the existing structure. Over the course of two weeks in late June and early July of 1578, the Lion and his helpers performed the dishonorable task of pulling down and disposing of the old gallows and

Raven Stone. Since anyone who touched an execution structure—
even a completely new, untainted one—risked lifelong pollution and
bad luck, all the city's masons and carpenters worked on the building
project together, thereby dissipating the danger. On the morning of
July 10, 336 masters and journeymen assembled to launch an all-day
"gallows festival." It began with a colorful and noisy procession of pipers, drummers, and representatives of all the city's patrician families
and crafts, as well as assorted clerics and many others. After solemnly
circling the site of the former gallows three times, the craftsmen
brought in several wagonloads of stone and wood and set to work.

The infamous site of Nuremberg's gallows (left) and Raven Stone (right)
(1648).

With the combination of efficiency and cooperation seen in a modern-day Amish barn raising, they completed both the gallows and Raven Stone by late that afternoon. Then they sat down with their fellow Nurembergers to enjoy great quantities of food and drink, with the entire day's activities—including the wages of every craftsman—paid for by the city treasury. Twenty-seven years later, in 1605, the ritual would be repeated, as it would every generation or so for the next two centuries.[27]

Maintaining the gallows between such public festivities was a decidedly less festive proposition. Despite the evil spirits and infamy

Nuremberg's gallows, as drawn by a court notary (1583).

associated with the execution grounds, miscreants regularly robbed or otherwise violated the cadavers that hung from the gallows. One nocturnal vandal might slice off the hand, the thumb, or even "the manhood" of an executed man, each believed to possess magical powers. Another would pry loose a head from its stake, perhaps to take home as a gruesome souvenir. Still others broke the ancient taboo for reasons much more mundane. In the fall of 1588, someone cut down Georg Solen after eight days and later Hans Schnabel after fourteen days, both times in order to remove and make off with the corpse's vest and pants. Leinhard Bardtmann (aka the Horseman) had only been hanging for three days when *someone cut through his neck, so that the head remained hanging and the body fell to the ground.* Theft was the apparent motive here as well, but in this instance it was triggered by a rumor that the condemned himself had cleverly planted, so as to spare his corpse an extended indignity: *Some wantonous fellows found out and believed that he had much gold sewn in his clothes and thought to get good booty. Nothing was found, however.*[28] The Horseman subsequently received a proper burial, just as he had intended.

Apparently even Meister Frantz and his superiors recoiled at the excessive humiliation of a hanged thief's cadaver. In Solen's case, only the bottom half of his corpse had been removed *and the rest left hanging,* so that *the body was finally thrown into the gallows pit the next day, as it looked too horrible.* And after word circulated that hanged thief Matthes Lenger had been *stripped naked the first night, except for his stockings,* there was such a surge of curious onlookers—especially "cheeky females," according to the prison chaplain—that the city councilors ordered Meister Frantz *to put a shirt and trunk-hose on him.*[29] Whether the executioner delegated this distasteful task, like so many others, to his Lion is not recorded.

A good name

Twenty-four-year-old Frantz Schmidt entered Nuremberg society as an unmarried foreigner, working in a despised profession. That he would confront more than the usual wariness that longtime residents accorded outsiders is an understatement. Even after he took a bride and became locally known, Frantz recognized that to be accepted by the citizens and leaders of Nuremberg, he would not only have to satisfy their standard of propriety but also find incremental ways to formalize and thereby secure his status as an honorable man. "In an honor-based society," the legal historian William Miller has observed, "there is no self-respect independent of the respect of others," and thus every personal interaction remains fraught with the danger of lost honor.[30] Frantz could probably never completely overcome the local animosity toward a foreign-born professional killer, but at least he could grind down the resistance, dim his father's stain of dishonor, and above all provide no ammunition for those who would push him back down into the gutter of society. The campaign would be long and require much patience and perseverance. The young executioner from Hof would need to prove himself as deliberate and precise in this enterprise as he was in his sword strokes on the Raven Stone.

Meister Frantz's deliberate construction of a reputation for himself simultaneously embraced and repudiated the existing social order. He was no rebel; his vision for himself remained framed within the somewhat narrow confines of the conventions of the day. Yet his journal reveals that, like many ambitious individuals, he possessed a social imagination capable of adapting those conventions to fit his own unique circumstances. For most people of the era, one's reputation was inextricably bound up in one's identity, and much of that identity was inherited, including place of origin and social status. For Frantz Schmidt, the importance of such identity was undeniable, but character and deeds—two factors within his own control—determined reputation, not birth. This sharp distinction, while far from universally accepted, at least provided the young foreign executioner with a fighting chance.

The first obstacle Frantz had to overcome was his own foreignness. Specific place of origin—one's town or village—constituted an important part of an early modern person's identity. This made sense, in an era when travel was slow, customs varied widely from region to region, and dozens of distinctive dialects flourished within the boundaries of what we now call Germany, many of them unintelligible to visitors from as little as a few days' journey away. In his journal, Frantz consistently identifies each culprit at the outset by his or her home village or town— *from Bürg* or *of Ansbach*. He himself was long known in Nuremberg as "the executioner from Hof" or "from Bamberg" (even though he had only lived briefly in the latter). A person who could not be literally placed was not only harder for others to remember but also immediately suspect. Although Frantz occasionally forgets or misremembers a proper name in his journal, never—except in the instance of a few itinerant prostitutes—does he fail to record a person's hometown.

Frantz also recognized that geographical origin always carried a political dimension, identifying an individual as either a native—born in Nuremberg or its surrounding territory—or "a foreigner"—born anywhere else regardless of distance, language, or current residence. Thus, the cowherder Heinz Neuner, who worked as a potter in the Nuremberg suburb of Gostenhof, remained a subject of the nearby margrave of Ansbach and thus just as much a foreigner as *Steffan Rebweller from Marshtall in Savoy . . . and Heinrich Hausmann of Kalka, fourteen miles below Cologne.*[31] Frantz frequently notes—forty-five times in 778 cases—when an individual is not only from Nuremberg but also a citizen, a special legal status granted only to certain residents. Citizenship carried several prerogatives, most notably the right to execution by the sword for capital crimes (as in the instance of swindler Gabriel Wolff) or even mitigation to flogging in the cases of Nuremberg forger Endres Petry or the incestuous Barbara Grimmin (aka Schory Mory).[32] Citizen Margaretha Böckin, convicted of a particularly treacherous murder, merely enjoyed the privilege of being beheaded while standing, having already been *nipped thrice with red-hot tongs and afterward her [decapitated] head was fixed on a pole above and the body buried under the gallows.*[33]

Of course, a busy metropolis like Nuremberg was filled with immigrants, some of them resident for decades. This aspect of identity was not in itself debilitating, particularly at the lower levels of society. Did Frantz's foreignness exacerbate his isolation? What did he consider home? It's not exactly clear. "The young executioner from Hof" had not lived in his native town for many years and did not display any hesitation whatsoever about flogging malefactors from Hof—some of whom he might even have known. But neither did he express any personal affinity with the city on the Pegnitz that now employed him.[34] Only after ten years on the job in Nuremberg did he begin to refer to *our town* or the murder of *the son of one of our citizens*, and even after that, when it is obvious that he has settled for life, such explicit signs of allegiance remain rare in the journal.[35] The transformation into "Frantz Schmidt of Nuremberg" required time, patience, and more tangible signs of mutual acceptance in his relationship with the city fathers.

Social status, based on family and occupation, obviously posed a much greater problem for the young journeyman. Here Frantz's interpretation of honor and status appear simultaneously alien and familiar to modern sensibilities. Although the victim himself of a capricious prince's life-altering command, he seems not only to accept the idea of upper-class privilege but also to actually believe in its sanctity at a profound level. He invariably writes about his social superiors with a reverence that bespeaks more than mere habit and more even than the caution of a man who knows that his employers might someday read his words. In fact, when Frantz writes of a crime in which a lower-class culprit harms a patrician or noble, he often seems as offended by the mere effrontery of a cross-class transgression as he is by the misdeed itself. He becomes visibly outraged, for instance, when the con artist Gabriel Wolff has the impertinence to defraud the wealthy and highborn of Nuremberg and other cities.[36] And in another entry he seethes with indignation as he describes the murderer of *the nobleman and soldier Albernius von Wisenstein* by *Dominicus Korn, a citizen's child, a mercenary, and whoreson of a tavern keeper.*[37]

For many of us on this side of the French Revolution, it's difficult to understand Meister Frantz's apparently deep belief in the innate superiority of the rich and the noble. Our modern culture of envy presupposes that the inherited wealth and privilege of others can be resented or coveted, but certainly not respected as divinely ordained. For Schmidt and his contemporaries, though, the hierarchy of birth existed as a natural force, like the weather or the plague—capricious, even destructive, but inevitable. It's hardly remarkable that Meister Frantz embraced this status quo. After all, he served as one of the key guardians of this stratified society—and he believed that he had the wit and resolve to achieve his own social ends within its confines. The cost was not negligible: the young executioner suffered daily reminders of his own low status, ranging from casual slights or veiled insults to his formal exclusion from every festival, dance, procession, and other public gathering except those that were directly connected to his unsavory profession.

A chronicler's portrayal of the 1605 execution of Niklaus von Gülchen, Nuremberg privy councilor, for embezzlement and other offenses (1616). In reality, von Gülchen was seated in a judgment chair, not kneeling.

The very men who worked with him on criminal cases—the city physician, the examining magistrates, the court notary—could not freely converse with him in the street or show any other signs of social intimacy. These and other indignities were simply to be borne by Meister Frantz, who likely saw them as the natural lot of someone in his unique social station. Whether these daily affronts caused him anger or shame or despair is known only to him.

One dramatic incident later in Frantz's career reveals the depth of his innate respect for authority and high birth. In December 1605 the noble privy councilor Doctor Niklaus von Gülchen (spelled *Gilgen* by Schmidt) was convicted of defrauding and betraying many prominent Nurembergers and the city itself, in the most infamous governmental scandal in over a century. Though condemned to death, Gülchen received all the privileges of a first-class execution: a comfortable cell in the Luginsland Tower rather than the Hole, special meals, exemption from torture during interrogation (the noble right of *non torquendo*), an honorable death by the sword, and burial in his family plot in Saint Johannis Cemetery.[38] Frantz's deep revulsion seethes throughout the lengthy passage he devotes to Gülchen's diverse *evil deeds*, which included breaking his oaths as a privy councilor, advising opposing parties in many affairs, embezzling from the city treasury, raiding municipal supplies of beer and wine, siring five children by his wife's servant, raping his undermaid, attempting to rape one daughter-in-law and bribing the other one to enter into a long-standing affair, cheating many noble and patrician families, and passing himself off as a doctor by means of a false seal. As in the case of the wellborn swindler Gabriel Wolff, it was Gülchen's easy willingness to abuse his privileged position and disgrace his family's honor that particularly outraged Nuremberg's executioner, almost constituting a kind of sacrilege. Yet the prerogatives of rank once more prevailed. Meister Frantz found himself having to negotiate with the condemned nobleman in his cell over the appropriate execution clothing. Schmidt's superiors finally lost patience with Gülchen and provided him a long mourning cloak and a hat from the municipal armory, which the condemned man burnished with regal aplomb during the public procession to the judgment chair, itself gently draped with a fine black silk cloth.[39]

For the great mass of humanity beneath the aristocracy and patriciate, Frantz Schmidt considered the linking of social status and reputation even more dubious. He was particularly wary of attempts by the craftsmen's guilds to shore up their members' deteriorating rank and influence by vilifying those with dishonorable professions—such as executioners—or with no profession at all. Frantz knew from early on that training or employment in a so-called honorable craft did not in itself make a person honorable. So although he subscribed to the then-universal convention of identifying each culprit in his journal by profession—*a furrier; a farmer; a wire-drawer*—he never states that a particular craft or guild is honorable. In fact, the word "honorable" itself appears only in reference to nobles or patricians, and its counterpart, "dishonorable," is entirely absent from the journal. For Frantz, craft, like hometown or name, served merely as a neutral way to situate an individual in physical space. In his mind, formal identity of this sort carried no implication of character, good or bad—so that even serial murderer Nickel Schwager's primary designation remains simply *a mason*.[40]

Frantz's distinction between social status and reputation is frequently evident in his combination of a person's professional and criminal identities, as when he writes of *a grocer and murderer, a horseman . . . and a thief, a peddler and thief*, or more impressively, *a tiler . . . a thief and a cheat at gaming, who also took three wives.* This tendency becomes especially prominent during Frantz's early years in Nuremberg, though he is inconsistent at times, such as in his identification of Georg Götz as *a [municipal] archer, thief, and whoremonger,* and later simply *an archer*—a perfectly understandable omission given the spontaneous nature of his journal keeping.[41] (It's unlikely that the ultimately beheaded Götz developed less of a taste for stealing and loose women during the time between his convictions.) Frantz's growing preference for compound identities—*Michel Gemperlein, a butcher, mercenary, murderer, robber, and thief*—also indicates the maturing executioner's recognition that the old order of identity by craft alone was increasingly meaningless in any moral sense.[42]

Those few instances where Frantz identifies perpetrators exclusively in terms of their offenses reveal even more about his own views of morality and character: *a child murderess* (for infanticide); *an arsonist;* or *a heretic* (for incest and for bestiality). Unlike simple fornication or even homicide, crimes of this nature completely obliterated all other aspects of an individual's identity in the executioner's mind. Individuals who had become full-time criminals are thus also sometimes exclusively designated by their chosen professions of *thief* or *robber*—hardly value-neutral terms.

Frantz's refusal to conflate social status and reputation obviously had much to do with his own situation. Even the appellation "Meister Frantz" might reduce him in other's eyes to the level of his odious craft. In general, though, a person's name revealed little about one's identity, let alone reputation. Noble and patrician names were of course generally self-evident, especially when accompanied in the journal by telltale antecedents, such as "the honorable" or "His Excellency." Jewish names were also easy to identify, as they typically featured first names of Hebrew origin (e.g., Mosche or Moses) and last names intended to serve as a label, such as Judt ("the Jew"). Otherwise, appellations in themselves told little. A Protestant woman might be named after the Blessed Virgin or a saint; a cobbler could be known as Fischer, a longtime Nuremberg family by the name of Frankfurter. Obviously, in actual life certain family names carried more weight than others in some localities, but even the surnames of many Nuremberg patricians also surfaced in the poor rolls and even criminal records.

The one major exception to this ambiguity was when an individual was identified by a nickname or alias. Not everyone who had a nickname engaged in some disreputable activity, but virtually all disreputable individuals had at least one alternate identity. By the time they had become professional criminals, almost all the juvenile thieves Meister Frantz encountered had acquired colorful street names, such as Frog Johnny, the Black Baker, Red Lenny, Corky, Hook, and Shifty. Popular monikers might be based on occupations (the Grocer, the Mason, Baker's Boy), places of origin (the Swissman, Cunz from Pommersbrun), clothing (Green Cap, Cavalier Johnny, Glove George), or combinations thereof (the Fiddling Cobbler, the Woodsman from Lauf, Baiersdorf Blacky). They could be comical (Chicken Leg, Rabbit, Snail), patronizing (Gabby, Stuttering Bart, Laddy), or even insulting (Horse Beetle, Raven Fodder). In a decidedly less politically correct age, nicknames often focused on an individual's appearance—Pointy Head, the Long Brickmaker, Red Pete, Lean George, and Little Fatty—or on personal hygiene, such as Dusty.[43] A nickname might also be a play on a given name, as in the case of Katherina Schwertzin (Black) who was known as the Coal Girl.[44] But whatever their origin, nicknames also served an eminently practical purpose: They avoided confusion in a society that overrelied on a few first names (particularly Hans).

For Nuremberg's experienced executioner, the sheer existence of a nickname often implied some association with "loose society," if not the criminal underworld itself. It's less clear that nicknames in themselves carried the same social taint for most common people—depending of course on the nickname. Contemporaries might have been understandably wary of the violent tendencies of men known as Mercenary John, or Scabbard, or somewhat apprehensive about their purses when introduced to the Tricky Tanner or Eight Fingers. There were surely few respectable social or work opportunities for women once their nicknames were revealed to be Playbunny, Furry Kathy, Grinder Girl, or, most jarring, Cunt Annie.[45] No doubt Meister Frantz was aware of a few uncomplimentary, or at least undignified, nicknames for himself, but he declined to preserve them for posterity.

Whatever the circumstances of one's birth or profession (or one's nickname), all of Frantz Schmidt's contemporaries would have agreed that the most reliable indicator of reputation was the company one kept—a fact of considerable comfort to Nuremberg's executioner, who could not choose his origins or even his colleagues but who could choose his friends. But who was included in what must have been a small circle of intimates, given the still pervasive social constraints he faced? And where did they meet? Certainly not the most frequent site of male sociability, since taverns were generally off-limits to executioners, especially one who didn't himself imbibe or gamble. Public festivals, wedding celebrations, and the like also remained closed to him, as did the homes of learned colleagues or acquaintances, who risked losing their reputations if they were known to associate with an executioner. Given his long tenure, Frantz clearly enjoyed at least an amiable working relationship with some of the city's magistrates, jurists, physicians, and apothecaries. He also maintained a correspondence and perhaps friendship with some other executioners in the area.[46] His relationship with the prison chaplains, by contrast, does not appear to have been particularly close: in their journals, Magister Hagendorn and Magister Müller rarely refer to him by name, instead calling him "the executioner" or "the hangman." Schmidt himself similarly writes impersonally of *the priests*. Whoever Frantz's closest companions were—and we may hope that he enjoyed some of the joys of friendship—their social encounters likely took place in the privacy of the executioner's house, although being seen there also carried some reputational risk to visitors.

Simply avoiding bad company was a more straightforward matter and one in which the son of Heinrich Schmidt had become well practiced. Thanks to the efforts of his Lion, Frantz had minimal direct contact with the municipal archers and other low-level law enforcers, so he avoided the popular animosity roused by their perceived corruption and general thuggishness. The new executioner disciplined without hesitation any begging beadles or municipal archers who consorted with prostitutes or raped young girls in their charge, either by flogging or execution.[47] He impassively notes his own execution of four former colleagues for murder and theft, including the knacker Hans Hammer (aka Pebble; aka Young Cobbler) and the archer Carl Reichardt (aka Eckerlein), who *stole here and everywhere from the executioners and their assistants, also at the knackers' yards where he lodged*. Given the further dishonor such associates indirectly brought on his profession,

Frantz's eagerness to distance himself is understandable. Tellingly, he makes no attempt to convince himself that such miscreants were exceptions among employees of this rank, but to the contrary remarks with surprise when a former beadle convicted of murder strikes him as an otherwise *reputable man*, the condemned man's wheel sentence accordingly mitigated to decapitation.[48]

Among men, association with loose company was an expansive concept but generally implied consorting or even working with professional criminals. Merely casual affiliation with known outlaws might itself provide sufficient grounds for torture in some serious cases. Acknowledged membership in a large robber band was even more damning, so that Meister Frantz can convey with a few words the notoriety of Joachim Waldt (aka the Tutor), *who cruelly stole much and broke into [homes] with some thirty companions*, or Hennsa Walter (aka the Cheesecutter), who was associated with *fourteen of his companions and two whores*. More typically, it is sufficient for him to note that a convicted robber *had many companions*, thereby establishing with one stroke a man's dark reputation as *a rogue* and his subsequently well-deserved execution.[49]

Excessive drinking, gambling, fighting, and consorting with prostitutes were also typically part of a bad male reputation, as was more simply "lewd and lousy language."[50] Given such behavior's frequency in the larger population, however, it indicated an inclination toward crime but did not constitute evidence in itself. Instead, Frantz used such details to contextualize criminals and frequently to pile on, further underscoring the bad character and just deserts of a man he had just executed. Hans Gerstacker (aka Red) *stole a lot [and] also beat a woman during an argument*. The bag maker and tollkeeper Andreas Weyr is justly flogged *because he committed lewdness with three common whores; he already [had] a wife; also embezzled from the tolls*.[51]

The executioner remained just as conventional on the question of female reputation. Like males, many of the women Frantz flogged or executed were tainted by their association with known criminals, often as the consort or wife of a notorious robber. If direct complicity in theft or murder was established, the sentence could be more severe, ranging from chopped-off fingers to death by drowning, as in the case of Margaretha Hörnlein, who acted *as an accessory to the murder of the newly born babies who were killed in her house, and gave the murderers and thieves food so that they might not inform about anything.* Frantz considered women who chose such a lifestyle already immersed in a separate, shady society made up of thieves, robbers, and murderers. Maria Canterin had already been flogged several times and disfigured for being the consort of two executed robbers—*Handsome* and *Glove George*—when she and her current lover, *the Scholar of Bayreuth,* were both executed for new thefts.[52]

Yet whatever her level of involvement in acts of theft or violence, a woman of ill repute was invariably defined principally by her sexual deviancy. With a single word, Frantz and his contemporaries could transform the reputation of any female suspected of promiscuity— much more effectively than with the frequent curse of *rogue* or *whoremonger* for men. Professional prostitutes, "soldiers' consorts," and other "loose females" (many of them victims of rape or incest) are regularly identified in the executioner's journal as *a common street whore, a thief-whore,* or simply *a whore.*[53] Like men who beat their own mothers or who swore at their betters in court, women believed to sleep around were automatically suspect of still graver offenses. Sometimes this results in a compound designation in Frantz's journal—*three citizen children and whores; a plumber's daughter [and] a whore; a cook and whore,* even *an archer's wife and whore*—but more often such women lose all other identity in the executioner's memory, sometimes even including their very names.[54]

The Reformation's preoccupation with sexual deviance made all women—married as well as single or widowed—increasingly vulnerable to accusations of promiscuity and its damaging consequences. In the worst scenarios it was a contributing factor in accusations of witchcraft and infanticide, the two most common grounds for female execution during the early modern era. More commonly, any detected extramarital activity by women led to flogging and banishment or in a few rare cases—usually exacerbated by theft—execution. While women overall made up only 10 percent of the individuals Frantz executed during his career, they constituted over 80 percent of those he put in the stocks and then *whipped out of town with rods* for sexual crimes.[55]

Frantz clearly recognized the double standard applied to men and women, even noting when men convicted of sexual misdemeanors received lesser punishments than their female counterparts, including for incest.[56] Yet he appears more amused than compassionate in quoting the lines scrawled on a church wall by the distraught husband of a woman executed for *lewdness and harlotry . . . with twenty-one married men and youths*, including a father and his son: *"Father and son should have been treated as she was, and the panderers also. In the other world I shall summon and appeal to emperor and king because justice has not been done. I, poor man, suffer though innocent. Farewell and good night."*[57] For Nuremberg's executioner, you were the product of your actions, and if those included *losing [your] honor [i.e., virginity] to a mercenary five years ago* or having *three whore's children*, you were *a whore*.[58]

Surprisingly for the era (and for a pious Lutheran executioner), religious identity remained a completely neutral factor in Frantz Schmidt's assessment of personal reputation and character. He shows no open animosity toward the Catholics he executed (whom he never refers to as papists), remarking only upon a special prayer or communion request on the scaffold.[59] Hans Schrenker (aka the Crawler) cheekily attempted to use his Catholic faith as grounds for postponement of his execution, asking at the scaffold to be permitted *to go on a pilgrimage . . . to his confessor, after which he would return (his request was denied)*. Schmidt's unique uses of *heretic* and *godlessness* each refer to the culprit's particular deed, not his or her religious denomination.[60]

Even Jews, who had been ritually humiliated every Good Friday in the Hof of Frantz's youth and officially banned from the city of Nuremberg since 1498, are mentioned more often sympathetically as victims of executed thieves or robbers than as perpetrators.[61] When Meister Frantz was ordered to publicly strangle (out of mercy) the spy and thief Moses the Jew from Otenfoss, he meticulously notes that *it is fifty-four years since a Jew (named Ambsel) was executed*. There is no reference to the "blood pollution" accusations put forward by modern anti-Semites or any suggestion of more serious punishment than flogging for Hay Jud, convicted of *overtak[ing] the Christian women from behind, in his wantonness intending to rape [them] and all the while pressing on them out of brazenness until his nature was satisfied*. Julius Kunrad—a Jew who had converted to Christianity and boasted several powerful sponsors, including the bishop of Würzburg—likewise received the standard flogging and banishment for bigamy and fornication, even though he also had an illegitimate child with *a common [Christian] whore . . . before he was baptized*. When later that same year (and now calling himself Kunrad from Reichensachsen) Kunrad was executed for robbery, multiple thefts, and murder, Schmidt makes no comments about his religious identity except to observe that on the scaffold he *would not receive the [Lutheran] sacrament, but [desired it] in the Catholic way*.[62]

Frantz Schmidt's careful construction of his own good name rendered him understandably sensitive to abuses of reputation. He became especially incensed when confronted with individuals who assumed a name or social status that was not their own—a fairly easy feat in an era before standard means of verifying personal identity.[63] What modern scholars admiringly call "self-fashioning" and what lawyers characterize as "fraudulent imposture" was a deeply serious and troubling matter for Nuremberg's executioner. He is chagrined that Lienhard Dischinger, who *with false letters and seals [passed himself off as] a transplanted schoolmaster or priest*, escaped with a briefly summarized flogging, and reassured that Kunrad Krafft, who committed numerous frauds under a false name and *giving himself out to be [both] a citizen of Forchheim [and] a councilor of Colmutz*, was ultimately beheaded for his lies.[64] Theft of a good name—as in the case of the notorious forger Gabriel Wolff—threatened the bedrock of Schmidt's worldview more than the stealing of money or property. When he writes about the weaver's daughter Maria Cordula Hunnerin, who was beheaded for her crimes, it is not her sizable thefts from former masters that take center stage but her shameful and scandalous imposture:

> [she] took up at Altdorf with the son of a cloth manufacturer from Schweinfurt, [and,] giving herself out to be the daughter of the innkeeper at the Black Bear in Bayreuth, hired a carriage, drove to the inn there with her betrothed and a soldier's wife, ordered food and drink to be prepared, pointed out an old man in the inn as her father, then left the inn to fetch her sister, leaving the others sitting in the inn, and the soldier's wife had to pay 32 fl.[65]

Of course the use of multiple identities was endemic among professional thieves, a practice that further reinforced their disreputable status. Virtually every one of these individuals whom Frantz encountered in the course of his career boasted at least one alias, and often more. The robber and mercenary Lienhard Kiesswetter *is also known as Lienhart Lubing, Lienhart of Kornstatt, Mosel Lenny, and Sick Lenny*; another young thief already had five aliases by the age of sixteen. An honest man, by contrast, has but one true identity, so Meister Frantz considers it a sign of genuine contrition that Fritz Musterer (aka Little Fritzie; aka Snail) *first told his real name just before being led out [to the gallows], that before he was known as Georg Stengel of Bachhaussen, a thief and robber.* The female consorts of robbers and other professional criminals were likewise known for having multiple aliases, sometimes changing their names as they changed their men. *Thief-whore* Anna Gröschlin (also known as Speedy's Woman) admitted to Frantz that three years previously she *had given herself out as Margaretha Schoberin*, taking the last name of her then consort Georg Schober (as well as assuming a different first name).[66]

Slander, another form of reputational theft, provoked an even stronger emotional response from the status-sensitive executioner, who was himself no stranger to the suffering caused by malicious gossip and prejudice. Many of Frantz's contemporaries shared this point of view, deeming a blow to one's good name more grievous than a wounding of the body. Bastian Grübel (aka Slag) *stole much and besides confessed to twenty murders,* but what most preoccupies Schmidt in his account is how he slandered an enemy, claiming he was an accomplice, which resulted in the innocent man's arrest and torture. Frantz is apparently even more outraged at the former executioner's assistant Friedrich Stigler *for having brought accusations against some citizens' wives here that they were witches . . . However, he wittingly did them wrong*—a serious crime for which Stigler was ultimately beheaded by a disgusted Meister Frantz. Aware of the emotional agony caused by false defamation, Schmidt renders especially harsh judgment on the attempted rapist Valentin Sundermann, who maliciously claimed to have witnessed the mistress of the house *have lewd relations . . . with several journeymen*, and bestows unexpected sympathy on the career thief Georg Mötzela, who languished *in prison for three-quarters of a year because his boy, his whore's nine-year-old brother, accused him of five murders . . . but there was nothing in it.*[67]

Honor could be bestowed or revoked by those in power, men who could be capricious, even cruel. Honesty—and consequently reputation—represented an act of self-determination. By rejecting the caste fatalism of most of his contemporaries and hewing to a path of forthright action that he hoped would lead to a more honorable position in life, Frantz Schmidt unwittingly embraced a more modern concept of individual identity. This was a strikingly humanist approach for a semiliterate autodidact. His subsequent speculations about human nature and free will shared some important insights with the greatest intellects of the day, despite their raw and fractured form of expression. For Frantz, though, philosophical speculation came in a distant second to his simple, practical objective, and in that respect, establishing an honest reputation was a priority without equal.

The victims' avenger

The essential ingredients for a good name were common knowledge at every level of society. An astute and unscrupulous young man might easily have built a public reputation by manipulating perceptions, achieving the semblance of propriety without actually embracing the principles themselves. As witness to so much human cruelty and deception, it would be understandable if Frantz had become apathetic or even cynical about the criminal justice enterprise and its moral ambiguities. After all, as he well knew, not all evildoers got caught or punished and not all victims were completely blameless in their own misfortunes. Satisfactory performance of his duty, moreover, did not demand any passion for justice or profound belief in the righteousness of his daily work. Early on he might have decided to focus solely on his own self-advancement and the outward conformity it entailed.

A lifetime of journal entries confirms, to the contrary, that Frantz Schmidt was not only a willing executioner but also a passionate one. His outrage at the atrocities committed by robbers and arsonists appears genuine and his commitment to restoring social order likewise heartfelt, not grudging or calculated. His empathy for victims, especially those *robbed of all [their] worldly possessions*, is frequently and convincingly expressed. Rather than suppressing or denying his emotions, in other words, Meister Frantz chose to channel them, providing the only relief he could to the victims of crime—legal retribution.

Frantz's personal definition of justice was highly traditional, and thus distinctly different from that of the imperial law that supposedly guided him.[68] While invoking "ancient custom" and "divine commands," legal and religious reformers of the sixteenth century strove for a new conceptual coherence in criminal law, based on the respective authorities they represented. In this more abstract model, the principal injured parties in a crime were no longer a victim and his or her kin group, but the legal sovereign and God Himself. For Frantz Schmidt, by contrast, all crime remained in essence an act of personal betrayal, either of another individual or of a group. Trust, not obedience to God or state, was the more sacred bond criminals violated, and the greater the degree of that violation, the more infamous the criminal for Meister Frantz.

Learned jurists expanded the definition of treason, for instance, to include not just the betrayal of a superior but a variety of social transgressions they considered rebellions against divinely ordained secular authority itself—the subsequent focus of most new legislation. Yet for Frantz and most of his contemporaries, even political treason continued to be viewed in personal injuries rather than abstract terms. In the ongoing cold war between the city of Nuremberg and the margrave of Ansbach, for instance, both sides regularly employed rangers, spies, and other mercenaries to gather intelligence or to capture agents.[69] His journal entries on these various acts of "treason," however, show no emotion until he comes to the traitor Hans Ramsperger, who

> betrayed many citizens of Nuremberg and poachers, of whom some ten were executed and nothing found on them [i.e., no incriminating evidence]. Also betrayed the town of Nuremberg to the old margrave, revealing where the walls were weakest and most easily stormed and offering if possible to do his best to bring this to pass. Also offered to betray Herr Hans Jacob Haller, at Weyer's house, as well as Herr Schmitter and Master Weyermann or bring them to prison.

Although Ramsperger was ultimately *executed with the sword here out of mercy,* his executioner adds with evident satisfaction that *his body*

A court notary's sketch of the traitor Hans Ramsperger's dismembered limbs and head, publicly displayed at the gallows (1588).

[was then] quartered, and each limb attached to a different corner of the scaffold and the head stuck on a pole above them.[70]

Counterfeiting, another crime elevated by the jurist authors of the *Carolina* to a capital offense against the state (punishable by burning alive), was similarly gauged by Nuremberg's executioner in terms of personal injury. Beyond the insult to Nuremberg's magistracy, he thus finds it difficult to express much outrage at this nonviolent crime and reports the offenses in the same dry manner as other thefts. Even Nuremberg's leaders displayed some ambivalence about the officially prescribed punishment, consistently commuting the severe sentence of burning alive to decapitation and subsequent burning.[71]

By contrast, descriptions of violations of the master-servant relationship, still another crime the jurists redefined in terms of treason, consistently evoked an emotional reaction in Meister Frantz, but not because he thought they represented some profound threat to the social order. He writes approvingly that a maid who murdered her patrician mistress was given *two nips with burning tongs on both arms as she was led out on a wagon,* and after she was executed with the sword her body *thrown in the gallows pit and her head stuck on an iron over the gallows.*[72] Yet what has really most outraged the executioner was the personal betrayal of a trusting employer, an old lady the culprit stabbed in her own bed at night. Nuremberg's magistrates were predictably more severe with servants who stole large amounts from their masters, and here too Frantz appears more acutely attuned to the degree of personal betrayal involved, Maria Cordula Hunnerin not just *stealing 800 fl. worth in thaler and three kreuzer pieces from the safe box of her master,* but from one *she served for half a year.* Still more treacherously, Hans Merckel (aka Deer John), *who was in service for twenty-two years,* made a career of betraying various masters, *stay[ing] half a year to two years in one place and then leav[ing], taking away with him hose, doublets, boots, woolen shirts, and whatever money he could get.*[73]

Patricide, like regicide, represented the supreme act of treason in a patriarchal society, and here at last Meister Frantz was in complete agreement with the jurists. He was incredulous over the reprehensible behavior of Peter Köchl, who beat *his own father* severely and repeatedly over the course of many years before ultimately ambushing him on a street *and inflict[ing] seven wounds on him, leaving him for dead.* Köchl was spared the usual execution by wheel only because his father survived the last attack. The patricide Frantz Seuboldt had no such luck, having shown much greater premeditation and malevolence in first attempting to poison his father and finally shooting him from behind some bushes. The motives behind both attacks were never even mentioned by Frantz. Not until much later in life does he openly express sympathy with a woman who attempted to poison her own abusive father on account of the father's being a *violent, wicked man [who] treated her harshly.*[74]

Betrayal of a kinsman or kinswoman in general dismayed Meister Frantz to a much greater degree than all but the most heinous acts of violence, again indicative of a more ancient notion of justice in play. He was appalled that Ulrich Gerstenacker not only killed his own brother but *also drove out with [him] to the woods [where he] slew and murdered him with premeditation* and afterward pretended it was an accident. Hans Müllner similarly ambushed his own sister in the woods, with the still more disturbing aggravating factors that she was pregnant and he *committed lewdness with her [corpse]*. Can there be any doubt about the just fate for people who were so low as to steal from their own cousins or a young man who *threatened to burn down the houses of his relatives and guardians for refusing him money, though he had formerly squandered it on women and whores?*[75] Most disgracefully, Cunz Nenner

> *stole up to 60 fl. worth [of items] from one of his relatives at Perngau and when the latter thrashed him for it he threatened to burn his house, so that the relative had to agree to pay 50 fl. besides. Also threatened to burn the house of one of his relatives—who, out of pity, had brought up his young daughter in his house for four years—if he did not give the eight-year-old child some wages. Then also threatened one of his relatives at the Rockstock, from whom he had stolen a cow and who had recovered it, that if he did not give him 15 fl. he would burn down his house.*[76]

It was the shameless long-term violation of the sacred blood bond that was at the center of his description of *Laurenz Schropp, a miller's man from Lichtenau [who] worked for twenty-two years at his cousin's mill, stealing wheat from him, yet by his own account he* only [!] *gained about 400 fl.* (emphasis added)—a considerable amount of money even over the course of more than two decades.[77] "At what price honor or decency?" is the unspoken question of Nuremberg's repulsed executioner.

Always identifying with the victims, Meister Frantz reserved his greatest sympathy for people of inferior status who were abused by those in positions of authority and trust. Attacks against children in particular filled him with a fierce loathing and indignation. Amid the otherwise laconic entries of his early days, Frantz carefully details the thoroughly reprehensible assault of Hans Müllner (aka the Molder), *who raped a girl of thirteen years of age, filling her mouth with sand so that she might not cry out*. His shock at a similar betrayal of childish trust by Endres Feuerstein is conveyed by listing the respective ages of the five girls the young man raped at his father's private school (six, seven, eight, nine, and twelve) and pointedly adding that *two among them he damaged so [severely] that one could no longer hold any water [and] the city midwives nursed [the other] for a long time, believing she would die.* The more disturbing the outrage, the more specific Frantz becomes about the age of the victim, as in his description of a farmhand who *tried to rape a girl of 3½ [but] the mother came in and prevented him.*[78] The executioner notes with relish that he repeatedly nipped with fiery tongs the robber Georg Taucher, who broke into a house and *murdered a tavern keeper's son . . . cutting his neck and throat, [and] tak[ing] money from the till,* and years later gives the same torturous execution to Georg Müllner (aka Lean George), who, with his companions, broke into a farmer's house at night, cut his throat, and *attack[ed] the same farmer's son (whom the father had hidden in the oven), stabbing him in the thigh and stealing much, so that the farmer's son died eight days later.*[79]

Beyond the brutal violation of childish trust and innocence, the unnatural contrast in age between perpetrator and victim troubled the empathetic executioner. He first establishes that Gabriel Heroldt was *a tailor and citizen and warden of the Frog Tower here at Nuremberg [and] a man of advanced age* before describing Heroldt's full offense, namely that *he violently raped Katherina Reichlin, who was under his charge as a prisoner, and committed lewdness with her. The year previously he tried several times by force to commit lewdness with a girl of thirteen but could not take her honor from her because of her youth.*[80] It is the final blow against the forger and confidence man Kunrad Krafft that he also swindled money from the wardships of children, and likewise fully appropriate that the carpenter Georg Egloff be executed for *deliberately kill[ing] his apprentice, who owed him 9 fl., with his carpenter's file in a beech wood.*[81]

Violence against children in any form was hard enough for Meister Frantz to forgive; violence against one's own flesh and blood remained utterly incomprehensible and unpardonable to him. Throughout his long career, Frantz executed twenty women for infanticide; in every instance he showed himself especially sensitive to the unnatural horror of the deed. Most commonly, he refers to the mother *squeez[ing] [the child's] little neck,* or *crushing the little head,* and in one instance *murderously stabb[ing] [the male child] with a knife in the left breast.*[82] As in Frantz's descriptions of vicious robbers, the contrast of innocence and brutality remains a consistent theme. He vividly re-creates how

Dorothea Meüllin *stopped up the mouth with earth and made a grave with her hand in which she buried the struggling child.* Other *heartless mothers* appear no less brutal: Margaretha Marranti gave birth during the night near a shed by the Pegnitz River and *as soon as [the child] stirred its arms and struggled, she threw it into the water and drowned it.* Other equally disturbing means of disposal included burying in a barn, locking in a trunk, casting into a heap of garbage, or, most shocking, throwing alive into the privy.[83] Having participated in the interrogations of each of these women, some of which included the threat of torture, the executioner knew that many of them were emotionally or mentally disturbed, particularly the murderers of older children, such as Anna Strölin and Anna Freyin. Yet he made no pretense of being concerned about issues of medical or legal competence, and was instead preoccupied with rage at the grisly vision of Strölin, who with *premeditation slew her own child, a boy of six years of age, with an ax,* only sparing her other four children at the last moment.[84]

Attacks on old people and the sick similarly outraged Meister Frantz's sense of basic social trust, as they would anyone in any society. It's not hard to imagine his shock at two drunken journeymen's assault and attempted rape of *an eighty-year-old woman* or other violent incidents where the victim was elderly.[85] Frantz is surprised yet pleased when Hans Hoffman, already banned six times from Nuremberg, was *caught in the act of stealing clothes from the infected people at the Lazareth [hospice] . . . and the Honorable Council ordered the sentence to be read in front of the Lazareth by a town beadle,* after which *he was then led out of the Lazareth and executed here at Nuremberg with the rope.* Such a proceeding, the executioner adds for emphasis, *had never been heard of or seen before.* Yet one week later, on October 21, 1585, four thieves were hanged for the related crime of breaking into the houses of recently dead people, and all but one such offender in subsequent years were similarly dispatched.[86] No such extreme consequences followed for the convicted thief and adulterer Heinz Teurla, but Meister Frantz registers his personal disgust that *he made a child with a poor maid who had no legs.*[87]

Given Frantz's deeply felt sentiments about betrayal and kinship, it is slightly jarring to read his muted account of Georg Preisigel, who *killed his wife and afterward hanged her to make it look like she had*

The cover illustration of a broadsheet account of a father who strangled his own wife and two small children, then hanged himself (*right*). His corpse was later dragged through the streets of Schaffhausen and then placed atop a wheel at the execution grounds (*left*) (1561).

hanged and killed herself. Also formerly stabbed a man with a skewer; or, still briefer, of Hans Dopffer (aka Schilling) *who with premeditation and for no cause on her part, stabbed and murdered his wife, who was very pregnant.* Meister Frantz by no means condoned spousal murder, but he also showed little interest in probing the basis for domestic disputes (especially during this phase of his career), summarizing crimes of this nature with the same brevity normally reserved for mundane thefts. In what should be a sensational case, we hear only that Margaretha Brechtlin *gave her husband, Hans Prechtel (a carpenter in Gostenhof), insect powder in a porridge, also in eggs and lard, although he did not die at once of it.*[88] The drama of plots interweaving infidelity and greed were left entirely to the popular press and theater, where they predictably enjoyed great success.[89]

When no threat to life or limb was involved, Meister Frantz's level of interest in victimized spouses sagged even more perceptibly. Adultery, a personal betrayal of a profound nature, might be expected to have raised the executioner's ire. In the sixteenth century, the offense was punishable by flogging and banishment; bigamy was even defined by the *Carolina* and a host of contemporary German law codes as a capital crime (although uniformly punished in Nuremberg the same as adultery). Meister Frantz's flagrant lack of interest in this kind of infidelity, however, is obvious in his terse journal entries, such as *whipped out of town here with rods Peter Rittler from Steinbühl who took two wives,* or—as the case may be—*took three wives;* or *took four wives and impregnated two [of them];* or *took five women in marriage and committed lewdness with them.*[90] In each passage, this supposedly shocking transgression is summarized in a sentence or two, with no attempt on Frantz's part to include the names of all the parties, let alone any of the circumstances. The only time he's moved to write another line of description is when children are known to be involved.[91] Occasionally, in fact, he seems to mention bigamy only as an afterthought, as in the conclusion of the long list of crimes committed by one executed offender, *lastly, tak[ing] a second wife during the life of his first wife, and a third wife during the life of the second, after the death of the first.* He cannot even remember the name *of a farmhand who stole a chain from the gallows at Statt Hilpoltstein and took two wives.*[92]

Should we read into Frantz's seeming indifference to adultery some unhappiness or even strife between the executioner and his own wife, Maria? Or could it suggest implicit evidence of his own infidelity? In view of Frantz's burning preoccupation with appearances, the latter scenario seems unlikely, especially since even a casual relationship could undermine all his years of reputation building quite literally overnight. As for the happiness or unhappiness of his marriage to Maria, it remains impossible to gauge. The executioner never mentions his family life in the journal, and all we can learn from other sources is that the union produced seven children and lasted twenty-two years, until Maria's death at the age of fifty-five. Whatever form his own marital relationship took, Frantz shared in the common belief of his time that whatever happened within a household—short of murder or potentially fatal violence—remained a strictly private matter. Whether a cuckolded husband wanted to take his adulterous wife back several times or have her imprisoned repeatedly, Frantz considered it their business, requiring official intervention only when it became a public disturbance.[93]

Becoming a Nuremberger

Establishing a good name among wary locals remained a lifelong endeavor for Meister Frantz. Establishing his family's financial security, by contrast, took nowhere near that long. In December 1579, not yet two years into his initial contract, Frantz requested a New Year's bonus—a custom he knew of from his late brother-in-law—which his superiors readily granted. When he returned the following winter asking for a significant raise of 0.5 fl. per week, he was rebuffed, first with the promise of another annual bonus and later with an additional gift of 6 fl.[94] Four years later the young executioner made another attempt at securing a permanent raise and was again turned away, although this time with a one-time bonus of 12 fl., equivalent to more than a month's salary. Undeterred, the young executioner continued to press his claims and on September 25, 1584, finally achieved his next major career goal: a guarantee of lifelong employment at the requested higher salary, as well as a modest pension upon his retirement. By the terms of the contract, Frantz promised

> to be true, obedient, and dutiful to my gracious lords all the days of my life and to serve their needs and protect them from harm to the best of my abilities . . . never to serve anyone outside of this city, no matter where, without permission of the Honorable Council, in return for which my lords graciously grant me 3 fl. weekly and a New Year's bonus of 6 fl . . . until on account of age or other illness or infirmity I can no longer carry out my office.[95]

More to his superiors' relief, the ambitious executioner also swore "never again to seek any increase in salary"—an oath he assiduously kept for the next thirty-four years.

Frantz's negotiating talents aside, there are several explanations for his employers' generous concessions. For many years before Schmidt's arrival, the city had struggled to find an executioner who was at once skillful, honest, and reliable. Meister Frantz had proven himself to be all three, and was still only thirty years old. Nor had it escaped the city councilors' attention that Meister Heinrich of Bamberg was ailing and that his exceptionally capable son was a likely candidate to be his successor.[96] At a time when Nuremberg's courts were on average sentencing a dozen people a year to death and ordering corporal punishments for twenty more, city leaders dreaded the backlog and legal headaches that would ensue if they lost Schmidt and had to search for a replacement. Whether an outside offer was actually proffered by Bamberg's chamberlain (whom Frantz knew well) or merely implied by the young executioner himself, he achieved his desired outcome.

As is often the case, Frantz's greatest professional success to date was followed by an exceptionally difficult year. First, he was confronted with the unenviable task of torturing and executing his own brother-in-law. Friedrich Werner (aka Potter Freddy) was, by his own account, "bad from youth on," even though his late father had been a well-known citizen and his stepfather a respectable potter. It's not clear from the surviving records how or when such a "truly evil" character ended up marrying Frantz's widowed sister, but the unhappy union does underscore how severely limited the marriage options were for an executioner's daughter. For years the "strong and handsome" mercenary Werner had roamed the countryside "with evil company, committing multiple thefts, burglaries, and home invasions, as well as many robberies."[97] More gravely, he confessed to three murders, including that of *a boy alone in the Fischbach Wood*, and several attempted murders, the most shocking being the brutal robbing of *a wife in the Schwabach Wood, [whom] he left for dead.*[98]

When finally arrested and brought face-to-face with his brother-in-law in the Nuremberg interrogation chamber, Werner implausibly claimed "he [had] no idea why he [had] been imprisoned." If he was truly an innocent man, the magistrates countered, why then would he be operating under an alias, as he had been in Hersbruck, using the name "Jorg Schmidt"? Meister Frantz's reaction to this particular charge is not recorded, but his anger and shame must have been palpable. On the heels of more denials from Werner, he placed the culprit in the strappado—without the usual warning—and began interrogation "with the small stone." After a torture session of unspecified length, Werner's bravado faded and he eventually confessed to numerous crimes.

It's not hard to infer how Frantz felt about his notorious brother-in-law, a man who had not only committed heinous crimes but also one whose ties to the Schmidt family threatened to destroy the executioner's own carefully nurtured reputation. It's telling to note that although several eyewitness accounts confirmed the kinship between the two men, Frantz himself never once mentions it in his journal entry about the execution. Yet perhaps out of deference to his sister, Frantz dissuaded his superiors from carrying out the unprecedented sentence of "six nips with glowing tongs . . . two in front of the town hall, two in front of St. Lorenz Church, and two by St. Martha's at the [city's] gate," to be followed by a prolonged death beneath the wheel. So many nips, Schmidt argued, would likely kill the condemned man before he arrived at the execution grounds. The magistrates accordingly consented to only two, as long as the executioner agreed to make "a horrifying example" of Werner. They rejected, however, "with gentle words," the petition of Werner's stepfather and sister to mitigate the wheel sentence to beheading. Thus they compelled the executioner to treat his brother-in-law like any other murdering robber, administering the prescribed two nips while riding the tumbrel to the Raven Stone and then carrying out a brutal execution with the wheel.

On the day of the execution, as Meister Frantz stowed the hot tongs and prepared to stake Werner out, the chaplain asked the poor sinner if he had "any other evil deeds to confess," both to ease his own soul's passing and to prevent suspicion from falling on an innocent person. One chronicler records that Werner then "spoke for a long time at the execution stone with the priests and also with the hangman, who was his brother-in-law." Another account re-creates some of that conversation, reporting that "Meister Frantz, who was his brother-in-law, reassured him that he wanted to help him get through it as quickly as possible," if only Werner would reveal more about his crimes. Instead, the condemned man merely repeated the names of previously executed companions and then declared that he had spoken enough. He directed his final words to Meister Frantz, who stood by, wheel in hand, cryptically asking the executioner to remember him to the daughter of butcher Wolf Kleinlein. Whatever Werner's intended meaning, his brother-in-law swiftly proceeded to administer thirty-one blows with the wheel, demonstrating to all those assembled his complete repudiation of this notorious *murderer and robber*. Frantz Schmidt had worked too hard and come too far to be dragged back into the gutter by such a man.[99]

Within a few months of Werner's execution in February 1585, Frantz

A city chronicler's portrayal of Meister Frantz executing his own brother-in-law, the robber Friedrich Werner (1616).

himself suffered several profoundly personal blows. In the spring, his father, Heinrich, died. No precise record of the death or burial has survived; we know only that it was after February 22, Meister Heinrich's last public execution, and before May 1, when his estate was subsequently divided between his daughter in Kulmbach and his son in Nuremberg. Meister Heinrich's long-serving assistant, Hans Reinschmidt, succeeded his master as executioner of Bamberg.[100] Before the month of May was out, Heinrich's widow had also died and Frantz returned to Bamberg to take care of his late stepmother's affairs.[101]

What did it mean to Frantz that his father had died before their shared dream of restored family honor could become a reality? At least Heinrich had survived long enough to witness his son's contract for life with the famous city of Nuremberg, as well as the births of three grandchildren. Unfortunately, Frantz scarcely had time to grieve for his father and stepmother before another calamity struck. That summer, yet another epidemic of the plague hit Nuremberg, this one killing more than five thousand people over the course of the next several months.[102]

Tragically, Frantz's own four-year-old Vitus and three-year-old Margaretha were among the victims. Child deaths were a much more common occurrence in premodern Europe than today, but that did not make them any less painful for their parents. The precise dates of Vitus's and Margaretha's deaths were lost in the confusion of the epidemic, but we do know that sometime in 1585 Frantz bought a family plot in Saint Rochus, one of Nuremberg's more prestigious cemeteries, located just outside the city walls.[103] Perhaps he felt this was as much honor as he could attain for his two little children, lost before their young father could even hope to complete his quest to restore the family name. More we cannot say.

Work for the city's executioner, meanwhile, continued to mount. In 1585 alone, Schmidt would execute eleven people and flog nineteen, as well as undertake numerous interrogations. Overall, during his first decade of work for the city of Nuremberg, Meister Frantz performed 191 floggings, 71 hangings, 48 beheadings, 11 wheel executions, 5 finger-choppings, and 3 ear-clippings. His busiest year was 1588 (13 executions and 27 corporal punishments); his slowest was his first, 1578 (only 4 executions and 13 floggings). On average he put to death 13.4 people annually during this period and administered 20 corporal punishments. The great majority of executions took place in Nuremberg, but Frantz also traveled once or twice a year—always with official permission—to work in rural locations, particularly the towns of Hilpoltstein and Hersbruck, or to perform the occasional freelance interrogation or execution.[104]

At home, grief over the two early deaths gradually yielded to the joys and hectic pace of a newly expanding family. On January 21, 1587, Frantz and Maria were blessed with the birth of a daughter, whom they christened Rosina. Soon "Rosie" and her older brother, Jorg, who had survived the plague, were joined by Maria on June 8, 1588, Frantz Steffan on July 16, 1591, and finally, on December 13, 1596, the baby of the family, Johannes, also known as Frantzenhans.[105] The now bountiful Schmidt household was itself a proclamation of the *Hausvater's* growing prosperity and prominence in the community. Most artisanal families and a still larger share of poorer households remained considerably smaller, with incomes that could support on average only two or three children.[106] Aged parents also lived with their children in some wealthier households, and the Schmidt family could have certainly afforded this had any of Frantz or Maria's parents still been alive.

The culminating social achievement of Frantz's first two decades in Nuremberg came on July 14, 1593, almost exactly forty years after his family's disgrace at the hands of Margrave Albrecht. Citizenship in an imperial city was a cherished privilege, requiring both significant property and a stellar reputation. It was thus out of reach for most residents of sixteenth-century Nuremberg, including of course all officially disreputable individuals. Shortly after celebrating his fifteenth anniversary as the city's executioner, Frantz Schmidt made the bold move of petitioning the city council for that very status. Taken aback, the magistrates exclaimed that no executioner had ever held citizenship in Nuremberg, to which Meister Frantz countered that he sought the legal status less for the present than for the future, when he hoped his children *would take up another trade* and he himself could retire to pursue a second career. "Since he has to this point performed his office irreproachably," the council declared, the executioner's request was approved and he became one of only 108 individuals granted the status of citizen in Nuremberg that year. Still considered dishonorable, Frantz was ordered to take his oath separately, on the day after thirteen other new citizens. But this was a slight that he could readily endure, given the wide range of legal protections that the ever-more-confident and prosperous executioner had just secured for himself and his progeny.[107] Seven years later, the forty-five-year-old Frantz Schmidt could enter the new century as a full-fledged citizen of one of the greatest cities in the empire, assured of a lifetime of lucrative employment and free housing for himself, his wife, and their five children, aged four to fifteen. It was a remarkable achievement for a hangman's son, but in Meister Frantz's eyes it still fell far short of the ultimate goal.

4

THE SAGE

Just as the Stoics say that vices are introduced for our profit, to give value and assistance to virtue, we can say with better reason and less rashness, that nature has given us pain so that we may appreciate and be thankful for comfort and the absence of pain.   —Michel de Montaigne, "On Experience" (1580)[1]

> This my long sufferance, and my day of grace,
> They who neglect and scorn, shall never taste;
> But hard be hardened, blind be blinded more,
> That they may stumble on, and deeper fall;
> And none but such from mercy I exclude.
> —John Milton, *Paradise Lost*, book 3: 198–202 (1667)

It did not take the veteran Meister Frantz long to conclude that the barber-surgeon Hans Haylandt was *a very bad character*. Shortly before his beheading on March 15, 1597, Haylandt had been convicted of a particularly cold-blooded murder, recounted by his executioner in vivid detail:

> *[Haylandt] and his companion, Killian Ayrer, went out with a youth from Rotenfels who had been servant to a gentleman at Frankfurt, and when they stopped at midnight to drink at the fountain near Eschenburg, Ayrer asked the youth for a ginger, which he gave him, and as the youth was combing his hair, Ayrer slipped something into his own food and gave it to [the youth]. When [the youth]*

*couldn't stand out of weakness, [Ayrer] knocked him on the head,
so that he fell and said ouch. Haylandt, however, proceeded to cut
his throat and robbed him of 200 fl., which money his master at
Frankfurt had given him in their presence and asked them both to
go with the youth so that he might come safely with the money to
Rotenfels, since he knew them both, one from Hamburg, the other
from Rotenfels. While home in Frankfurt, they together planned
this murderous assault, before they departed, and when they carried out the murder by the fountain they took a stone from a vineyard and tied it with [the youth's] belt to his body, carried the same
over a meadow and threw it in the Main so that it sank into the
water; the bloody cudgel [they] buried. The next day the lord of
Eschenburg wanted to go into his vineyard, thus [his] dogs dug the
bloody cudgel back up. He also saw that a stone had been torn from
his garden wall, [whereupon] he went in search of the trail and saw
that something very bloody had been dragged across the meadow and
tossed in the water, and thus found the murder victim. After the two
[murderers] divvied up the money, the barber had journeyed to
Nuremberg (believing that if he hadn't helped or been present, the
deed wouldn't have become public). The murdered youth's father
went after him and had him arrested here [in Nuremberg] so that
he then had to confess.*[2]

This account features all the hallmarks of infamy that Meister
Frantz most reviled: a coldly premeditated murder for the sake of money,
betrayal of the trust of both the youth and his master, a cowardly ambush, and deliberate desecration of the youth's corpse. It also bears
several literary embellishments—in striking contrast to the terse journal
entries of Schmidt's youth. The now middle-aged executioner begins
his account by setting the scene, intentionally drawing a tranquil picture of three traveling companions stopping for a midnight snack at an
outdoor fountain, in order to heighten the reader's shock over the violent act that comes next. He conveys the sheer perfidy of the deed by
choosing details that heighten the contrast between good and evil: the
youth readily shared his provisions and innocently combed his hair as
Ayrer went about poisoning the food. The blow on the head, the
youth's exclamation, and the quick slashing of his throat all vividly re-

created a moment of intense violence. To be sure, Meister Frantz was no literary genius—his dialogue ("ouch") could particularly use some work—but by the second half of his life, he had clearly begun to apply his imagination as he recorded the culprits and crimes he encountered. Most significantly, he began to explore in writing the motives behind various actions that in his early days were simply ascribed to bad character or not probed at all.

Why do people do cruel things to one another, and why does God permit it? Frantz did not need to be a theologian, conversant in teachings on theodicy and divine providence, to wonder about the seeming capriciousness of human suffering and death or the inadequacies of human justice. As the executor of that justice, he could take some satisfaction in the punishment, and perhaps even redemption, of evildoers, but he realized long before that the solace offered to victims or the surviving family and friends of those killed was short-lived, incomplete, and often entirely elusive. By the age of forty-six, he had already spent nearly three decades immersed in the dark side of the human condition and was frequently compelled to resort to violence and deceit himself in the interrogation and punishment of those individuals who happened to get caught. Subjected to unceasing cruelty and suffering, Frantz, like any law enforcement official, had to marshal a significant degree of either detachment or personal faith to be able to carry on for so many years. Yet the source of that inner strength, beyond a fervent determination to restore the family's honor, remains the most elusive part of the man's identity.

In addition to his soul-killing work, Frantz Schmidt had other reasons to grow more pessimistic, bitter, and even cynical as he aged. Despite having achieved lifelong economic security and even citizenship, he and his family still suffered exclusion from respectable bourgeois society in ways both subtle and stark. More tragically, the new century had scarcely dawned when the horrors of the world struck at him directly. On February 15, 1600, during the coldest winter on record in Nuremberg, a new outbreak of plague claimed sixteen-year-old Jorg, Frantz's oldest surviving son. Five days later, the grief-stricken Schmidt family followed a funeral cortege to the family plot in Saint Rochus Cemetery, Jorg's coffin borne by his classmates from the Saint Egidien Latin School. Within three weeks, Frantz's wife of just over twenty years, fifty-five-year-old Maria, herself expired, probably felled by the same epidemic that had taken her son and would eventually rob more than twenty-five hundred area residents of their lives. This time "several of [Schmidt's] neighbors, voluntarily, out of goodwill," carried the coffin to the cemetery, indifferent to any dishonor this final act of respect might bring to them. Perhaps such tender, long-desired signs of communal acceptance mitigated the sting of these successive personal blows to Nuremberg's executioner. When Frantz Schmidt walked away from the fresh graves of his wife and young son on March 12, 1600, he was a forty-six-year-old widower with four surviving children between the ages of four and thirteen.[3]

The emotional impact of these two losses must have been staggering, but the bereaved father and husband did not leave a record of his grief; there are no personal references at all in the journal. Whatever his degree of emotional or religious turmoil, Meister Frantz pushed on in his work, six weeks later beheading two thieves and resuming his other duties. Most widowers in his era remarried within a year of their spouse's death, especially if there were still young children at home. Out of grief—or the simple lack of willing prospects—Frantz Schmidt never wed again, relying instead on thirteen-year-old Rosina and twelve-year-old Maria, with the help of a domestic maid, to run the household and look after their younger brothers. The family's isolated mini-society, saddened and diminished in numbers, persevered.

What do faith and redemption mean in such a harsh and unjust world? What roles do divine providence and individual choice play in it all? During the years that follow Frantz's own personal tragedies, a growing fascination with the hows and whys of human behavior began to dominate his journal entries. As his attempts to find order and meaning among the world's seeming chaos intensified, Frantz increasingly relied on the literary techniques common in the popular crime literature of the day, which he undoubtedly knew well.[4] Seemingly random events became coherent stories, evoking both pathos and resolution. His villains—most commonly bloodthirsty robbers and murderous relatives—were the same as those of the tabloid press of the day. Unlike the writers of cheap broadsheets and popular sermons, however, he neither moralized nor generalized about motives. For Meister Frantz, sin and crime remained profoundly personal, the product of character and choices, not cosmic external forces. His personal interactions with culprits and victims alike undoubtedly reinforced this preference for the concrete over the abstract. They also sensitized him to the individual nature of both sin and redemption. In his full embrace of the Lutheran teaching of salvation by faith alone, the middle-aged Frantz paradoxically became both more judgmental and more forgiving of the poor sinners before him. Would this belief in an ultimately merciful God—the solace of so many converted felons he executed—provide the executioner himself with some comfort amid his many personal travails and solitary quest?

Crimes of malice

As Meister Frantz's journal entries begin to grow in both length and complexity, it becomes clear that there are two standards by which he judged the severity of a crime: first, the degree to which both personal and social trust had been violated, and second, the level of malice that was shown by the perpetrator. Crimes that were premeditated, gratuitously cruel, or otherwise indecent indicated to the executioner that the perpetrator had voluntarily rejected the norms of civilized behavior and placed himself (or occasionally herself) outside society—had become, in a moral as well as legal sense, an outlaw. Highwaymen and other robbers were, in that respect, the most dramatically antisocial, and therefore culpable, of all the poor sinners who came before Meister Frantz—and subsequently merited the worst torture and punishment when caught. Seemingly ordinary individuals, however, were also capable of exceptionally malicious acts, as Frantz continually discovered throughout his long career. Though not professional outlaws, they were nonetheless guilty of the same willful rejection of divine and human laws. Like Cain and Satan before them, malicious criminals were defined by their deliberate self-isolation from the norms and comforts of "decent" society—a choice that was incomprehensible to the involuntarily outcast executioner.

The most recurrent example of malice in Frantz's journal is the coldly calculated violation of trust represented by the act of ambush or surprise attack. More dangerous than people who pretended to be something that they were not or those who slandered the innocent, the ambushing murderer repudiated the most basic level of human trust, and therefore decency itself. Whatever the relationship between the individuals in question or the degree of violence involved in such an attack, the reprehensible combination of malice and deceit hit a special nerve with Meister Frantz. The young executioner had encountered this brand of treachery during the first year of his career in the case of the robber Barthel Mussel, who *cut the throat of a man who was sleeping with him on the straw in a stable and took his money.* Thirteen years later, Frantz is equally appalled that Georg Teurla *struck a puppet maker apprentice on the head with a club in a meadow when he told the other there was something in his shoe, [then] stabbed him in the neck with a dagger and quickly covered him up.* In the same vein, Hans Krug *deceptively asked his companion, Simon, to see what kind of shirt he had on and then stabbed him in the neck with a knife he had brought there and hidden on him.*[5] The utter treachery of the act is often underscored by the mundane setting: a man turns and attacks his pregnant sister *on the*

A dastardly ambush of an innocent traveler by two robbers. Note the glee of the perpetrators and the fear of the victim (1543).

road as they returned from their usual work; a forester kills his brother *while driving a sled in the woods*; a woman strikes her friend on the head from behind with an ax, *when [supposedly] looking for lice and stroking her hair.*

As in broadsheet accounts of crime, Frantz's inclusion of descriptive details lent his stories dramatic verisimilitude, while simultaneously conveying the stark cold-bloodedness of the murderers. When a messenger was sent to collect a debt from Lienhard Taller (aka Spit Lenny), the farmer immediately handed over the payment and invited the servant *to spend the night with him, sleeping on a bench in the parlor. While he was sitting and talking to him, [Taller] seized an ax from the wall and gave him two blows on the head, killing him immediately and taking back the money.* Even more chillingly, the mercenary Steffan Stayner calmly *stabbed [a companion] on the left side so that it came out on the right side, [then] afterward cleaned off his foil before [the other] fell.*[6] One of Frantz's most detailed accounts of an ambush juxtaposes the violence of the attack itself and the perpetrator's ultimate punishment, thereby establishing the familiar equilibrium in cruelty that was the executioner's mainstay:

> *Georg Franck from Poppenreuth, a smith's man and a soldier, persuaded Fair Annala to let him escort her to meet Martin Schönherlin, her betrothed, at Bruck on the Leuth in Hungary. When he, with Christoph Frisch, also a mercenary, had brought her into a wood—the two having made a plot [about her]—Christoph struck her on the head with a stake from behind, so that she fell. [He] then dealt two more blows as she lay there. Franck also struck her once or twice and then cut her throat. They stripped her of everything except her shift and left her lying there, selling the clothes at Durn Hembach for 5 florins . . . Executed here with the wheel, first both arms, the third stroke on the chest, as decreed.*[7]

In these and other ambushes, Schmidt consistently underscores that the evil deed was done *with premeditation*, with malice aforethought—a distinction also stressed by the legal codes and judges of the day.[8] As in most societies today, legal authorities always deemed premeditated murder to be worse than simple manslaughter and accordingly punished it more harshly. The journeyman executioner is clearly appalled when the thief Georg Taucher *murdered a tavern keeper's son [during a break-in] at three o'clock in the morning . . . cutting his neck and throat*, but the crime is made still more reprehensible in that it was done *intentionally with a knife he carried about him for this purpose*. Similarly, when Anna Strölin *slew her own child, a boy of six years of age, with an ax*, or Hans Dopffer *stabbed and murdered his wife, who was very pregnant*, Schmidt feels compelled to stress in each case that the shocking murder was committed *with premeditation*.⁹

For Meister Frantz, the ideal man was honest, pious, loyal, respectful, and brave. Calculating murderers, such as the patricide Frantz Seuboldt, represented the perfect inversion of this heroic type. It was bad enough that Seuboldt, *out of premeditated hate and desire, killed his own father*, but his chosen method was particularly cowardly and unmanly:

> *[He] lay in wait for his very own father (a steward at Osternohe in the castle) upon his fowling ground, hiding behind a rock [and] covering himself with brushwood so that he couldn't be seen. When his father climbed a pole (which they call the ambush tree [underscoring the irony]) to take down the decoy-bird, he shot him with a round of four bullets, so that he died the next day. Although no one knew who had done it, as he fled from the place and while running [he] dropped and lost a glove, which a tailor at Gräfenberg had patched for him the day before. This [glove] was found by a woman, thereby revealing the deed.*

Seuboldt's treacherous and unnatural deed, despite his careful planning, was uncovered thanks to his own carelessness, a bit of early modern crime detection, and perhaps divine providence. Following his full confession (including that *the year before he had tried to poison [his father] twice, but had not succeeded*) the convicted father-killer *was led out in a wagon here, his body nipped thrice with red-hot tongs, then two of his limbs shattered with the wheel and finally executed with it*—once more, the additional procedural details convey the executioner's sense of justice accomplished.¹⁰ (See the illustration near the beginning of chapter 2, page 47.)

Where and when an ambush took place could further intensify the deed's infamy in Meister Frantz's estimate, again because of the blatant disregard for social norms. His journal entries tend to decry attacks in the woods more for the particular violence involved than for the degree of surprise, perhaps because the area itself was already presumed dangerous. Home invasions by armed bands, by contrast, clearly upset the executioner on a visceral level, and his accounts of these crimes reveal the same sense of personal grief as his anguished descriptions of attacks on children. He accordingly considers nocturnal burglary more serious than simple theft, especially since it might lead to an assault on a startled homeowner. "The night is no friend," warned a contemporary proverb that underscored the particular vulnerability created by darkness in this era before the advent of streetlamps. Within the city, the complete curfew after sundown meant that even a thief who snatched people's cloaks from them in the street by night could receive a death sentence. Meister Frantz deplored the murder or assault of a sleeping victim as an especially despicable act that provided compelling evidence of a perpetrator's cowardice and indecency.[11]

Unlike the accidentally fatal blows incurred in the heat of an argument, the violence of malicious murderers also tended to be excessive. Here too, Frantz relies on a few details to convey the cruel nature of such assaults. Elisabeth Rossnerin, *a day laborer and beggar, strangled in a pea field and stabbed with a dagger her [female] companion, also a field worker at Gebersdorf,* all for the sake of 4 pounds 9 pfennigs (approx. 1 fl.). Peter Köchl, eventually convicted of attempted murder, *severely beat his own father with a manure shovel.*[12] Still more brutal, Michel Köller *intentionally threw a rock at the head of a carter servant from Wehr . . . so that he fell from the nag, and took his money from him, but the throw hit him in the shoulders, and when the carter servant armed himself, [Köller] stabbed him repeatedly 32 times in the head with a pocket knife.*[13] Frequently, Meister Frantz employs the number of wounds inflicted as a shorthand for the gratuitous violence of such criminals: Elisabeth Püffin *entered at night the bailiff's house at Velden where she had served for 16 weeks and then the room of his brother-in-law Detzel, a gouty old man with an ear trumpet, giving him about eleven wounds on the head with an [iron] bar.* In a similar act of brutal betrayal, Michel Seitel, a shoemaker's man, broke into *the house of his grandfather's brother, a joiner, and attacked him while he slept, inflicting thirty-eight wounds and holes on his head with a jagged stone and one in the neck with a shoemaker's knife, intending to cut his throat and take the money.*[14]

Like the sensationalist broadsheets that attempted to exploit such atrocities, Frantz's accounts use timeworn dramatic techniques to evoke the terror of the victim, as well as the infamy of the perpetrator. In describing the outrageous assault on the aged patrician spinster Ursula von Ploben by a man and woman let into the house at night by her complicit maid, he succinctly re-creates the perspective of the unwitting victim, startled in her bedchamber by the intruders, who *accosted and smothered her with two pillows over her mouth and wretchedly stabbed her, which lasted almost a half hour, [Ploben] struggling so that they had to smother her three times before she died.*[15]

The father of two teenage girls, Frantz Schmidt was understandably attuned to the terrifying effect of two unrelenting would-be rapists on their victims. Hans Schuster, a barber journeyman,

> *during Holy Week met a married woman from Rückersdorf in front of the village, and accosted the same, attempting to force himself on her. When [she] resisted, [he] struck two blows on her head with his hatchet, threw her to the ground, [and] as she screamed held her mouth shut and stuffed it with much earth or sand until someone came to her assistance; otherwise he would have brought her to his will [i.e., raped her].*

Fifteen-year-old Hans Wadl, arrested on the same day, was just as merciless,

> *accost[ing] four girls in a small wood behind Ostenfoos who were collecting wood, falling on the biggest one, who was in her eleventh year . . . throwing her to the ground and attempting to bring her to his will. When the girl screamed and said she was too young, he replied, "By the sacrament, you have a good sturdy pussy." Throughout her mighty screaming [he] held the girl's mouth shut, took out his knife, [and said] if she would not stop he would stab her, thereupon knocking the girl around, so that two barbers were [later] needed, and he made the girl swear not to tell anyone—not even the devil— anything of it.*[16]

The *Carolina* defined rape as a capital offense, but the crime was both underreported and underpunished. Nuremberg's execution of six rapists during the entire course of the seventeenth century was actually an imperial record.[17] More commonly, as in the case of Wadl, an attacker escaped with mere flogging *out of mercy for his youth.* For Meister Frantz, though, the brutality, vulgarity, and sheer malevolence of these assaults provoked the same profound disdain that he usually reserved for murderous robbers.

To the younger Frantz, the distinction between intended and un-intended violence had been a stark one; later in life, the more seasoned professional showed more interest in weighing and analyzing the tangled motives of the unfortunates who came before him. The most common motive for premeditated murders and other attacks, especially among professional robbers, was of course money. Schmidt enjoys pointing out, however, that the hoped-for material gain is often meager, or occasionally entirely elusive—further emphasizing the sordidness of the crime. The tailor Michael Dietmayr *went for a walk with [a farmer acquaintance] and gave him a blow on the head from behind so that he fell, then gave him two more blows*—all for a total of the 3 fl. 3 pfennigs he found on the dead man. Two industrious robbers repeatedly attacked carters, female bread carriers, and peddlers *although not getting much from them.* Another killed a messenger for 5 orths (1¼ fl.) and some packages with unknown contents (that turned out to be worth little), and embosser Hans Raim was dismayed to find a similarly paltry amount on the woman he had just murdered in cold blood.[18]

Among nonprofessional criminals, Nuremberg's executioner found a history of personal enmity to be a more common motive for calculated acts of vengeance. Georg Praun (aka Pin George) *was at feud with a farmer and lay in wait for him,* while butcher Hans Kumpler, *on account of a quarrel with the watchman over the village commons, entered [the latter's] house at night to make peace and slew him with his own "dispute hammer"*[Streithammer], *which [Kumpler] took out of his hands.* In his ongoing dispute with a fellow barber journeyman, Andreas Seytzen *threatened to get back at him and give him something to remember, whereupon he stuck his [skin] scraping iron [i.e., razor] into an onion, also cooked plain peas, and breathed on the iron,* presumably intending to infect only his enemy at the public bath where they worked, but instead *over 70 persons in the bath were injured and received French [i.e., syphilitic] sores; [many] also passed out.* Frantz does not note the nature or origin of their feud but he does remark, with some sense of poetic justice, that the vindictive bathman *himself [also] got the sores and lay 8 weeks at home.*[19]

The perceived injustice behind vengeful acts, like the money sometimes gained in murderous assaults, often proved to be quite petty in Meister Frantz's experience. The maid Ursula Becherin *burnt a stable belonging to her master, a farmer on the Marelstein, because the old peo-*

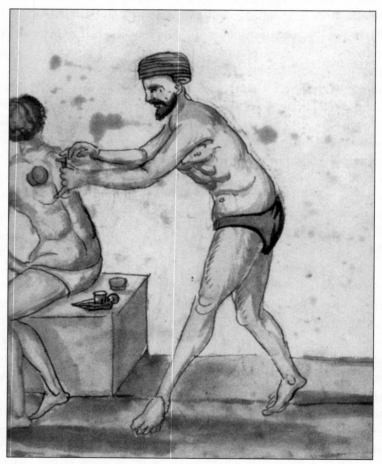

Public baths offered a variety of medical treatments in addition to opportunities for social interactions, including with prostitutes (c. 1570).

ple were harsh [to her], and in this year 1582 she did the same to her farmer master at Haselhof, burning down a stable because she could do nothing right in their opinion. Anna Bischoffin *burned down a stable at the Kützen farm . . . on account of a purse, which she had mislaid and thought had been stolen from her,* while Cunz Nenner similarly threatened arson *on account of some pigeons taken from him.* Other damning crimes sprang from even pettier origins. Is Schmidt decrying human folly or disproportionate violence when he notes in passing that premeditated assaults might be triggered by *a dispute over a lit torch, on account of a missing spoon,* or because of *a quarrel in a wood about a brooch?*[20]

Money, revenge, and perhaps love were all motives in the plot Kunrad Zwickelsperger and Barbara Wagnerin made to murder her husband:

> *Three times [Zwickelsperger] prompted [Wagnerin] to put insect powder in her husband's food, which she did, putting it in some porridge and even eating three spoonfuls herself, but the husband remained unharmed. He vomited six times and she twice, for—as Zwickelsperger had told her—if she gave him too much he would die, if a little he would only vomit. Zwickelsperger also pledged himself by going to communion not to have relations with any other woman than with her, the carpenter's wife, and she was to go and promise him the same. Also Zwickelsperger gave two fl. to an old sorceress that she might cause the carpenter to be stabbed, struck down, or drowned.*[21]

Whatever the sincerity of the conspirators' affection for each other, the intended victim survived all attempts on his life and saw both of his would-be assassins put to death at the hands of Meister Frantz. Love, or lust, possibly also played a part in Georg Wigliss's deadly assault on a peddler in the Nuremberg forest, as he not only stole 8 *gulden from him,* but *afterward took to himself the murdered peddler's wife, living at Leinburg, and was married to her.*[22] A mutually hatched plot, a murderer's attempt to assuage his own guilt, or a bizarre instance of genuine attraction—Schmidt does not reveal his own take on the murder-marriage, only that Wigliss, a three-time murderer, was executed *with the wheel* next to two hanged thieves.

Bandits and highwaymen embodied the most extreme exemplars of self-indulgent, gratuitous cruelty—evil for its own sake. Though making up less than a tenth of the people Meister Frantz executed, these murderous outlaws dominate his longer accounts and are by far the most vividly drawn characters of the journal.[23] Their attacks on people along the road or in their own homes look less like carefully planned heists than excuses to indulge their sadistic impulses—binding and torturing victims with fire or hot grease, raping them repeatedly, and killing survivors in gruesome ways. Even after encounters with human violations of almost every nature, Frantz is still shaken by a group of sixteen bandits who *attacked people by night . . . bound them, tortured them, and did violence to them, robbing them of money and clothes.*[24] He writes with obvious empathy of two of their victims, *one woman [who] received seventeen wounds, blows, or stabs, of which she died after thirteen weeks; the other had her hand hacked off and died on the third day.*[25] In Frantz's accounts, the stolen property often seemed an afterthought

An eighteenth-century French engraving graphically conveys the cruelty of home invaders and the terror of their helpless victims, particularly in isolated mills (1769).

to the spree of barbarism that preceded it. Men like this reveled in their defilement of all social norms, attempting to outdo one another in their audacity—most inexcusably for Frantz Schmidt when they engaged in the cold-blooded torture and killing of pregnant women, whose fetuses were cut out and murdered before their mothers' eyes. Once more, we should be attuned to the executioner's own need to justify the cruelties he himself later inflicted on such criminals. Although this may sometimes have led Frantz to exaggerate—whether consciously or unconsciously—the violence he describes was indisputably real, as was the genuine terror such outlaws left in their wake.

Nor did atrocities end with the deaths of their victims. Professional robbers, by Schmidt's accounting, were also the most likely to desecrate a corpse. This may seem like a surprising issue of concern for a professional executioner whose job required him to do the same at times, but in fact it's an indicator of the profound seriousness of Christian burial for Meister Frantz and virtually all his contemporaries. Leaving a cadaver hanging from the gallows, exposed on the wheel, or burned to ashes deeply disturbed those who believed in an afterlife and the physical resurrection of the dead. Intentional abuse or neglect of the recently deceased was just as reprehensible. The early image of robber Klaus Renckhart forcing a murdered miller's wife to serve him fried eggs on the dead man's corpse remained unsurpassed in shock value, but typical of such men's disregard for basic human decency.[26] Frantz remarks with dismay whenever murdering robbers stripped their victims' bodies and left them lying by the roadside, sometimes covered with brushwood, other times thrown into a nearby body of water. In the case of Lienhard Taller (aka Spit Lenny), however, it's not clear whether Schmidt is relieved or troubled that the murderer first hid the body of his victim *under some straw in a stable [but] on the next night, with the help of his wife, he carried the [man's] body to a little wood and buried it.*[27]

For Meister Frantz, the ultimate proof that these individuals spurned all social norms could be seen in the way that they treated one another. Unlike some of their literary counterparts, the outlaws in Schmidt's accounts followed no self-imposed code, exhibited no lasting loyalty, and in fact regularly turned on one another. Sometimes the motive was revenge, as when the robber Hans Paier was *betrayed and given to* capture by the banished Adam Schiller (whom [Paier] claims no memory of having hexed in the New Forest so that he would immediately die). More often it was greed that triggered the conflict, especially during the division of spoils. Hans Georg Schwartzmann (aka the Fat Mercenary; aka the Black Peasant) *quarreled over the share of the booty with his companions at Fischbach, so that they beat him up and cut up his whore who helped him.* Michel Vogl similarly fought with a longtime accomplice *about a robbery they had committed [together] and tried to stab him, whereupon [Vogl] seized [his associate's] gun and shot him, so that he instantly fell dead.* To demonstrate the utter lack of any honor among thieves, Meister Frantz adds that in this instance the victim's former companion *afterward stripped and plundered him, taking 40 fl.* Even the robber Christoph Hoffman's accidental shooting of his own companion similarly ended with the former stripping the corpse and dumping the body in some low water.

The infighting among robbers could also be vicious, as when Georg Weyssheubtel *chopped off one hand and almost hacked in two the other arm of one of his companions and then [gave him] a head wound so that he died.* The notoriously brutal Georg Müllner (aka Lean George) not only robbed and killed one former companion but also the next day ambushed and killed the man's wife in a nearby woods, *suffocating her with a kerchief she had round her neck, murdering her, and robbing her of her money and clothes.* Not to be surpassed, the robber Hans Kolb (aka the Long Brickmaker) *stabbed his [own] wife at Büch two years ago [and] later stabbed one of his companions on a road in Franconia . . . Likewise he also cut the ear off his companion's consort in the field.*[28]

Schmidt's anger toward amoral highwaymen was fueled by the deep frustration that he and other law enforcement officials experienced in preventing or punishing their attacks. His palpable jubilation at the capture and execution of such outlaws is thus understandable. Whenever possible, he cites the names of confederates, particularly if they had already been caught and executed. In his account of the crimes of the robber Hans Hammer (aka Pebble; aka the Young Cobbler), there is a hint of boasting in Frantz's aside that Hammer's numerous accomplices in one especially brutal home invasion had all been executed by him, along with obvious chagrin that *Pebble had still many more companions*, presumably still at large. Frantz records with similar satisfaction that the companions of Hans Georg Schwartzmann and *his wench* Anna Pintzrinin—namely Chimney Michael, the Scholar of Bayreuth, Spoon Kaspar, Curly, the Scholar Paulus, Clumsy, Six, and Zulp—*have also since received their due*. In describing the crimes and executions of the robbers Heinrich Hausmann and Georg Müllner, he goes so far as to provide the full names and/or aliases of forty-nine accomplices. His rationale for compiling such a list remains mysterious, since all but four of the culprits remained at large. Perhaps he is making notes in anticipation of future arrests, a kind of wish list for himself and his partners in law enforcement. It remains in any event an idiosyncratic and unique gesture.[29]

Crimes of passion

There was a major distinction for Frantz Schmidt between such malicious violations of basic human decency and mere capitulation to human weakness. Nonfatal and nonviolent crimes accordingly received much less coverage or analysis in his journal. Unless he could identify individuals who were intentionally harmed, Frantz devoted little space or reflection to property or sexual improprieties, even though together they composed over three-quarters of the punishments he administered over the course of his career.[30] Of course Schmidt continued to play the role of communal avenger in such cases, but the visceral satisfaction so obvious in his accounts of executed robbers is notably lacking. In other words, containing his outrage did not present much of a challenge in the majority of his executions and other punishments. In that respect, Frantz Schmidt came closer to the legal ideal of the executioner as a steady and dispassionate instrument of state violence.

Frantz's attitude toward nonmalicious crimes allowed him to show greater compassion for the people who committed them. The most forgivable crimes in his view were those of passion—which by definition lacked premeditation or malice—particularly onetime explosions of violence in a moment of rage. Most men in that still tumultuous era, including Frantz Schmidt, carried a knife or other weapon at all times. Not surprisingly, drunken or otherwise heated disputes over male honor regularly led not only to fistfights, but also to stabbings or duels, some of them fatal. The *Carolina* and other criminal codes narrowed the definitions of self-defense and "honorable killing," but as in the American Wild West (or certain parts of the modern United States), a verbally or physically injured man bore no duty to retreat—to the contrary, self-redress remained an imperative.[31] Victims who had suffered nonfatal wounds typically sought compensation through the age-old practice of private financial settlement (wergild).[32] When angry words led to a dead body, Frantz recognized that justice had to be served, but he tended to treat homicide in the heat of anger as an unfortunate but understandable fact of life.

In his earliest entries, Schmidt laconically notes that a farmer *stabbed a forester*, or a furrier *stabbed a son of the Teutonic Knights*. Occasionally he makes note of the particular insult (*traitor, thief, rogue*), the weapon in question (*knife, ax, hammer, bolt*), or the source of the dispute, often trivial: *for the sake of [a] whore over the payment for a drink; over a kreuzer [0.02 fl.]; or because [his friend] cursed him as a traitor*.[33] Otherwise these accounts have the bored affect of a traffic report.[34] In a world where men must be ever ready to defend their honor, Frantz intimates, there are bound to be accidents, as when the municipal archer Hans Hacker *disarmed [another] archer's son on watch because of cursing, came to words with one another and gave [the other] an accidental blow with a hammer so that he died*.[35] Hacker escaped with a flogging, but Peter Planck's escalating brawl with a prostitute had an even more tragic ending for both. The series of regrettable events, writes Meister Frantz, began when Planck returned home after an evening of heavy drinking:

> As he was walking near the Spitler Gate toward the pig stalls he saw a woman, who was a whore, walking in front of him along Sunderspühl Street and hurried after her. According to his account, she addressed him, asking him to go home with her, and when he refused she said he had to swear by the sacrament or something of this kind. Then, as he sat down, she took away his hat, apparently trying to make a fool of him, and said he had concealed it. He tried to take the hat back from her and they struggled with each other. When he gave her a blow in the face, the whore drew both her knives and stabbed at him. As she went at him, he

picked up some sand and threw it at her; she did likewise, but when she refused to stop trying to stab him, he drew out his knife and stabbed at her, wounding her eye, so that she fell and his knife broke in the act, leaving the shaft in his hand. He knelt on her and snatched the knives from her hands, but his hand was cut by the blade and in rage he drove the knife through her left breast as she lay there.[36]

Sudden anger, fueled by alcohol and injury (to either honor or person), sparked the violence in cases like these—heat, as opposed to the iciness of calculated treachery.

Succumbing to other passions, particularly sexual desire, likewise appeared inevitable and less grave to Nuremberg's longtime executioner. Flogging for fornication, adultery, or prostitution made up nearly one-quarter of Meister Frantz's 384 corporal punishments, yet his records of these events are typically the briefest in the journal—probably

In a universally armed society, even a house servant sweeping away cobwebs kept his personal dagger close at hand (c. 1570).

because they were so very commonplace. His most frequent victims were professional prostitutes, denizens of the shadowy world Frantz repudiated at every opportunity. Unlike his clerical colleagues, though, he displays less discomfort over what he terms *lewdness* (*Unzucht*; lit. "undiscipline") than any other form of public scandal. It seems unlikely that the pious Schmidt would have ever denied the sinfulness of extramarital sex, but it is hard to detect more than mild disgust when he writes about the offense, particularly when the activity in question was purely consensual. To the contrary, his language is coarse and very matter-of-fact, his references the briefest in the journal. He even shares a few ribald Chaucerian moments, such as when

> *Sara, a baker at Fach, daughter of the tavern keeper at Heilbronner Hof, called the Furrier, allowed her maid to commit lewdness. Also incited a smith to have a go with the maid and made him bring her proof of it, giving her some hairs ripped from [the maid's] little bush. When the maid cried out, [Sara] held her mouth shut by sitting with her ass on the mouth and afterward poured a cold [glass of] water into it.*[37]

Another passage, part of a digression on the subject of past reprieves, could be right out of the bacchanalian world of Boccaccio's *Decameron*:

> *A farmer from Hersbruck who, after drinking with another farmer in an inn, rose from his drink to take a piss but [instead] went to his drinking companion's wife by night, as if he were her husband coming home, lay down in bed and committed lewdness, then got up and left her, but was recognized as not her husband by the woman when she looked after him.*[38]

The earthy humor of an executioner who spent most of his time with criminals and lowborn guards should come as no surprise. It also reminds us that Meister Frantz's piety was not equivalent to prudishness and that the rigid sexual standards of his clerical colleagues were not necessarily endorsed by the rest of society, even among the faithful.

Public scandal, more than private sin, remained the graver offense for the status-conscious Schmidt, who considered reputation the most precious possession imaginable. Accordingly, the only flashes of disapproval or even anger over sexual offenses come when a perpetrator brought shame on his or her family and community through improper behavior. Georg Schneck did not just commit adultery but *took in marriage a whore in the New Woods called Dyer Barbie and had a wedding with her.* The thief Peter Hoffman *also deserted his wife and took a consort, then when she died took another and had the banns published at Lauf; when he wasn't permitted [to marry] he took Brigita.*[39]

Surprisingly to modern readers, wedding vows in this era did not have to be pronounced before a pastor or priest to be legally binding. A simple promise exchanged in private or before a few witnesses, followed by sexual consummation, could be considered official. Predictably, a common scandal involved a man who made false vows in order to lure a young woman into bed and then later abandoned her. A young woman who became pregnant in this manner faced a grim set of options: acknowledge the pregnancy and bring shame on herself, her family, and her child; seek an abortion, which was illegal and often deadly; or hide the pregnancy and then abandon the baby. Some women who chose this third option—most of them young, poor, and without family support—labored alone and in desperation committed infanticide, a crime that if discovered meant certain execution.[40]

In cases of false vows—at least those that did not involve infanticide—Schmidt's sympathies invariably lay with the dishonored young women and their families, particularly once the affair became public. Meister Frantz writes with contempt of scribe Niklaus Hertzog, who *impregnated a maid at Hof in the Vogtland* [Schmidt's hometown], *promised [her] marriage and had public banns announced, then absconded and left her behind,* adding, *also impregnated a maid here at Wehr [and] had a wedding with the same.* He has no patience with the equivocations of the farmhand Georg Schmiedt, *who admitted courting a farmer's daughter, lying with her twenty times, committing lewdness, claiming that he intended to marry her but later denied it.*[41] As in all crimes, deceit and cowardice particularly aroused the executioner's wrath, and he records with satisfaction the few occasions when such cads received their just due from his birch rod.

Other sexual references reflect the same abiding concern with propriety over morality, public embarrassment over private sin. Violating the privacy of the bedchamber, for instance, appears merely distasteful, as when Schmidt flogged the tailor journeyman Veit Heymann and his bride, Margaretha Grossin, *because they committed lewdness and let other maidens watch.* He is somewhat more disgusted with Ameley Schützin and Margaretha Puchfelderin, who prostituted their respective daughters, and Hieronimus Beyhlstein, who pimped for his own wife.[42] Still more scandalously, the clerk Hans Brunnauer

> *during his wife's lifetime committed lewdness with Barbara Kettnerin (also during her husband's life); promised her marriage, consorted with her for three years, went about the country with her for half a year, and had a child with her. Similarly committed lewdness twice with the woman Kettnerin's sister, also several times with the stepmother of the Kettnerin sisters. Also boarded and slept with the wife of a joiner named Thoma for half a year, and promised her marriage and cohabited with her. Also had twin children by a servant during his wife's lifetime.*[43]

And even the world-weary Meister Frantz is taken aback to learn that *Apollonia Groschin provid[ed] her marriage bed for [the confectioner Elisabeth Mechtlin] and herself commit[ted] lewdness—she in a bed with the confectioner and a barber journeyman, called Angelhead, [he] lying in the middle and committing lewdness with both [of them].*[44]

The most serious sexual offenses, according to Christian doctrine, were incest and sodomy, both traditionally considered crimes against God and subject to death by fire. The abomination of incest, in particular, supposedly threatened an entire community with divine retribution if not punished. Yet only the case of seventeen-year-old Gertraut Schmidtin, *who lived in lewdness for four years with her own father and brother*, appears to have genuinely shocked Meister Frantz, uniquely prompting him to call her a *heretic*. Still, even here, out of sympathy (and perhaps in recognition of her victim status), he does not dispute the mitigation of her punishment to beheading, while noting that the executioner of Ansbach burned the father and brother alive eight days later at nearby Langenzenn.[45] Frantz also refrains from including any prurient details of the relationship, even though he knew them well from his participation in Schmidtin's interrogation.

One reason for Frantz's exceptional response in this instance was that it was the only case of incest between biological relatives he encountered during his career. Cases of this nature rarely escaped the conspiracy of silence within the early modern household, and thus genuinely shocked most people when they became public. More commonly, incest convictions involved stepfathers and stepdaughters or even one person having sex with two people related to each other (e.g., one woman with two brothers; one man with a woman, her sister, and her stepmother, etc.).[46] Though incomprehensible to most modern sensibilities, incest defined in this second manner was still considered a kind of profound blasphemy and thus usually led to death sentences, though always mitigated in Nuremberg to beheading and occasionally even to flogging.

Typical for the day, the only individuals to escape an incest conviction with banishment were men. Meister Frantz undoubtedly noticed this double standard—which prevailed in virtually all sexual matters—and in fact likely shared it. Sometimes he excuses the discrepancy by distinguishing the level of complicity, as in the case of a father and son who had each been sleeping with their maid: *[they were] unaware of each other's doings*, and therefore merely flogged while she was executed. Kunigunda Küplin, conversely, had been fully cognizant *of what was happening [between her second husband and daughter] and herself [even] arranging it*, and was thus justly condemned to decapitation and posthumous burning. Particularly scandalous behavior provided a similar justification for magisterial severity. Frantz carefully noted that when Elisabeth Mechtlin *committed lewdness with two biological brothers, [both named] Hans Schneider*, it had been *among the butchers' stalls* (an especially dishonorable place), or that Anna Peyelstainin (aka Cunt Annie) not only *committed lewdness and harlotry with a father and a son, called the Cauldrons, who both had wives and she a husband, [but] similarly with twenty-one married men and youths, her husband helping her.*[47]

Sodomy in the early modern era comprised a variety of offenses, ranging from homosexuality to bestiality to other "unnatural" sexual practices (and even heresy).[48] Frantz's first judicial encounter with homosexuality came in 1594, when he burned at the stake Hans Weber,

> *a fruitier, otherwise known as the Fat Fruiterer . . . who for three years had practiced sodomist lewdness [with Christoph Mayer] and*

*was informed on by a hookmaker's apprentice, who caught them
both in the act behind a hedge off a Thon lane. The fruiterer had
practiced this for twenty years, namely with the cook Andreas, with
Alexander, also with Georg in the army, and with the baker Toothy
Chris at Lauf, and otherwise with many other baker servants that he
couldn't name. Mayer was first executed with the sword and then
the body burned next to the fruiterer, who was burned alive.*[49]

Two years later, tradesman Hans Wolff Marti, though apparently even
more prolific in same-sex partners and also accused of stabbing the wife
of one of his lovers, was spared burning alive (although the grounds for
such mercy remain unclear).

Contrary to his pervasive fear of robbers and their criminal
underworld, Schmidt's acknowledgment of an apparent homosexual
underground does not appear to have caused him any anxiety. Curiosity, rather—as well as the need to establish an unreformable character—
drives his compulsion to itemize the many alleged partners of both
condemned sodomites. In Marti's case the list is even lengthier:

*having committed sodomist lewdness with [said] mason, also with a
carpenter . . . Also committed such lewdness here and there
throughout the countryside, first with a bargeman at Ibis, also with
another at Brauningen, with a bargeman at Frankfurt, and with a
farmer at Mittenbrück, with a cartman at Witzburg, with a locksmith at Schweinfurt, with a farmer at Windsheim, and with a cartman at Pfaltza, also with a man at Nördlingen, and with a straw
cutter at Salzburg, lastly with a small city guard at Wehr, named
Hans.*[50]

Even though Marti identified his partners in only the vaguest of
terms—either to protect them or because he did not himself know their
names—Meister Frantz did not apply torture to force the suspect to
finger his confederates as witch hunters of the era did. In both instances, Schmidt's tone also remains markedly nonjudgmental and free
of derisory language—a sharp contrast to his obvious disgust for *Georg
Schörpff, a heretic who committed lewdness or had relations with four
cows, two calves, and a sheep* and was consequently *executed with the*

sword as a cow pervert at Velln [and] afterward burned together with a cow
with which he'd had sexual relations.[51] Schmidt even mentions a farmer
who was accused of *assault[ing] people [and] attempting to commit sodomist lewdness with them* who was merely flogged, his sentence apparently reduced because of the perpetrator's *great drunkenness*.[52] The
restraint that Frantz shows when he deals with sodomy shouldn't be
interpreted to mean that homosexual activity was either widespread or
generally condoned in Meister Frantz's Nuremberg. The severe clerical
injunctions against such "abominations" and their cosmic repurcussions
remain, however, notably absent in Schmidt's writing.

Even if Frantz did consider incest and sodomy to be crimes against
God, there's no evidence that he shared the supposedly common belief
that such acts invited divine punishment of the entire land (*Landstraffe*) by epidemic, famine, or some other disaster. Outright blasphemy
was another matter. Like any other early modern male, God the Father
was likely to lash out when His honor was directly challenged, whether
by *a common whore* speaking in jest, an archer's son ranting in the
midst of an altercation, or a bitter glazier, who *during a great storm, with
mighty thunder, blasphemed God in heaven and swore, calling Him (God
forgive me for writing it) an old rogue [and saying] the old fool had gambled and lost money at cards [and] now wanted to win it back with dice.*
The pious executioner, who even seeks to appease the angry deity in his
own private journal, uneasily reports on the blaspheming glazier's *merciful* treatment: merely *placed in the stocks for ¼ hour [and] a piece of
the tip of his tongue taken out on the Fleisch Bridge.*[53]

Thefts from a church or monastery, offenses that in the Catholic
tradition were considered sacrilegious and blasphemous, did not by
contrast trouble the Protestant Meister Frantz. He identifies, for instance, Hans Krauss (aka Locksmith John) as *a church thief [who]
broke into the church at Endtmannsberg, stole the chalice, and broke
open four trunks, stealing the vestments.* But Krauss was hanged the
same as any other thief, even despite the additional disclosure that *he
also helped ambush and attack people in their houses at night.* The executioner displays the same tone of indifference with the even more prolific church thieves Hans Beütler (aka Skinny) and Hans Georg
Schwartzmann (aka the Fat Mercenary). Throughout his journal, rather,
it was the thieves' level of activity—*stole often in many places*—that

earned them the gallows, not any special reverence for the purloined items themselves.[54]

Crimes of habit

The great majority of the criminal offenders Meister Frantz punished were motivated by neither malice nor other passions. In his experience, most habitual criminals, principally thieves, were not even driven by avarice, the presumed incentive to stealing. Unlike violent robbers or onetime offenders, nonviolent thieves in fact tended to display a distinct emotional detachment vis-à-vis their offenses. Frantz accordingly displays a similar detachment in his brief journal accounts of the same, only taking pains to note the degree of financial loss entailed. The variety of stolen items is vast, ranging from several hundred gulden in cash to small amounts of money, clothing, bed mattresses, rings, household objects, weapons, chickens, and even honey from unprotected beehives. The rustling of horses and cattle proved the most lucrative form of theft; trading in stolen clothing the most common. That all these thefts might be considered equal in severity, let alone punished by death, appears incomprehensible to the modern observer. How could an allegedly pious executioner possibly condone such harshness in punishing nonviolent offenses, let alone justify his own role in carrying out such severe sentences?

Once more, we must look to Frantz's deep empathy for the victims of crime. In a generally poor society, the loss of a few mantles or a relatively small amount of cash could represent a significant, even devastating loss for a struggling household. Accordingly, the executioner records thefts of under 50 fl., roughly the annual salary of a schoolmaster, not just more precisely but also with more visceral alarm—reflecting their more immediate implications for specific victims. Clearly Meister Frantz did not consider all thefts equal and he did recognize a greater gravity with large amounts, but his journal's pervasive emphasis on the victim's suffering led to some revealing juxtapositions. While smaller numbers are always specific, sometimes to the pence—reflecting the significance of even a minor amount to a victim who possessed little—large numbers are almost always rounded off into hundreds of florins. In

1609 he recounts how Hans Fratzen *stole ten bed blankets about eigh-teen weeks ago and broke into the hut makers' shelter at Bamberg, stealing 26 fl. worth of clothes*, while in the next passage he simply writes that a well-known cat burglar *stole about 300 fl. worth of silver jewelry*. Frantz similarly devotes a long passage to describing how Maria Cordula Hun-nerin fraudulently ran up an unpaid tavern bill for 32 fl. before noting in passing that later on she stole *800 fl. worth in thaler and three kreuzer pieces from the safe box of her master*.[55]

In another journal entry, the executioner's seemingly compulsive list-ing of multiple thefts in fact serves to underscore both the bad charac-ter of the perpetrator and the great number of his victims: *Simon Starck . . . stole money six times out of the purse of one servant, 1½ fl. from the cooler, and from his farmer 29 fl., which he took back from him, and at Schweinau 5 fl. from a peddler, about 2 fl. from his cartman, about 1 fl. in sum from an Italian*.[56] Even more bizarre to modern eyes, Frantz's personal identification with crime victims moves him to write passages like the one about Sebastian Fürsetzlich, *who stole money from the purses of carters while they slept at night in inns, namely 80 fl. 6 schilling, 45 fl., 37 fl., 35 fl., 30 fl., 30 fl., 20 fl., 18 fl., 17 fl., 8 fl., 8 fl., 7 fl., 6 fl., 3 fl., 2 fl*.[57] Rather than simply totaling the amounts or copying them in chronological order, Schmidt carefully restructures the thefts in de-scending order of value to convey the crimes' individual financial im-pact on multiple carters as well as the moral case for Fürsetzlich's punishment—albeit in a highly idiosyncratic manner.

Thieves and other nonviolent offenders indisputably deserved pun-ishment in Meister Frantz's moral universe, but their crimes, like those of prostitutes and pimps, usually represented the conscious lifestyle choices of weak, rather than malicious, individuals. This attitude repre-sented a divergence from the more sweeping approach of jurists and clerics to all crime. Despite the executioner's exceptional attunement to the losses suffered by their victims, his primary emotional response to the 172 thieves he hanged during his career was less anger than weary resignation. Their own selfish choices had brought them to this moment, and Schmidt never once excused the circumstances behind their thefts. The man born into a gutter-status profession predictably had little sympathy for the many hard-luck stories he encountered in the interrogation chamber. Yet it is neither triumph nor guilt that tinged his accounts of hanging recidivist small-time thieves, but head-shaking sadness. "How could a society hang a man for stealing honey?" we ask from our perspective; "Why does a man repeatedly risk hanging to steal some honey?" wonders Frantz.

The answer to both questions is that stealing had evidently become an unshakable habit for the offender in question and Frantz Schmidt's superiors had simply reached their point of exasperation. The crucial issue was usually not what a thief had stolen but how often. Virtually all those condemned to die were multiple offenders; many had been arrested, imprisoned, and banished several times. Put another way, most of the individuals ultimately hanged by Meister Frantz had irreversibly transformed themselves in his eyes from people who stole once or twice into professional thieves, "accustomed to the deed."[58] "Obstinate" was the characterization most common among Nuremberg's obedience-craving magistrates, but the modern language of compulsive behavior would be closer to the executioner's assessment of many recidivists. He observed that the affluent farmgirl Magdalena Geckenhofferin, *again and again borrowed several mantles, brassieres, and other clothing [and] she even went to communion or to a wedding to snatch the same,* clearly indicating from some kind of internal rather than external stimulus. Meister Frantz thought it obvious that Farmer Heinz Pflügel and his wife, Margaretha, who *had a property worth about 1000 fl. but often busied themselves with thievery,* were likewise motivated by something other than outright deprivation.[59]

Stealing, according to the veteran executioner, was always a choice, but also for many—to use an anachronistic term—an irresistible addiction. Too often, the habit was acquired at an early age. Balthasar Preiss, *child of a [Nuremberg] citizen . . . lay eleven times in the Hole, went several times into the chain gang, was for half a year in the Frog Tower, and [spent] a year in irons in the tower, but would not abandon thieving. When put to some handicraft, ran away and stole.* Meister Frantz himself repeatedly flogged and reprimanded his former colleagues, the municipal archers Georg Götz and Lienhard Hertl, who each spent several years rowing in Venetian galleys; yet both men continued to steal and rob until finally stopped at the gallows. Even career offenders who wanted to rehabilitate themselves were often pulled back into the criminal life against their will. The *old thief father* Simon Gretzelt forty

years ago *forswore his thieving*, Frantz writes, and longtime thief Andreas Stayber (aka the Minstrel) *stole many things besides here and
there but had given up these practices for five years and wanted to reform*
[literally, "become pious"]. The executioner takes no apparent pleasure
in recording that in both cases the former thieves' pasts caught up
with them: Gretzelt eventually returned to an immoral life, and the
Minstrel was sentenced to hang as a consequence of the incriminating
testimony of his former companion, the infamous highwayman Hans
Kolb.[60]

Habitual stealing by no means equaled skillful stealing. Many thefts
were purely crimes of opportunity—a street vendor who turned his
back for a moment, clothing left unattended on a washline, a house left
vacant because of a wedding feast. The farmhand Hans Merckel (aka
Deer John), *who was in service for 22 years,*

> *used to stay half a year to two years in one place and then leave,
> taking away with him hose, doublets, boots, woolen shirts, and
> whatever money he could get. When he drove some sheep to Augs-
> burg for his master and obtained 35 fl. for them, he ran away with
> the money. Did the same to his master at Amburg, who sent him
> with 21 fl. and a horse and cart to fetch some white beer from Bo-
> hemia; left the horse and ran away with the money. Also stole a
> pair of hose and a doublet, in the pockets of which were 15 fl.,
> which he was unaware of.[61]*

More simply, a messenger called the Cabbage Farmer *was given a
satchel containing silver cutlery and 200 fl. worth of Groshen to carry to
Neustadt, [but] he broke into it and sold the silver to the Jews at Furth for
100 fl. in cash,* spending all his proceeds on eating and gambling.[62]

Burglary, because it both violated the home and risked personal
contact, presented a greater threat. By late middle age, the veteran executioner had become a connoisseur of such break-ins, rarely the well-
conceived and skillfully executed heists of legend. He was amused by
the ineptitude of some amateurs, such as Anna Pergmennin, who
*sneaked into the house of a schoolmaster at Saint Lorenz [Church], in-
tending to steal but was caught and imprisoned; eight days earlier had
been locked in the cellar of Hans Payr, [also] intending to steal.* Erhard

Rössner *one night broke open the locks of twelve stores but couldn't get inside*, while Lienhard Leydtner, a padlock smith, *in the last two years broke into forty-two shops in this town with keys he made for that purpose, thinking to find money, but stole nothing special.*[63] Still more embarrassingly, the shepherd Cunz Pütner

> *had twice concealed himself in Master Fürer's house and tried to break into the office and steal money, but when he had bored seven holes in the door the first time he achieved nothing. [So] he again hid in the house and tried to break into the parlor. When the master heard him and cried out there was a search and [the shepherd's] shoes were found sitting on the floor, he having removed them so as to move silently. He was still hiding in the parlor, though, where he was captured.*[64]

Even the professional burglar Lienhard Gösswein, who *was in possession of many tools, was caught in the cellar of the innkeeper Wastla's house at the Fruit Market, intending to steal.*[65]

Bungled break-ins could also lead to more serious consequences. Lorenz Schober—who, according to Meister Frantz, *stole trifles, namely 12 loaves of bread, 6 cheeses, a shirt and a doublet—*

> *broke into the house of a poor woman at Gründlein, and when she caught him in the act and held him, screaming for help, he drew a knife and stabbed her thrice, the first time in the head, the second time in the left breast, the third in the neck, and left her lying for dead, so that she recovered with difficulty.*[66]

Only the prolific cat burglar Hans Schrenker (aka the Crawler) appears to earn the executioner's professional respect, though not without a hint of mockery:

> *Climbed into the castle at Freienfels, [first] using a ladder over the cowshed, then by a ladder against a tower to the roof, then again by another ladder through a window into a parlor. Broke open a safe box with his cooper's knife and stole about 300 fl. worth of silver jewelry. Then, descending by the ladders as he had climbed, went*

out in front of the castle and hid the jewels under a stone on the other side of the hill. Entered again by the ladders, broke open a desk, and stole a bag with 40 fl. Although a sack with 500 fl. lay close to it, when he was about to take the money such a fear overcame him that he ran away, thinking for certain that someone was running after him.[67]

Perhaps in part to relieve the tedium of writing about mediocre bumblers, Meister Frantz made note of especially ingenious or industrious thieves. One wire-drawer *over the course of a year and a half, used specially forged keys to break into the shop of an ironmonger, once or twice a week, stealing about 21 Ell [approx. 52 feet] of wire, 14 Ell [approx. 35 feet] of steel, and 40 thousand nails.* The determined Anna Rebbelin *entered houses here more than forty times, and always went up two or three flights of stairs into the rooms and stole a great quantity of goods.*[68]

Small-time grifters, a favorite of picaresque literature, particularly intrigued Meister Frantz, probably because of their brazenness. Christoph Schmiedt (aka Cooper Chris), a longtime thief, most recently *entered eight rooms at the public baths, wearing old clothes, and when he went out put on the best [ones] of other people, leaving his old ones in their place.* Margaretha Kleinin, who also regularly worked as a burglar, *approached people with glasses clattering in small bags, as though it were money, [and] convinced people to trust her so that she could steal from them.* Georg Praun *stole 13 thaler [approx. 11 fl.] from the bag of a youth from Gräfenberg who was traveling with him, putting stones in their place,* and Hans Weckler similarly *stole 200 fl. from the saddlebag of a [fellow] tailor sleeping next to him in a room at an inn in Goldkronach, afterward putting sand through the rip so that it had the same weight again.* Fittingly, Meister Frantz adds, Weckler quickly *gambled away the money here, being cheated out of it by the roof workers Grumbly and Rosie, for which he sued them both, and on that account they were both whipped with rods out of the city*—whereupon the two cardsharps notified the authorities of their mark's previous theft.[69] Frantz clearly delights in the picaresque staple of thieves who subsequently have their money stolen by other thieves, and he repeats it often.[70] It wasn't difficult to cheat trusting people, he realized, nor did it require any special cleverness, just an indifference to other people's suffering.

Large-scale, successful swindlers consequently caused Meister Frantz more consternation, particularly when they audaciously cheated the wellborn, most notably the forger Gabriel Wolff and the treasure hunter Elisabeth Aurholtin. Though scrupulously nonviolent, these con artists were also much more calculating—and thus malicious—than common thieves. They also coolly lied, which exacerbated their thefts still further in his eyes. Anna Domiririn, who *often lay in the pesthouse*, nonetheless *intentionally deceived people with fortune-telling and treasure-finding* and thus received a full flogging, even though she *could not walk; had to be led out under the arms of two beadles*. Margaretha Schreinerin, an *old hag about 60 years old, likewise deceived people here and there, by claiming that she had inherited a great fortune* and making multiple bequests to notables around town in exchange for food, drink, and small loans (which she promised to pay back shortly). Despite her age and apparent ill health, she was *burned on both cheeks as a deceiver*. Nor was there any leniency from Meister Frantz or his authorities for Kunrad Krafft, a longtime court clerk whose forgeries and embezzlements over the years ultimately cost him his life.[71]

Mercy and redemption

Whatever the motive or nature of the crime, in Meister Frantz's scheme of justice all offenders had hope. As a believing Lutheran, he accepted that the world was a profoundly evil place and that all men and women would repeatedly succumb to sin over the course of their lifetimes. Admittedly, some fell into much graver transgressions and crimes than others, but the essential message of Christianity for Frantz was the good news of divine forgiveness for all those who sought it. This should not be confused with rehabilitation in the modern, secular sense—after all, sixteenth-century Lutherans believed that the corrupting effects of original sin remained powerful even among the faithful. What Schmidt and his colleagues, both magistrates and chaplains, sought from convicted offenders was acknowledgment of guilt and submission to the authority of God and the state. In return, both the temporal and divine judges held out the promise of absolution and thus redemption.

Mercy, consequently, was the powerful counterpart to punishment in the early modern notion of justice. Frantz shares this reverence, intoning the word ninety-three times in his journal, more than *God* (sixteen times) or *justice* (twice) or *law* (none). Virtually every use of *mercy* in the journal refers to the mitigation of a criminal punishment, but clearly the pious executioner was determined to help poor sinners attain heavenly as well as earthly redemption. The precondition to both was genuine contrition.

Visible signs of remorse thus went a long way with Meister Frantz. He notes with approval that the murderer Michel Vogt *was already out in the woods [and] came back here*, and also that the child murderer Anna Freyin, the thief Hans Helmet, and the murderer Matthias Stertz all voluntarily turned themselves in to authorities (as well as that Stertz *had been a Catholic but turned Lutheran* before his execution). Frantz repeatedly recognized in his journal those souls who *took leave of the world as a Christian*, particularly in his later years.[72] Both the executioner and the prison chaplains took heart that the repentant thief Hans Drechsler (aka the Mountaineer; aka Mercenary John) not only "learned more in the last three days from the chaplains and jail-keeper than in all his life," but also left the world in an exemplary manner, proclaiming on the scaffold to all assembled, "God bless you and the leaves and the grass, and everything I leave behind! Say a Paternoster for me. Today I shall pray for you in paradise."[73]

Embittered prisoners, particularly violent robbers, who adamantly "didn't want to pray" earned scorn from the chaplains and the executioner.[74] A rebuffed Magister Hagendorn was not above remarking that one recalcitrant thief "carried [a violent fever] with him to the gallows, from which he was not recovered until Meister Frantz hanged a cure about his neck."[75] Both the chaplain and Meister Frantz also knew that condemned culprits frequently exploited their captors' spiritual concerns to forestall the inevitable. After repeated visits to twenty-five-year-old jewel thief Jakob Faber, Magister Hagendorn began to lament the desperate man's obvious insincerity and continued resistance:

When I came to him, he was ready with all of his old tricks. He mentioned his honorable family, particularly the pleas of his old and helpless mother, and put forward all manner of excuses why he should continue to live and escape the death penalty. He cared more for his body than his soul and he was troublesome before the council, as with us, though not in the matter of instruction and comfort, for he had studied and learned the catechism in his tender youth, and knew certain psalms likewise, particularly the 6th and 23rd, as well as other prayers, but adhered obstinately to his old ways. Whether we told him sweet or bitter things, his only purpose was to go on living.[76]

Meister Frantz likewise had no tolerance for malefactors who had yet to come to terms with their situation and refused to display the appropriate submission. The notorious Georg Mayer (aka Brains)

often pleaded epilepsy. When he was about to be examined by torture, he fell into a fit and pretended the illness tormented him. As he had been excused three days before on this pretext, he taught his companions to do likewise, so that they would be let off, but when Knau also tried to do this he could not pull it off and when he was detected he admitted [the truth].[77]

Perhaps because of such feigned illnesses, Schmidt displayed no apparent sympathy for condemned poor sinners on account of mental disabilities, even while acknowledging obvious symptoms ranging from confused mumbling at execution to outright psychotic episodes.[78] He was outraged when convicted criminals attempted to game the system for clemency or merely delay, such as the robber Katherina Bücklin (aka Stammering Kathy; aka the Foreigner), who *should have been executed twelve weeks earlier but obtained a respite because of pregnancy, which turned out to be nothing*; or Elisabeth Püffin, also convicted of robbery and attempted murder, who *obtained a respite of 32 weeks on the plea of pregnancy, the committee of sworn women visiting her 18 times* before she was ultimately *executed with the sword.*[79]

In some instances, submission to divine judgment inspired worldly clemency—the judicial *mercy* to which Frantz's journal regularly refers. "In response to his supplications and prayers, and in view of his sufferings under torture," the thief Hans Dietz saw his sentence of hanging mitigated to beheading.[80] More typically, Nuremberg's magistrates showed little concern over spiritual conversion or pain endured, instead exercising their power to forgive only when it would bolster their own standing in the community. When city councilors assembled the morning of an execution to consider whether to punish "by the book" or "by mercy," it was the social standing of the individual before them that carried the most weight, not the apparent state of the poor sinner's soul.[81] In the case of Hans Kornmeyer, "an especially handsome young person of twenty . . . his mother, together with her five children, two of whom are his siblings proper . . . interceded on his behalf, as well as his master [who'd had him arrested] and the entire guild of compass-makers," successfully securing the young thief execution with the sword instead of with the rope.[82] In an even more stunning example of social influence at work, the earring maker Hans Mager and the goldsmith Caspar Lenker, both citizens, received full pardons from their homicide convictions following the intercession of the local guild, the leading goldsmith of Augsburg, and a passing emissary from Lorraine, as well as many friends and relatives.[83]

Nuremberg's criminal records are also filled with pardons of especially well-connected (or especially lucky) prisoners granted at the request of various *illustres personae* passing through town, ranging from the eminent theologian Philipp Melanchthon to the duke of Bavaria.[84] Even children of low-level city employees might benefit from their parents' official status. It probably helped Margaretha Brechtlin, convicted of poisoning her husband, that she was a daughter of the tax collector at the Spitler Gate, so that in the end she was *executed with the sword out of mercy*. Despite their multiple thefts, both a night huntsman's son and a bailiff's son likewise escaped with floggings, and even Georg Christoff (aka Shank), an oft-arrested *thief and chain gang youth*, was aided by his father's position as a municipal archer.[85]

Obviously this magisterial tendency to favor the well connected put poor and foreign individuals at a disadvantage, since they rarely had the same social capital to draw on as citizens and local craftsmen. It also weakened the chaplains' arguments for religious contrition among condemned malefactors, who presumably saw nothing to be gained by even feigning religious conversion. But as the magistrates gradually recognized, any act of leniency on their part invariably made for a smoother and more successful execution ceremony, and eventually their hard position began to soften. Young Hans Kornmeyer repeatedly threw himself down before the court in gratitude for the commuting of his hanging sentence to beheading, while Niklaus Kilian enthusiastically praised the judges for their commutation and left praying Psalm 33, then singing, and in the end "dying joyfully." When the prison chaplain brought the thief Hans Dietz news of his sentence's commutation to beheading,

> he was so delighted and comforted that he kissed the hands of both of us, and also the jailer's, and most diligently thanked us. Before the court, during the reading of the judgment he wept bitterly, and returned thanks for the merciful sentence. On his way out he sang almost continuously, so that the people, and even the executioner himself, were moved to pity.[86]

The ultimate word on clemency meanwhile became an even more jealously guarded prerogative of the city council itself. Gone were the pre-Reformation days when a nun or young virgin had the power to rescue any condemned person from a deadly fate. Pregnant women still might influence judges in other German lands but the last such account in Nuremberg is the pardon of one bigamist soldier in 1553 because of the intercession of "his [pregnant] first wife and sixteen other women besides."[87] Even in the exceptional 1609 case of Hans Frantz, whose two daughters pleaded with the magistrates that "their bridegrooms would not keep them or marry them if they had to watch their father-in-law hang on the gallows," the result was commutation to beheading, not a full pardon.[88] Folk stories abounded about women who agreed to marry condemned men—most notably the Swabian account of one condemned thief who took a good look at his prospective one-eyed bride, then turned to mount the gallows—but governmental authorities from the mid-sixteenth century refused to cede such power to anyone in actual practice. This included, apparently, the executioner, who in earlier days—as recently as 1525 in Nuremberg—could save a condemned woman by marrying her.[89]

That said, it's likely that Meister Frantz, especially during these later years, had some influence on the mitigation of sentences. Certainly by this time in his life he had become freer in showing his disdain for previous naive acts of official generosity. As a young man,

Frantz merely remarks in a neutral way that a thief *twelve years before had been spared the gallows at Kulmbach.*[90] Over the years, as he saw more of the same people coming before him, his bitterness over misspent mercy came increasingly to the fore. He follows his 1592 lament that convicted robber Stoffel Weber *should have been executed with the sword but he begged off as he was being led out and was punished at a customs house* with a lengthy discourse on other ill-considered reprieves in Nuremberg's recent past. He notes in 1606 that the two Widtmann brothers, ultimately hanged for multiple thefts, *should have been executed two and a half years ago, for they had been condemned to death—and I was at the time sick—but were reprieved.* He never liked that Gabriel Wolff *should have had his right hand cut off first, this being decided and ordered, but was subsequently spared this,* and appears genuinely stunned that *a farmer from Gründla who killed two farmers (he lay in wait for) with an ax was spared by petition.* Not only did such favors cheat the victims, but in the case of professional robbers—such as Michel Gemperlein, who *three years ago should have been executed with the rope for theft but was pardoned*—they led to the suffering of more innocent victims before the criminals were definitively stopped.[91]

The only potentially mitigating factor that moved the mature executioner other than genuine contrition was youth, an increasingly common attribute among those condemned for theft. As a result of the new severity in punishing crimes against property during the second half of the sixteenth century, Meister Frantz's professional tenure coincided exactly with the only period in early modern German history during which minors were executed for crimes other than murder or "crimes against God," such as incest, sodomy, and witchcraft. Nonviolent burglary and common theft frequently involved juveniles, with fifteen- to seventeen-year-olds accounting for as many as one in three thieves in some areas. Occasionally the youths, who sometimes operated in organized bands, stole large sums of money, but usually they snatched relatively insignificant items—a bracelet, a pair of pants, some loaves of bread.[92]

The *Carolina* left much discretion to criminal judges on the question of age in capital punishments, explicitly forbidding only the execution of those under fourteen, but even there permitting some exceptions if the offender was deemed "mature in evil."[93] This appallingly extreme punishment for juvenile theft also shocked Frantz's contemporaries, and Nuremberg's leaders, like those elsewhere in early modern Europe, continued to invoke the mitigating factor of youth in most decisions.[94] In 1605 a seventeen-year-old thief, Michel Brombecker, had his death sentence commuted to two years on a chain gang, but only in response to the appeals of his master "and the entire butcher craft"—once more evidence of the social connections that vagrant and destitute youths crucially lacked.[95] The capital punishment of the scholar youth and citizen's child Julius Tross was similarly reduced to flogging, as were those of the two thieving Wechter brothers and two other youths convicted of brutal rapes (a capital crime).[96] The coach-boy Laurenz Stollman, meanwhile, even though *he had not enjoyed the proceeds of his [latest 150 fl.] theft*, had no apparent local patrons and thus was still executed, albeit *out of mercy with the sword.*[97]

Still, even among those minors with no social capital whatsoever, clemency remained the norm. Eighteen-year-old Hans Beheim had indeed been hanged by Frantz's predecessor for "great thievery." But as recently as the year before Schmidt's arrival in Nuremberg in 1578, three different groups of condemned boy pickpockets aged seven to sixteen years were deemed "too young to hang" and had their sentences reduced to work in a chain gang, followed by flogging and banishment. To drive home both the seriousness of the offense and the generosity of the commutation, the magistrates had one group of boys, "none older than eleven," actually climb the gallows ladder before being pardoned and then forced to stand by and watch their eighteen-year-old leader hang for real. Almost twenty years later, Frantz would hang the adult Steffan Kebweller for running a similar group of young cutpurses, whom he paid the extravagant weekly wages of one thaler (0.85 fl.) plus room and board for their labors; once more, the youths themselves were released.[98]

In fact, all the juveniles ultimately executed for theft in Nuremberg were serial offenders, some having been arrested and released as many as two dozen times. Benedict Fellbinger (aka the Devil's Knave) *had been in the chain gang and lain fifteen times in the Hole, also defied his banishment eleven times.* Every member of one particularly active group of young thieves had supposedly spent at least ten detentions in the begging stockade or dungeon, sometimes followed by a public flogging.

Most important, all juvenile thieves eventually condemned to death had previously received the penultimate punishment of permanent banishment, usually at least two or three times. In every case, final verdicts noted that "such warnings and mild treatment had been received with disdain," and the juveniles continued to return to Nuremberg and steal. At some point, magistrates concludeed that "no improvement is to be hoped for" and clemency on account of youth abruptly ended.[99]

As a result, over the course of his long career, Meister Frantz would himself hang at least twenty-three thieves who were eighteen or younger, including one thirteen-year-old.[100] At Frantz's very first execution in the city of Nuremberg, when he was not yet twenty-four himself, the condemned was in fact one of the youthful pickpockets pardoned just the year before—"a very handsome young person of seventeen," according to one chronicler.[101] How did Frantz feel about this and the many other youthful hangings that would follow? Ever restrained in his expression of outright sentiment, he nonetheless conveys both his initial discomfort and, later, an evolving understanding of human character that provided him with some reassurance in such difficult cases.

During his own youth, Frantz never mentioned the age or youthfulness of any offenders he executed. If it weren't for the city chronicles, which do note the precise ages of the young thieves he hanged, we would not even know that he encountered any juveniles at the scaffold. This reticence is even evident in his account of the extraordinary hanging of seven young thieves, aged thirteen to eighteen, on February 11 and 12, 1584. These five boys and two girls had each been banished multiple times for burglary, and one of the girls, Maria Kürschnerin (aka Constable Mary), had even had her ears cropped by Meister Frantz the year before. The shocking group execution of such young offenders attracted an enormous crowd and made a particular impression on local chroniclers, who recorded the ages of the youths as well as multiple other details (see illustration on page 176). Twenty-nine-year-old Frantz Schmidt, by contrast, notes only that the thieves *had broken into citizens' houses and stolen a considerable amount.* He then adds a single, apparently uneasy observation: that the hanging of women *had never before happened* in Nuremberg. On the equally salient detail of the girls' youth, the journal is silent.[102]

A decade later, Meister Frantz readily acknowledges that the two thieves Hensa Kreuzmayer and Hensa Baur were *both about sixteen years old,* and presumably on that account *out of mercy executed with the sword.* From that point on, he regularly includes the ages of all juveniles executed, without feeling compelled to add any exceptional justification

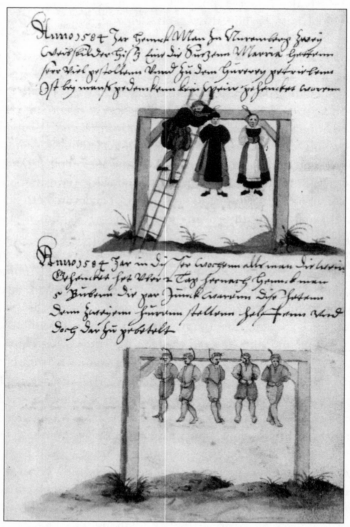

A Nuremberg chronicle records the unprecedented 1584 hanging of two young women, followed the next day by the hanging of five male youths, all part of a local burglary gang (1616).

other than *stole much*.[103] Both sixteen-year-old Balthasar Preiss and fifteen-year-old Michel König, Schmidt adds, had been given multiple opportunities to reform, but in each instance *would not abandon thieving or could not stop [stealing]*.[104] His 1615 account of another group hanging, this time involving five slightly older thieves, aged eighteen and nineteen, is even less sympathetic:

> The Big Farmer [aka Klaus Rodtler] stole much with the con-
> demned Devil's Lad and Farmer Cunz, had many other compan-
> ions, and lay often in the Hole [but] always lied his way out.
> Bruner [aka Junkman] only gathers purses; since he was released
> fourteen days ago has stolen about 50 fl. When the three [cut-
> purses] were executed [last month], he stole two purses during the
> execution. Riffraff [aka Johann Bauer] also belonged to this com-
> pany, was often in the Hole and the chain gang. The Weaver [aka
> Georg Knorr] also lay several times in the Hole, always released on
> account of his piety. All five thieves executed with the rope.[105]

What do we make of the mature Frantz's justification for torturing and executing teenagers? Should we read his lengthy protestations of their unreformability as an attempt to convince his own uneasy conscience that the punishments are just? Or had he, like some of the magistrates, grown so frustrated by the young men's repeated offenses, so outraged at their disregard for the council's many acts of mercy, that he truly believed they deserved the gallows? Is this evidence of a darkening, even cynical view of human nature?

Like most people, Meister Frantz appeared to be uncertain whether nature or nurture exerts more influence in the development of children who become career criminals. Clearly he didn't consider lack of access to respectable craft training—a fact of life for him and his own children—to be an acceptable explanation for why a young man might turn to crime. And he had no sympathy at all for those who did have access to training but squandered it. Laurenz Pfeiffer, described by Schmidt as *a grocer and a thief*, was *a young person who attempted to learn the tailor craft but did not do well*, and subsequently took to stealing, as did the burglar Pangratz Paumgartner, *who learned the compass-making [craft] here from Peter Ziegler*.[106] In fact, the great majority of the juveniles he encountered at the scaffold had received some artisanal training, as had the majority of all the men he executed. Whatever the actual opportunities for employment, these individuals all started out with advantages never enjoyed by an outcast executioner.

Consorting with "bad company" was another frequent catalyst to crime, often establishing a bad or even criminal reputation before the fact. Frantz considers it relevant but not exculpatory that the servant Hans Dorsch was incited to steal large amounts from his long-term master by his cousin and circle of male friends.[107] Spending days and nights with drinking, gambling, and quarreling men could rarely end well. A youth who wanted to live an honest life had to possess enough self-discipline to avoid the company of dishonest men—a choice the executioner himself had made long before. Military service apparently offered an especially effective education in vice. After serving multiple campaigns in Hungary, the local sons Hans Taumb and Peter Haubmayr fell among professional robbers, and despite multiple arrests and reprieves *both again kept whores as before, putting them in the way of people. As soon as anyone was interested or spoke to them, they pulled [the women out] and blackmailed [the would-be customer], taking all his money or clothes.*[108]

Then as now, Frantz and his contemporaries most often traced the roots of criminal behavior back to the parents, sometimes attributing the child's perfidy to a faulty upbringing, and other times to an inherited predilection for crime.[109] While Frantz always notes when he flogged or executed a relative of a previously punished criminal, he refrains from interpreting the connection.[110] Given his fierce beliefs about self-determination, and despite his regular encounters with pious and law-abiding parents of deviants, Schmidt appeared to fall more on the nurture side of the debate, blaming some parents for bad upbringing but still holding their grown children accountable. He is clearly disgusted that Hans Ammon (aka the Foreign Tailor) not only robbed churches but also *taught his daughter to steal*, or that Cordula Widtmenin *helped both of her sons in thievery, taking the stolen goods from them.* Parents who prostituted their own daughters or involved their children in counterfeiting were equally reprehensible.[111] And although victimized children might be pitied for their unfortunate backgrounds, that didn't absolve them of responsibility for their own actions, even if they were still relatively young. Bastla Hauck, who was flogged and eventually executed for theft, had watched his own *father and brother [hanged] and [another] brother whipped out of town with rods* for the same crime, yet he refused to mend his own ways.[112] Nor did it make any difference to Meister Frantz that the con artist Elisabeth Aurholtin as a child had been abandoned by her deranged father in some snowy woods, after he had drowned her mother and hanged her brother.[113] Schmidt's genuine sympathy for the little girl of the past would always be outweighed by the undeniable culpability of the present-day woman before him.

Schmidt's insistence on personal accountability did not make him oblivious to the apparently innate origin of some bad character. The robber Hans Rühl *some years ago, while yet a boy, killed another boy of ten by throwing a stone at him and was sent to the chain gang for it, [yet] when he was released he consorted with the knacker [until] he was banished from the town for his evil ways.*[114] Many condemned thieves, despite multiple apprenticeships, continued to steal from an early age, most notably the prolific burglar Jörg Mayr, *who was 17 years old [and] had begun [to steal] eight years ago.*[115] Other young men likewise appeared to Meister Frantz to be overwhelmed by their own violent dispositions, a vulnerability merely exacerbated by drink, bad company, and loose women. Such ne'er-do-wells established their character early in life, including Frantz's own executed brother-in-law Friedrich Werner, who "was bad from youth on and consorted with bad company."[116]

Whatever the respective influence of nature and nurture among criminal offenders, the veteran executioner steadfastly held to his fundamental principle of self-determination. How could it be otherwise for a self-made man who himself had come so far from his cursed origins? Fates were made, not inherited. It was ironic that the notorious *whoremonger and great traitor* Simon Schiller escaped stoning by an angry mob by *jump[ing] into the water [and] crawl[ing] under the millwork*, only to be stoned to death in the same place a year later—but it was his continued wanton ways that determined his end, not the stars, as so many condemned criminals claimed. Frantz's Lutheran acceptance of radical original sin and divine providence in no way released a sinner from personal responsibility in accepting or rejecting God's grace.

Frantz's most recent personal tragedies had the potential to weaken or strengthen his religious faith. The same might be said of his decades of immersion in the world of crime. Frustratingly, we have no idea whatsoever of the religious or philosophical works the self-taught executioner might have turned to for inspiration and consolation, other than the Bible. The most revealing clue we have to the state of his piety at this point of life is a text dated July 25, 1605. The Meistersinger (master singer) schools of German cities represented guild versions of the medieval minstrel tradition, comprised of male members ranked by their respective compositional abilities as apprentices, journeymen, or masters. Composers had to follow strict rules about rhyming, meter, and melody, as well as perform their works a cappella before a panel of master judges. Nearly thirty years after the death of Nuremberg's most famous Meistersinger, Hans Sachs, the city's song guild continued to hold annual open competitions for nonmembers. Remarkably, the long-time executioner himself, undoubtedly with some assistance, made his own submission. Although his song was likely never actually performed, it was later included in a published Meistersinger collection of 1617, the year of Meister Frantz's last execution.[117]

Not all historians have accepted the song as the work of the famed executioner, particularly given its linguistic fluency relative to his journal. Upon a close reading, however, the evidence for authorship appears incontestable. The text itself is signed "Meister Franz Schmidt at St. Jacob's," the latter a church near the executioner's residence. Schmidt was admittedly an extremely common name of the day, but Franz or Frantz—German for Francis, in veneration of the saint of Assisi—was not, at least not in a Protestant city like Nuremberg. It was also unusual among the Meisterlieder for a text to be signed with "Meister" (Frantz's popular honorific) rather than "Magister." The crowning proof that "our" Frantz Schmidt indeed composed the Meisterlied is the poet's choice of subject: the alleged correspondence between King Abgar of Edessa and Jesus, a story with particular resonance for the executioner-physician.

According to legend, the Syriac king Abgar V, a contemporary of Jesus, heard stories about the Galilean miracle worker and wrote to him requesting a personal visit. Suffering from leprosy, gout, and other painful ailments, Abgar professed his belief in Jesus' divinity and offered to host the Messiah if he would travel to Edessa (modern-day Şanlıurfa, Turkey) and heal the ailing ruler. Jesus, the received story goes, wrote back to Abgar that he was unable to come himself, but that in recognition of the king's faith, he would send a disciple—Thaddeus Thomas, or Addai in the local tongue. And indeed, shortly after Jesus' ascension, Thomas arrived in Edessa, as his master had promised, and miraculously healed Abgar, who was immediately baptized. The story circulated widely in the ancient world, with the purported letters themselves published in the fourth century by the church historian Eusebius of Caesarea. Over time, an image of Jesus on a cloth, "made not by human hands," became part of the legend and was venerated in the eastern part of the Roman Empire, where it took on still greater liturgical significance.

The story of Abgar and Jesus—which most modern scholars dismiss as spurious—never experienced the same popularity in the western part of the empire, which makes Frantz's selection of it unusual. At the very least, it suggests he had some familiarity with Eusebius's *Ecclesiastical History* (c. 323), which the song both names and closely follows in the wording of the two letters. Its central theme of healing clearly appealed to the executioner-physician, who repeats the word *illness* more than any other in the song, both in the physical and spiritual sense. *Impure spirits*, as much as blindness and lameness, *torment people with pain*, and it is *faith*, not *herbs or medicine*, that heals the suffering king. The words *wonders* and *power* also recur frequently, again recalling the spiritual nature of Jesus' healing. Whatever stylistic or theological assistance Frantz received in the composition of the song, the thematic thrust remains entirely his own, fully in keeping with his other writings. If anything, his lifetime of exposure to human cruelties and suffering had merely confirmed the foundational Protestant belief in salvation by grace and faith alone. Sin was inevitable among the fallen human race, but so was divine forgiveness—if one sought it. Criminal punishment offered not just an opportunity for legal expiation but for spiritual redemption, making the executioner a priest of sorts (although, as a Lutheran, Meister Frantz would have rejected identification as a intercessor who had the power to convey divine forgiveness himself).[118] Like a life of sin and crime, submission to divine forgiveness was for him a question of individual choice.

Among the many gospel stories about forgiveness, two in particular apparently found resonance in the pious executioner's journal. The first was that of the Prodigal Son, the well-known parable of a son who immorally squanders his inheritance yet is taken back and embraced by his compassionate father (Luke 15:11–32). Like his biblical counterpart, the thief Georg Schweiger made several regrettable choices, most notably

in his youth, together with his brother, first stole 40 fl. from his own flesh-and-blood father. Later, when his father sent him to settle a debt, he kept the money and gambled with it. Lastly, discovering that his father had buried a treasure in a stable behind the house, stole 60 fl. of it. He also had a lawful wife, whom he deserted, and attached himself to two whores, promising marriage to both.

A popular broadsheet version of the story of the Prodigal Son, with the title character taking his leave on the left, enjoying the high life in the center, and reduced to feeding swine on the right (c. 1570).

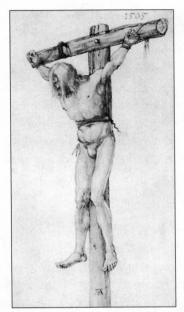 

Albrecht Dürer's evocative drawings of the bad thief (*left*) and the good thief (*right*) (1505).

Yet rather than forgive his errant offspring, *his father himself had [his son] imprisoned and desired and insisted that his right be exercised, in spite of the fact that he had recovered his money, and paid 2 fl. from it [for the jail time].*[119] Clearly Frantz believed that Schweiger's father had justifiable grounds for his anger, and the executioner himself does not question the thief's subsequent beheading for his crimes. That the injured father's heart remained hardened against his own prodigal son, however, appeared to him both unnatural and unchristian—an offense of a different order.

The second example comes from the year before Frantz made his submission to the *Meisterlied* contest, following a double execution of thieves. Although also implicit, the contrast in the two malefactors' display of repentance and faith clearly suggested to the evangelical executioner an analogy to the good and bad thieves crucified with Jesus (Luke 23:29–43). Like Dismas, the good thief, who asked the adjacent Christ "to remember me when you come into your kingdom," the shepherd Cunz Pütner showed all the requisite signs of remorse and *died as a Christian*.

His gallows companion Hans Drentz (aka Stretch), by contrast, was a virtual reincarnation of the bad thief (traditionally known as Gestas) who mocked and cursed Jesus as a false prophet from his own cross:

> *[He] would not pray or say a word about God nor confess the name of Christ. When questioned [about God] he always said he knew nothing about Him and could say nothing nor repeat any prayer. A young maid had once given him a shirt and since then he had been unable to pray. The sacrament was not administered to him, therefore he died in his sins and fell down near the gallows as if tormented by a fit. He was a godless man.*[120]

These men had all made their choices, Frantz seems to say, and their subsequent fates were thus of their own design. Every person was destined to sin; to seek or to bestow mercy was a choice. As the widowed father of four persevered in the odious occupation chosen for him—and in his slow but relentless campaign to achieve a status he had chosen for himself—this thought must have offered some reassurance and comfort.

5

THE HEALER

This policy and reverence of age makes the world bitter to the best of our times; keeps our fortunes from us till our oldness cannot relish them. I begin to find an idle and fond bondage in the oppression of aged tyranny; who sways, not as it hath power, but as it is suffered.

—William Shakespeare, *King Lear*, act 1, scene 2, 46–51 (1606)

The word virtue, I think, presupposes difficulty and struggle, and something that cannot be practiced without an adversary. This is perhaps why we call God good, mighty, liberal, and just, but do not call Him virtuous.

—Michel de Montaigne, "On Cruelty" (1580)[1]

Over nearly a half century as an executioner, Meister Frantz Schmidt confronted a bewildering array of human vice and cruelty. Yet in all that time, no culprits provoked a more primal revulsion in Meister Frantz than the sociopathic highwayman Georg Hörnlein of Bruck and his equally depraved henchman Jobst Knau of Bamberg. The executioner's meticulous recounting of their myriad offenses—a mere sampling by his own acknowledgment—constitutes the single longest entry in his journal. In the company of other unsavory associates, most frequently Georg Mayer (aka Brains) from Gostenhof, Hörnlein and Knau roamed the back roads and forests of Franconia for years, assaulting, robbing, and brutally murdering scores of peddlers, wandering journeymen, farmers, and other travelers, including women and youths. After itemizing more than a dozen known examples of their perfidy, Meister

Frantz prepares to end the day's entry. But then—we can almost see him shake his head in exasperation—he changes his mind and goes on to record still more damning examples of the duo's infamy, including that *they attacked people on the Mögeldorfer meadow and everywhere that citizens went for walks . . . as well as attacked eight people on the streets of Heroldsberg, severely wounding a man and a woman and chopping the hand of a carter in two.*

His disgust almost palpable, Schmidt continues with a blow-by-blow account of what he obviously considers to be the most disturbing incidents of the robbers' long rampage:

> *Six weeks ago [Hörnlein] and Knau, together with their companions, were consorting with a common whore, when she gave birth to a son in [Hörnlein's] house, whereupon Knau baptized it, then cut off its little right hand while alive. Afterward his companion, called Blacky, who acted as godfather, tossed the baby in the air, so that it fell upon the table, and said, "So big must my little godchild grow!" Also exclaimed, "See how the devil runs his trap!" then cut its throat and buried it in his little garden. Over eight days later, when Knau's whore bore a baby boy, Knau wrung its little neck, then Hörnlein cut off its little right hand and later buried it in his shed.*

The sheer horror of both moments comes through in Schmidt's writing, as he contrasts the diminutive terms *baby, little neck,* and *little right hand* with the drunken men's cold-blooded mockery of baptism and godfatherly affection. For Frantz, the incident epitomizes the pair's utter depravity, and he recalls with undisguised satisfaction the two burning nips that each man received on his arms and legs before suffering a painful execution on the wheel "from the bottom up" on January 2, 1588. Nine days later he executed their accomplice Brains, also with the wheel, and a week after that, he dispatched Hörnlein's wife and accomplice, Margaretha, employing the supposedly abolished *death with water,* revived one final time by the council—without protest from the executioner—for this especially heinous offense.[2]

But why were these men chopping off babies' hands in the first place? It was not a random atrocity. During Knau's interrogation, which involved repeated applications of the strappado under the supervision of Meister Frantz, the robber claimed that the right hand of a newborn male was widely known to bring good luck, even invisibility, a useful asset for a professional thief. He said that Hörnlein told him he had cut off many babies' hands during his travels and successfully used the "little fingers" as candles during break-ins, "so that no one awoke." (In England this practice was known as the Hand of Glory.)[3] Hörnlein confirmed this account in his own confession under torture, elaborating that the hands must stay buried for eight days, preferably in a stable, after which they may be dug up and carried. He admitted instructing Knau in this practice and giving him one of the hands for his own use, but professed only a modest expertise in any other of the "magical arts." When pressed further, however, Hörnlein conceded that one old woman taught him how to carry a small sack of lead and gunpowder to three successive Sunday masses and thereby gain magical power. He also acknowledged stealing a piece of rope "in broad daylight" from the gallows at a nearby town and carrying it around with his other talismans as protection against gunshot. Challenged by skeptical interrogators, Hörnlein retorted that he even got his two companions to shoot at each other as a test of the charm's power, and since neither was harmed, he won five gulden from each of them.[4]

Magical spells and curses were ubiquitous in Meister Frantz's world. His contemporaries energetically disputed the nature and efficacy of such powers (not to mention their source). But virtually no one challenged the essential mysteriousness of the natural world—and thus the possibility that with certain occult knowledge, human beings might be able to wield some sort of magical power. This fluid and often contradictory quality of pre-eighteenth-century popular beliefs about magic presented Meister Frantz with a predicament. In his sideline as a man of medicine, Schmidt could benefit by exploiting ancient magical beliefs about the "healing power" of the executioner and his equipment. And yet with the European witch craze at its height, a practitioner who bore even a tenuous link to magic faced undeniable danger as well. At once feared and respected—not unlike a powerful wise man or tribal shaman—Frantz was sought out (and well paid) for his healing expertise. But he also risked accusations of incompetence or dark magic from dissatisfied patients or any of his numerous and diverse competitors in a ruthless medical marketplace.

This ambiguous and vulnerable position was of course nothing new to Nuremberg's executioner. Just as he turned governmental demand for pious and responsible state killers to his personal advantage, Meister Frantz also exploited the healing aura surrounding his craft to further advance his quest for respectability—all the while artfully avoiding the wrath of zealous "witch finders" and jealous medical rivals alike. But medicine—as he revealed later in life—had always represented much more to the longtime executioner than a means to an end or a reliable source of supplemental income. Unlike the odious profession foisted upon him, *the doctoring art* was his true vocation. *Almost every person,* Frantz writes, *has an enduring inclination toward a certain thing by which he might earn his keep,* and for him, *Nature [herself] had implanted in me the desire to heal.*[5] More than his role in the redemptive ritual of the execution, his lifelong work in physical healing provided the executioner with a sense of accomplishment, purpose, even restoration. His struggle to secure this professional identity for himself and his sons would in fact shape the final three decades of his life. Whether Meister Frantz's own painstakingly constructed and formidable reputation as an executioner would aid or hinder that final self-fashioning remained to be seen.

Live bodies

All premodern executioners were presumed to possess a certain amount of medical expertise. Some were even appointed to their posts explicitly because of their reputed skills in healing people or animals, typically cows and horses. Nuremberg's magistrates rehired one of Frantz's notoriously dissolute predecessors less than a year after angrily dismissing him expressly "because his doctoring greatly helped many injured and sick people to recover, and since Jörg Unger, the current executioner, is absolutely worthless [in that respect]."[6] In the day of Frantz Schmidt's father, medical consulting had constituted a minor supplement to the salary of most executioners. By the time Frantz himself became professionally active, fees for healing might constitute as much as half of an executioner's annual income.[7] Following his official retirement in 1618, Schmidt would become almost completely reliant on earnings from his medical work, which continued to flourish until his death, several years later.

The varied and sometimes shadowy array of medical and quasimedical services available in the premodern world represented market competition at its unregulated finest. Academically trained physicians boasted the highest level of official certification, but their small numbers and high fees made them inaccessible to the majority of the population. Guild-trained barber-surgeons, "wound doctors," and apothecaries enjoyed a similar aura of respectability and were at least ten times more prevalent than academic physicians in large cities such as Nuremberg.[8] Typically, these professionals trained as apprentices and journeymen several years longer than physicians studied at university. By the late sixteenth century, virtually every German state employed its own official physicians and barber-surgeons as well as apothecaries and midwives, imbuing each profession with still greater legitimacy and credibility.

Of course, institutional endorsements of this nature did not prevent most people from turning to any of a variety of nonsanctioned "empirics"—peddlers, traveling apothecaries, oculists, Gypsies, and religious healers—each hawking an assortment of curative powders, compounds, ointments, and herbs. Physicians of the seventeenth and eighteenth centuries routinely derided the healing abilities of such "quacks" and "charlatans," but at least some of these roving practitioners offered remedies that actually provided relief in certain cases. Sulfur salves did occasionally clear up skin conditions, and certain herbal concoctions did manage to soothe some aching backs. Obviously, the more sweeping and outlandish claims of itinerant healers were sheer hokum. But at least these traveling quacks advertised their wares with humorous songs, diverting theatrics, and even the occasional snake-handling show (to promote a tonic that provided immunity from any bites).

The healing reputation of Meister Frantz lacked any official backing or carnivalesque promotions, but it unquestionably benefited from the many folk beliefs surrounding his nefarious profession. Like the "cunning" men and women found in practically every village, executioners

allegedly knew secret recipes and cures for a variety of ailments—
ranging from cancer and kidney failure to toothaches and insomnia—
information typically passed down orally to their young acolytes. The
controversial physician Paracelsus (1493–1541), who publicly rejected
most of what he'd been taught in medical school, famously claimed that
he learned the bulk of his healing remedies and techniques from executioners and cunning people. The Hamburg executioner Meister Valentin Matz was widely reputed "to know herbs and sympathy [healing]
better than many learned doctors."[9] Whatever the efficacy of an executioner's treatments, the "sinister charisma" of Frantz and his fellow
practitioners gave them an invaluable advantage in the highly competitive (and highly lucrative) medical marketplace of the day. Sons of executioners frequently profited from the association as well, and were able
to operate prosperous medical practices even if they did not follow their
fathers into the execution profession. Many widows and wives of executioners also did medical work, sometimes competing for patients with
local midwives.[10]

But how much did Meister Frantz truly know about the art of healing, and where did he learn it? Meister Heinrich certainly would have
taught his son all that he could. But, having grown up as the son of an
honorable tailor, Heinrich would have had to learn the healing arts on
the job, as it were. Once the Schmidts had been accepted into the profession, other executioners probably shared some of their secrets, know-
ing that direct competition from a geographically distant colleague was
unlikely. The many criminals and vagrants Heinrich and Frantz encountered during their work provided another fecund source of information, often including magical incantations, but this type of healing
ventured into risky territory.

The most valuable resources for a literate executioner were probably
the numerous medical pamphlets and other reference works that
flooded the print marketplace from the early sixteenth century on.[11]
University-trained physicians just a few generations later would have
been scandalized by the do-it-yourself approach of most popular medical manuals in Frantz Schmidt's day. More shocking still, in many instances the popularizers were themselves members of the medical elite.
The respected physician Johann Weyer (1515–88), today famous as an
early vocal opponent of the witch craze, was better known to fellow

healers of his era for his *Doctoring Book: On Assorted Previously Unknown and Undescribed Illnesses*, which covered treatment for conditions ranging from typhus and syphilis (hardly "unknown" in 1583) to "night attacks" and diarrhea.[12] Weyer assumed his readers had little or no professional training and describes symptoms and cures in clear, specific, and jargon-free language, supplemented by illustrations of the relevant herbs, medicinal insects, and toads. He also sprinkles biblical references throughout the text, as did most popular authors of the era, beginning with an opening reminder that suffering and illness themselves were the result of Adam and Eve's original fall from grace.

Hans von Gersdorff's *Fieldbook of Wound-Healing*, reprinted several times after its initial 1517 publication, was an even more likely resource for Meister Frantz.[13] Based on the author's extensive experience as a military wound doctor, the 224-page compendium is practically a medical education in itself, beginning with a discussion of the respective roles in health of the four humors, the elements, and the planets, and then offering a step-by-step guide to diagnosing symptoms and applying treatments. Though Gersdorff focused more on external wounds, he also described basic human anatomy, and included several carefully marked illustrations. Like Weyer and other popular authors, he provided illustrations of herbs as well as schematics that show the reader how to construct scalpels, cranial drills, braces for broken limbs, clamps, and even a still. Just as crucially for any nonacademically trained healer, the *Fieldbook* included an extensive glossary of Latin medical terms and their German translations, as well as a thorough alphabetical index of symptoms, body parts, and treatments.

In accounting for Meister Frantz's medical success, we should not underestimate the sheer value of listening to patients.[14] A reassuring air of self-confidence and other interpersonal skills could go a long way, particularly since conversation constituted a much more important component of the early modern medical consultation than did physical examination. In the words of one popular manual, "A good case history is already half of the diagnosis."[15] Learning about a patient's occupation, family members, diet, sleeping habits, and more would be useful for any practitioner, but especially for executioners and other folk healers, who could draw on neither the official certification of physicians and barber-surgeons nor the entertaining showmanship of traveling empirics. Meister Frantz could succeed only by painstakingly building up a broad base of loyal patients who felt that he understood them and their ailments. The famed "executioner's touch" may have gotten some patients through the door, but given the abundance of healing alterna-

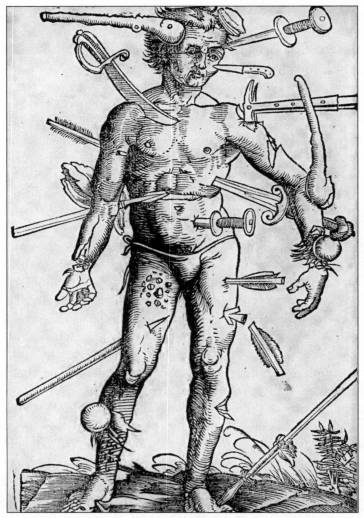

The much-reprinted "wound man" illustration from Hans von Gersdorff's *Fieldbook*, indicating the variety of human-inflicted injuries that executioners and barber-surgeons regularly treated (1517).

tives available, it would not have kept them coming back had not some successful healing actually occurred.

Genuine skill was especially essential in the executioner's traditional sphere of medical activity, namely "external treatments" such as resetting broken bones, treating severe burns, cauterizing the bleeding from amputated limbs, and healing open sores or gunshot wounds. More than a third of the wounds treated by wound doctors and executioners resulted from attacks with knives, swords, or guns.[16] These were areas of demonstrable expertise for Frantz, since his years of work in the torture chamber gave him extensive experience in how to avoid severely wounding subjects during interrogation as well as how to heal them before questioning or public execution. Frantz apparently received no supplemental fee for his work healing prisoners, but some of his fellow executioners earned three or four times as much for healing a criminal suspect as they did for the torture they had just administered.[17]

Schmidt's medical ledgers have not survived. But by his own estimate, in nearly fifty years of medical practice he treated more than fifteen thousand patients in Nuremberg and its surrounding territories.[18] Even accounting for some hyperbole as well as the occasional double-counting (Frantz was never good with numbers), this is a remarkable figure. It means that Meister Frantz saw on average more than three hundred patients a year—at least ten times as many individuals as he tortured or punished. Did this knowledge offer him consolation for the agonies that he intentionally inflicted? Did these nearly daily medical experiences reinforce his already deep compassion for the suffering of crime victims? Undoubtedly his widespread reputation as a successful healer helped mitigate the disdain normally reserved for executioners. But it was not enough in itself to make him or his family honorable.

In this context, the selective way that people of the era interpreted the effect of the executioner's touch appears especially mystifying and capriciously cruel to modern sensibilities. The very individuals who refused to share a table or drink with the publicly reviled executioner, much less allow him into their homes, apparently had no qualms about visiting Frantz in the Hangman's House and allowing him to lay hands on them there.[19] The privacy of such encounters in part accounts for the double standard, but there was apparently no secrecy or shame involved in consulting Meister Frantz for medical reasons. Admittedly,

A wound doctor performs an amputation on an inebriated but still conscious patient. Wound doctors and barber-surgeons constituted Frantz's main competition in the medical marketplace (c. 1550).

given the nature of his healing expertise, the majority of his patients were soldiers, manual laborers, and farmers. Respectable artisans, however, also consulted him on a regular basis, as did patricians and even some nobles, among them three imperial emissaries, the cathedral provost of Bamberg, and a Teutonic knight, as well as several patrician city councilors and their family members.[20] The steady flow of individuals from all ranks of society into the Hangman's House clearly gives the lie to any absolute marginalization of the executioner and his family. On the other hand, this regular contact with people who shunned them in public must have made the Schmidts' unique limbo-like social status even more difficult to bear.

Treating external wounds was also the provenance of barber-surgeons, and this predictably led to frequent disputes between them and executioners, conflicts that usually resulted in governmental intervention. Here too, Frantz's success at building both his personal and professional reputations appears to have staved off the wrath of competitors and the city council alike. He was never once censored by his superiors on this score, and in 1601 they actually referred one man, who complained about a local barber's unsatisfactory healing of his seven-year-old son's right knee, not to the municipal physicians but to Meister Frantz.[21] Eight years later, the barber Hans Duebelius claimed that because Meister Frantz had previously treated an injured innkeeper, the barber guild would consider him dishonorable if he attempted to cure the same man. Councilors reassured Duebelius that he could proceed without fear of contamination, but they also declined to reprimand the executioner for his own medical activity.[22] It's unlikely that Nuremberg's barber-surgeons embraced Frantz as a fellow professional, but neither did they openly challenge either his skills or his obvious clout with the magistracy.

Another potential threat to Frantz's medical success was the rapid ascendancy during his lifetime of the academically trained physician. These professional healers had long occupied the top rung in terms of both prestige and income, but their numbers remained small. Nevertheless, from the late sixteenth century on, they began to assert a new dominance in the medical marketplace. First, they consolidated in German cities, forming quasi-governmental bodies, such as Nuremberg's Collegium Medicum, established in 1592 under the leadership of Dr. Joachim Camerarius. At the same time, physicians convinced secular authorities that the diverse and often "ignorant" methods of "practical healers"—even including guild-certified barbers, apothecaries, and midwives—required closer regulation and supervision. In Nuremberg this meant more restrictions for licensed practitioners and large fines, possibly even banishment, for amateur "tooth breakers," alchemists, wise women, Jews, black magicians, and other empirics.[23]

Fortunately for Frantz Schmidt and his successors, the Collegium

Medicum did not assume oversight of their medical activity, but it did restrict them to treating external injuries, "about which they have some knowledge."[24] Meister Frantz also appears to have successfully avoided the open conflicts with physicians that were common among fellow executioners throughout the empire, including his immediate successors.[25] Surprisingly, Frantz's forensic work brought him into more direct and regular contact with these patrician professionals than with the artisanal barber-surgeons, who were much closer to him in training and expertise. Perhaps the respect Schmidt apparently enjoyed in official circles even encouraged him to daydream about one of his sons pursuing this noble—and as yet unreachable—profession. The day when such a social leap would be possible was closer than he imagined.

Dead bodies

Although much of Meister Frantz's work required him to engage with the living—prisoners, officials, patients, and the like—he also spent a significant amount of time with the dead or, to be more specific, with the cadavers of the poor sinners he had executed. Some of the bodies of those he dispatched received the same treatment as those of any other departed souls, including burial on consecrated ground.[26] The majority, however, met a less happy fate. The corpses of hanged thieves and murderers broken on the wheel of course remained exposed to the elements, their crumbled remains eventually swept into a pit under the gallows. Other cadavers were handed over to the executioner for dissection or other use. In no instance was the body of an executed criminal allowed to go to waste; it functioned instead as evidence of the court's mercy, a gruesome warning, or a useful medical object.

In premodern Europe it was commonly believed—by academic physicians and folk healers alike—that the bodies of the dead possessed tremendous curative powers. This led to a practice that strikes the modern sensibility as bizarre, even disturbing, but that enjoyed widespread acceptance in the era of Meister Frantz: namely the ingestion, wearing, or other medical use of human body parts to heal the sick or injured. Belief in the curative power of various types of human remains can be traced back at least to the time of Pliny the Elder (A.D.

23–79) and would continue to thrive into the eighteenth century.[27] Despite this tradition's obvious affinity with magic, virtually all medical professionals of the day insisted that the practice had a firm foundation in natural philosophy and human anatomy itself. According to followers of Paracelsus, also known as chemical doctors, human skin, blood, and bones possessed the same healing powers as certain minerals and plants and transferred a curative spiritual force to the ill person. Classically trained Galenist physicians scoffed at such "magical" explanations, and instead insisted that body parts healed the sick by restoring the internal balance of the four humors (blood, phlegm, black bile, and yellow bile). Virtually no healer, formally trained or not, disputed the received wisdom that a recently deceased human body provided a panoply of curative supplies.

Drinking blood, "the noblest of the humors," was considered an especially potent remedy with many uses, among them dissolving blood clots, protecting a patient from painful spleen or coughing, preventing seizures, opening up blocked menstruation, or even curing flatulence.[28] Since the medical establishment believed blood to be continuously concocted by the liver, its supply was also theoretically unlimited, thus diminishing any concern over frequent bloodletting, or phlebotomy, intended to restore the humoral balance. Because age and virility determined the potency of the fluid, the blood of suddenly executed young criminals, whose life force had not yet had a chance to escape, was especially prized. Epileptics, eager to drink the warm and fresh poor sinner's blood, frequently lined up next to the scaffold following a beheading—an alarming scene for us to envision, yet an unremarkable one for Frantz Schmidt and his contemporaries.

Before the mid-seventeenth century, Meister Frantz and his fellow executioners enjoyed a near monopoly on the various human body parts used for popular healing. Many of them ran side businesses supplying apothecaries and other eager customers. The official pharmacopoeia of Nuremberg, stocked largely by the cadavers of executed criminals, included whole and prepared skulls, "human grains" (from ground bones), "marinated human flesh," human fat, salt from human grains, and spirit of human bone (a potion derived from boiling bones). Pregnant women and people suffering from swollen joints or cramps wore specially treated strips of human skin, known as human leather or poor sinners' fat. The healing power of mummy, as preserved human flesh was generically known, even became the focus of a new devotional mysticism devised by the Jesuit Bernard Caesius (1599–1630). There is no way to know how much additional revenue Frantz earned from the human parts trade or to what degree he even engaged in this to-our-eyes ghoulish but lucrative practice.[29]

Inevitably, some healers of the era also promoted various explicitly magical uses for human body parts. One fellow executioner's recipe for treating a bewitched horse called for a powder made out of certain herbs, cow fat, vinegar, and burnt human flesh—all mixed with a shaved stick found on a river's bank before sundown.[30] Academically trained Protestant physicians, eager to debunk Catholic belief in the power of saints' relics, vociferously denied that human body parts had any such supernatural power. They accordingly dismissed as superstition such uncomfortably akin beliefs as the popular claim that the finger or hand of an executed thief would bring good luck in gambling or, if consumed by a cow, provide protection against witchcraft. Catholic authorities in Bavaria similarly professed shock "that many people dare to take things from executed criminals, and seize the chains from the gallows where the criminal was hanged . . . as well as the rope . . . to employ in certain arts," and forbade the use of any such object "to which superstition attributes another effect than it can have naturally."[31] Church leaders of both denominations were even more alarmed by some executioners' attempts to cash in on their magical notoriety. In 1611, for example, Frantz's counterpart in the Bavarian city of Passau began a long-running and especially lucrative practice by selling little folded pieces of magically inscribed paper, known as *Passauer Zettel*, which were reputed to protect the bearer from bullets.

A much more familiar (and still current) use for the cadavers at Meister Frantz's disposal was dissection for anatomical studies.[32] Artists such as Leonardo da Vinci and Michelangelo had long before requested the bodies of the executioner's victims for this purpose—decreed permissible by Pope Sixtus IV in 1482—but the medical interest in dissection did not really take off until the publication of Andreas Vesalius's remarkable drawings in *De Humani Corporis Fabrica* (Concerning the Construction of the Human Body; 1543). Accompanied by detailed commentary, the twenty-eight-year-old physician's graceful illustrations of skeletal, nervous, muscular, and visceral systems stunned the medical establishment. Almost immediately, medical faculties across Europe began to devote lectures and endowed chairs to the study of human anatomy, convinced by the observations of Vesalius and other pioneers that much of what they had previously taught—received

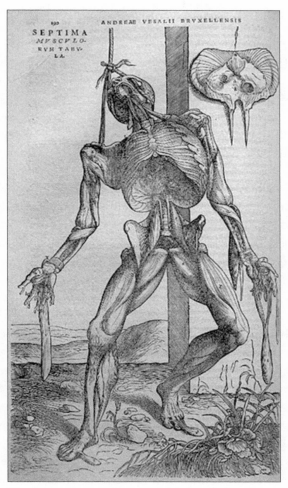

The human muscular system, one of almost two hundred detailed illustrations from Vesalius's 1543 *De Humani Corporis Fabrica*. Note that even the celebrated expert uses a recently hanged criminal as his model.

knowledge that dated back to the second-century Greek physician Galen—was inadequate or outright wrong. A century later, eleven German universities, including Altdorf near Nuremberg, boasted their own anatomical theaters, and the practice of medical dissection was ubiquitous.[33]

Demand for the corpses of executed criminals accordingly rose steadily over the course of Meister Frantz's lifetime. By the early seventeenth century, the trade in human cadavers and body parts had reached a feverish pitch. Shortly after Meister Frantz's death, the citizenry and councilors of Munich were scandalized to learn that their appropriately named executioner, Martin Leichnam ("cadaver"), before handing over the corpse of a beheaded child murderer to her parents for Christian burial, had first sold off various body parts, including her heart, which was ground into a curative powder.[34] Medical students from the University of Altdorf apparently always asked Frantz or his successors for permission before taking away executed bodies, but their less scrupulous peers elsewhere frequently staged unauthorized midnight raids of cemeteries and execution grounds. The most infamous body snatcher in the empire was undoubtedly Professor Werner Rolfinck (1599–1673), whose fondness for pilfering the local gallows led his medical students at the University of Jena to coin a new verb for the practice in his honor: "rolfincking."[35]

Meister Frantz's own keen interest in human dissection was uncommon among executioners and offers further evidence of his higher medical ambitions. Since 1548 the Nuremberg city council had restricted "the cutting up of poor executed victims" to a few physicians, and then "so long as only a few persons were present." Three years before Frantz Schmidt's arrival in Nuremberg, Dr. Volker Coiter was permitted to dissect two thieves and give the fat to the executioner for his medical supplies.[36] This traditional division of labor and body uses was probably what city magistrates had in mind when they granted the new executioner's request in July 1578 "to cut up beheaded bodies and take what is useful to him in his medical practice."[37] Yet in his journal's account of how he dealt with the body of beheaded robber Heinz Gorssn (aka Lazy Hank), twenty-four-year-old Frantz is careful to specify *I later dissected [the body].*[38] Schmidt rarely used the first-person pronoun in his journal, so it seems clear that in this entry the young executioner wished to commemorate a significant personal achievement. He explicitly records only three similar occasions—in 1581, 1584, and 1590—and the last time clarifies his intentions with the phrase *dissected* (*adominirt*) or *cut up*. It could be assumed that Frantz had simply appropriated the more serious language of anatomy to describe his own carvings, except that these are the same words he used when he handed over the body of the thief Michel Knüttel to the local physician Dr. Pessler for a full postmortem in 1594. His interest, in other words, was not merely in extracting usable body parts but in exploring human anatomy itself—the same as with any other physician.[39]

Of course there were serious limitations to the discoveries an amateur anatomist might make, even one aided by popular versions of Vesalius's work and his own healing experience—not to mention a reliable

Volker Coiter (1534–76), municipal physician of Nuremberg. Coiter, like his successor Joachim Camerarius the Younger (1534–98), was an anatomy enthusiast, at one point even temporarily banished from the city on account of grave robbing (1569).

supply of fresh cadavers. Frantz's curiosity about human anatomy was shaped by the time in which he lived, an era when most laypeople were fascinated by oddities and anomalies but uninterested in—or unaware of—the possibility of organizing their observations into any kind of theoretical system, a pursuit that was left to natural philosophers and theologians. His methodical observation of his victims' bodies, like his interest in their character, also does not surface in the journal until the second half of his life. In his early years, for example, Frantz might note that two brothers and their companion were *three strong young thieves* or note in passing that an executed robber only *has one hand*.[40] We also learn that the barber Balthasar Scherl *was a small person, had a hump in the front and back* and that the beggar Elisabeth Rossnerin *had a crooked neck*.[41] Years later, he writes with an earnest amateur's precision that the beheaded thief Georg Praun (aka Pin George) *had a neck two spans long and two handsbreadth thick [approximately nineteen by eight inches]*, that Laurenz Demer (aka the Long Farmer) *was two fingers less than three Ells in height [i.e., about 7'4"]*, and that the flogged Simon Starck *has 92 pockmarks*—all facts that could only have been ascertained by his own punctilious postmortem examination.[42] The only time that Meister Frantz's air of scientific dispassion eluded him was following the decapitation of thief Georg Praun, *when his head turned several times [on the stone] as if it wanted to look about it, the tongue moved and the mouth opened as if he wanted to speak, for a good half quarter of an hour. I have never seen the likes of this*.[43] Like most early modern chroniclers, the astonished executioner does not offer an explanation, only a wonder worthy of recording.

Black magic

The healing expertise of executioners, as well as their conversancy with the illicit practices of the criminal underworld, lent the profession an aura of authority on the subject of the dark arts. In popular folklore, executioners and their magical swords (drenched in the blood of recently executed young men) could prevail against vampires and werewolves as well as summon spirits of the dead or exorcise ghosts from houses. In one typical folktale of the day, the persistence of an especially vexing house ghost prompts a showdown between a Jesuit exorcist and an executioner, with the latter ultimately claiming victory by trapping the troublesome spirit in a sack and later releasing it into a forest. Dramatic performances of this sort appear but once in the chronicles of sixteenth-century Nuremberg, in 1583, with Frantz a mere spectator to an officially sanctioned demonic exorcism by a Lutheran cleric.[44]

Of course, in the frenzied atmosphere of the pan-European witch craze of approximately 1550 to 1650, any association with magic—even medicinal—could prove quite dangerous. Many people presumed executioners themselves to be "secret sorcerers" and "witch masters," particularly during the peak witch-panic years of the early seventeenth century, when all magical practices came under suspicion of diabolical origin. Though ultimately vindicated, Frantz's Munich counterpart never fully recovered from his 1612 imprisonment for illicit magic (based on evidence brought to the courts by a Jesuit accuser). Even Schmidt's own successor would be admonished for his involvement in "magical business" and threatened with banishment "or worse" should the council learn that he had made any contact with "the evil spirit." Other professionals were less fortunate, most notably the widow of a later Nuremberg Lion, who was convicted and burned alive for witchcraft in the city's only case involving an alleged diabolical pact and sex with the devil.[45]

More typically, professional executioners in Meister Frantz's day served as the indispensable allies of self-proclaimed witch finders. Johann Georg Abriel, Frantz's counterpart in Schongau, and Christoph Hiert of Biberach were themselves highly sought-out experts in finding the so-called witch's mark, and helped to advance many witch hunts in Bavaria and Upper Swabia during the 1590s. Other executioners played similarly pivotal roles in producing confessions under torture and spreading the panic. Southern Germany in fact saw more executions for witchcraft than any other region in Europe—perhaps 40 percent of the grand total of sixty thousand—and Franconia in particular was ground zero of the witch craze, most infamously as site of the Bamberg and Würzburg panics of 1626–31 that resulted in the executions of more than two thousand people.[46]

In this respect, Frantz and his city represented an oasis of restraint amid the enveloping madness. Until the late sixteenth century, Nuremberg had witnessed only one execution for magic ever, and that was more properly a case of accidental poisoning by what was intended to be a love potion, nearly six decades before Frantz Schmidt's arrival.[47] By July 1590, though, even the city on the Pegnitz began to show some vulnerability to the hysteria sweeping the region. The city council reacted swiftly, but in contrast to the leaders of other territories, by arresting and imprisoning Friedrich Stigler, a banished Nuremberger and former executioner's assistant in Eichstätt, *for having brought accusations against some citizens' wives here that they were witches and he knew it by their signs . . . also said that they gave magic spells to people.*[48]

Stigler, who boasted considerable expertise from his work with Frantz's counterpart in Eichstätt, claimed to have identified eleven witches just on the street where he resided, specifically five older women and six "apprentice girls." During his interrogation, which included a session on the strappado under Meister Frantz, the newly arrived witch-hunt veteran claimed that he had initially rebuffed all local citizens' appeals for help in detecting witches in Nuremberg, demurring that the city "had its own executioner" for such matters. If this remark was intended to incriminate Frantz Schmidt for being soft on witches, it had the opposite effect on his loyal employers, who likewise regarded all allegations of witchcraft with deep skepticism. Undaunted, Stigler next told how he was finally persuaded by the unrelenting petitioners to share his anti-witchcraft expertise, which he did by selling them small bags of blessed salt, bread, and wax for one ort (¼ fl.) each. According to Stigler, the bags, which he had been taught to make by his executioner master at Abensberg, both protected one from witches and could be used to find the devil's spot on a witch, which—as everyone knew—was impervious to the pain of a needle prick.[49]

The presiding magistrates gave no credence whatsoever to Stigler's "false accusations . . . made out of pure, brazen, wantonness," and showed more concern over his own familiarity with magic, not to mention his three wives. More than anything, it was their determination to prevent a local panic that ultimately led them to pronounce a death sentence for the "godless" Stigler, "on account of having given rise to all kinds of unrest, false suspicion, and strife among the citizenry as well as various superstitious, godless spells and conspiracies and other for-

The burning alive of three accused witches in Baden. The pan-European witch craze coincided almost exactly with Frantz Schmidt's lifetime (1574).

bidden magical arts and methods elsewhere."[50] On July 28, 1590, he was *out of mercy* beheaded by Meister Frantz.[51]

The Nuremberg government's decisive response to its first serious encounter with witch paranoia received the full support of its executioner. Given the popular association of executioners with the dark arts, Frantz Schmidt had special motivation to see such a disreputable fellow professional punished. That Stigler *wittingly did [the accused women] wrong* earned him still more disdain from the slander-sensitive Meister Frantz. Above all, Nuremberg's executioner appears to have shared the wariness of his superiors toward witch accusations in general, as well as their profound fear of the disorder and lawlessness that inevitably ensued. He followed with amazement and likely disgust the mass trials and burnings in the Franconian countryside where he had traveled as a journeyman. Like Stigler, Frantz knew from his experience in Bamberg about the methods of witch finders as well as the genuine danger of coerced confessions at the hands of a skilled torturer. The pivotal role of the professional executioner in such spurious proceedings must have been for him a source of discomfort, perhaps even shame.

Over the next two decades, Nuremberg's magistrates continued to fervidly resist the panics seizing neighboring territories. Less than eighteen months after Stigler's execution, the tortured confession of a suspected witch in the neighboring margravate of Ansbach led to the arrest of two women from villages in Nuremberg's jurisdiction. After a painstaking investigation of the charges involved in both cases, Nuremberg's jurists found insufficient justification for torture and recommended dismissal of charges. Upon receiving Meister Frantz's further assessment that both women were of too advanced an age to withstand physical coercion anyway, the city council ordered both women released. The following year, when officials of the margravate learned of the covered-up suicide of an alleged witch in Fürth (admittedly within their legal jurisdiction), they not only demanded that her body be exhumed and burned, but also that all her family's property be confiscated. Once more eager to avoid triggering a panic, Nuremberg's jurists countered that neither the charges against her nor the nature of her death could be definitively established, and thus continued to back the aggrieved widower and his son during several additional legal assaults from the margravate. In subsequent years, the council released three Altdorf men after confiscating their "magical books and decks of cards" and summarily dismissed two old women accused separately of employing magical healing. Only the convicted perjurer Hans Rössner, who repeated Friedrich Stigler's mistake of spreading false rumors and accusations of witchcraft, received punishment, although unlike his doomed predecessor he escaped with time in the stocks and lifelong banishment (under threat of execution, should he return).[52]

Neither Meister Frantz nor his superiors denied the efficacy of magic per se, but they focused instead on whether it had been used in conjunction with any harmful deeds, known as *maleficia*. Schmidt impassively notes that Georg Karl Lambrecht, the last poor sinner he executed, *also occupied himself with magic spells,* but since no *maleficia* were established, it was not one of the crimes mentioned in his official verdict.[53] He considers it relevant that Kunrad Zwickelsperger, who *committed lewdness* with the married Barbara Wagnerin, *gave two fl. to an old sorceress that she might cause [Wagnerin's husband] to be stabbed, struck down, or drowned,* but Zwickelsperger's ultimate condemnation is based on the more pertinent evidence that he also convinced his lover to poison her husband repeatedly (as well as that he slept with her mother and three sisters).[54] Often Frantz mentions "magical" curses to establish character and motive for subsequent violent action: a young knacker who publicly *hexes* his treacherous former companion *so that he would immediately die*; or a village bully who threatens his neighbors that *he would burn their house down [and afterward] cut off their hands and hide them in his breast.*[55] Anticipating the conclusions of historical anthropologists centuries later, Frantz recognized that such curses and threats often represented the empty bluffs of the powerless. When the arrested thief Anna Pergmennin threatened *that she would fly off next to an old broom-maker hag on a pitchfork,* Schmidt adds sardonically, *but nothing happened.*[56] His apparent openness to the possibility that something might have happened distinguishes his skepticism from ours, but his steadfast imperviousness to witch hysteria matches our own.

The similarity of Frantz Schmidt's outlook to that of contemporary physician Johann Weyer suggests that the executioner was familiar with the latter's *De Praestigiis Daemonarum* (On the Illusions of Demons; first German edition in 1567), either indirectly or through his own reading. The most famous (and consequently vilified) early opponent of the witch craze, Weyer likewise refused to rule out the efficacy of magic, but simultaneously argued that the great majority of self-proclaimed witches were either self-deluded or outright frauds. The remainder were intentional poisoners—a capital crime sufficient unto itself. Like their contemporary Michel de Montaigne, Weyer and Meister Frantz showed acute awareness of the power that emotions could exert on the human imagination, both in the case of alleged victims and alleged perpetrators.

Certainly Meister Frantz recognized the genuine psychological agony of some poor sinners who came before him and had convinced themselves of inescapable diabolical entanglements. During his imprisonment in the Hole, the thief Georg Prückner *gave out that he had received from the night watchman at Kreinberg something against wounds which he must eat—having sworn in return, however, never again to think of God nor pray to Him—which he did and gave himself to the devil. He tried to break out of the Hole and indeed behaved wantonly, as if the evil spirit tormented him.* The executioner's judicious *and indeed . . . as if* succinctly conveys his simultaneous acknowledgment of a diabolical power and his own conviction that Prückner was in fact delusional. Neither Frantz nor his chaplain colleague, Magister Müller—who complained of being kept awake at night two blocks away in the Saint Sebaldus parsonage because of Prückner's loud ravings—treated the tormented soul as an actual disciple of Satan, and indeed agreed that he *behaved in a Christian manner [in the end].*[57] Schmidt believed, in other words, that the temptations of a spiritual devil could prey on a weak mind, even if witches' sabbaths and other physical encounters remained pure fantasy. Another disturbed inmate, the thief Lienhard Schwartz, unsuccessfully tried to kill himself in prison, first with a knife and later by hanging with his torn shirt, saying *a voice spoke to him, though he saw nobody, telling him that if he surrendered to him he would soon help him.* Meister Frantz pointedly adds, *at this he fell into repentance, but if the voice had called again it might have happened [otherwise].*[58] On the source or reality of the voice, the executioner remains mute.

Any residual awe of so-called dark magic from his younger days was effectively demolished by Frantz Schmidt's lengthy experience in the torture chamber. He knew intimately of the persistence of countless spurious beliefs among professional criminals, despite not a single example of efficacy. Attempts to acquire invisibility or protection through severed body parts, pieces of the gallows, or other talismans were invariably presented in his journal as evidence of pathetic gullibility. Like disreputable companions and confiscated burglary tools, magical charms could also provide evidence of illicit activities and intentions. During one interrogation, the incorrigible honey thief Peter Hoffman claimed repeatedly that the skull and bones found on him during his arrest were not intended for nefarious purposes, but rather as a means of healing epileptics. (He also denied magically transporting his estranged female companion across great distances, but eventually acknowledged that he had appropriated her undergarments in a failed attempt at love magic designed to bring her back to him.) Schmidt notably declines to make use of such harmless "incantations and conjurations" to further blacken Hoffman's name in his journal, instead mentioning only his multiple thefts and adultery.[59] Even the notorious Georg Karl Lambrecht, pushed hard to admit that "he is himself a true sorcerer and conjurer of devils . . . addicted to the diabolical arts," in the end owns only to buying a charm and some enchanted slips of paper to protect himself against gunshot. Moreover, after having tested one "magically protective" skull on a dog (which promptly died from multiple bullet wounds), he concludes that "the deeds and boasts of these vagabonds were all pretended and imagined [and] he did not desire to have anything further to do with them"—a conclusion his executioner had apparently reached long ago.[60]

The great majority of the so-called magical experts that Meister Frantz Schmidt encountered during his career could be classified quite simply as frauds. He whips out of town Cunz Hoffmann, who *gave himself out as a planet reader [i.e., astrologer] and palm reader*, as well as four divining Gypsies, and *the fortune-telling and treasure-finding* Anna Domiririn, who *in one day [obtained] about 60 fl. and five golden rings from Frau Michaela Schmiedin*. Like many traveling folk, the thief and cardsharp Hans Meller supplemented his income with occasional commerce in magical objects: among other practices, he was convicted of coating yellow turnips in fat, sticking hair on them, and selling them as mandrakes for healing purposes.[61] The procuress Ursula Grimin (aka Blue) *said she was a cunning woman and could tell which man carried a child*, informing a customer that if he wanted to avoid an unwanted pregnancy, *he had to shove quickly into only her maid; otherwise he had to wait with his paramour until [Grimin] said, "Let's see what my little lamb chop or baby is doing," whereupon she stood before the men, uncovered herself, and said, "Hurrah cunt, gobble up the man."* Frantz's amusement over the gullibility of Grimin's clients is surpassed only by his obvious enjoyment of the relatively innocent fraud of a young shepherd at Weyer, *who for two years pretended to be a ghost in a house, tugging on the people's heads, hair, and feet while they slept, so that he could secretly lie with the farmer's daughter.*[62]

The most shameless—and successful—magical fraud Schmidt

encountered during his executioner days was undoubtedly the one-legged seamstress Elisabeth Aurholtin of Vilseck, who called herself the Digger. Claiming to be "a golden Sunday child," she amassed a fortune of over 4,000 fl. by convincing people of all ranks that she had the ability to locate hidden treasures and liberate them from the dragons, snakes, or dogs who guarded them.[63] The key to her success, in her executioner's assessment, lay not in the *devilish incantations and ceremonies [she employed]*—all ineffectual gibberish—but rather in her evident gift for making the most far-fetched stories sound credible. After listening to her tale of a sunken underwater castle and its iron chest full of treasure, three initially skeptical men spent an entire day digging for a white adder, with which "she would charm the treasure so that it would float on the water." Others wandered the countryside for days with her and her divining rod, apparently undaunted by their persistent lack of success and ready to pay still more for her special services.

Meister Frantz cannot suppress a hint of amazement at the sheer audacity of this gifted con artist or the gullibility of her greedy victims. He describes her most successful scheme in exceptional detail:

> *This was how she carried out her tricks. When she came into a house and wanted to cheat someone, she used to fall down as if she were ill or in convulsions, giving out afterward that she had a wise vein hidden in her leg, whereby she could foretell and reveal future events and discover hidden treasures, and that when she entered a house her veins never left her in peace until she announced these things. Also that the realms of earth were opened out before her, and that she saw therein gold and silver, as if looking into a fire. If any doubted, she asked leave to spend the night in the house, so that she could speak with the spirit of the treasure. When this happened, she behaved at night—with her whisperings, questions, and answers—as if someone were speaking to her, and gave out afterward that it was a poor lost soul in the house that could not enter into bliss until the treasure was dug up. Thus the people let themselves be persuaded by her, believing such tales because of the terrible incantations and assurances which she used, and caused the ground to be dug up. During this digging she would slip a pot full*

of coals into the hole and give out that she had dug it up herself.
Then she commanded them to lock it up in a chest for three weeks
and not touch it, and that it would turn to gold when she recovered
it, [but] the coals remained coals.

Predictably, Schmidt is most shocked by Aurholtin's fearless defiance of
the prescribed social hierarchy. She defrauds many well-to-do individuals and even convinces one noble to house her and her small daughter,
and two others to serve as the child's baptismal sponsors. On other occasions she cheekily invokes one of Nuremberg's patrician leaders as a
business reference, claiming to *have drawn a fountain of gold for Mas-*
ter Endres Imhoff out of his yard and had dug up a golden treasure, noth-
ing less than idols of pure gold. Meister Frantz never once takes her
claims to supernatural powers seriously, but he remains in awe of her
prowess as a conjurer of tales.

An executioner's legacy

Until his late fifties, Meister Frantz showed few public signs of weari-
ness in his duties. He traveled less often for work and apparently not at
all after 1611, but he continued to personally administer almost all floggings and other corporal punishments well past the age when most of
his fellow executioners handed over such physically demanding work to
their younger associates.[64] The first trace of decline came in February
1611 when he experienced his most dramatically miscarried execution
ever—requiring three strokes to decapitate the incestuous and adulterous Elisabeth Mechtlin. Spectators expressed shock at the fifty-seven-
year-old veteran's "shameful and very heinous" performance.[65] The
executioner's only written acknowledgment of this widely publicized
embarrassment was a single word at the end of the journal entry: *botched.*
The following year, a particularly reviled pimp and government informer
slipped from the executioner's grasp as he was being flogged out of
town and was subsequently stoned to death by an angry mob—resulting
in an official investigation and unprecedented scolding of the veteran
executioner.[66] Two additional botched executions followed, one later
that year on December 17, 1613, the other on February 8, 1614—neither

of them noted as such in Frantz's journal. There were no apparent calls for the elderly executioner's retirement, however, and he went on to dispatch eighteen more poor sinners over the next thirty-four months.

What turned out to be Meister Frantz's final year on the job began unremarkably, with two successful beheadings and a few floggings. Then, during the night of May 31, someone—more likely several people— tipped over the Nuremberg gallows.[67] Schmidt makes no mention of the occurrence in his journal, nor did he apparently assign it any significance, assuming it was merely an act of drunken vandalism. Less than a month later, however, he records a more unnerving event that took place during the hanging of rustler Lienhard Kertzenderfer (aka Cow Lenny) on July 29, 1617. According to one chronicler, the executioner's first attempt to mount the gallows was thwarted by "a sudden, stormy wind," which swept the two ladders from the gallows, so that they had to be retrieved and tied fast. Even then Meister Frantz and the *thoroughly besotted poor sinner* could hardly move forward amid the powerful gusts, which "roared and raged so terribly that it blew and threw people to and fro." But at the moment the condemned man, who had refused to pray, was finally dangling from the rope, "the wind calmed and the air became completely still." *Just then a hare came out of nowhere and ran under the gallows and through the crowd*, pursued by a dog "that no one recognized" (and that many spectators took for a demon pursuing the soul of the poor sinner). A shaken but more circumspect Meister Frantz demurred that *what kind of hare it was or what kind of end he had God knows best.*[68]

Seemingly undeterred by omens or by old age, Meister Frantz hanged three more thieves over the next five months and flogged two before coming to what would be the final execution of his career. The prescribed live burning of counterfeiter Georg Karl Lambrecht, on November 13, 1617, was a rare event for Nuremberg and only the second execution by this method that Frantz Schmidt had performed in more than four decades of service. Ever anxious to orchestrate the violence, Nuremberg's council ordered the executioner to speed the condemned man's death either by placing a sack of gunpowder around his neck or by strangling him first, "albeit unnoticed by the crowd."[69] Meister Frantz replied that he preferred strangulation since the gunpowder might either misfire or explode with such force as to endanger those nearby. As usual, the councilors deferred to his expertise, underscoring only that the strangulation had to be done in such a way "so that the crowd doesn't notice." Efficiency rather than mercy drove their decision; the spectators' terror of live burning needed to be preserved.

Lambrecht's execution should have been one of Schmidt's smoothest. During the previous five weeks, according to the prison chaplain, the poor sinner "had talked more with God than with humans," weeping and praying incessantly.[70] After making a full confession and receiving communion in his cell five days before his scheduled execution, Lambrecht had refused "to contaminate or stain his body with food or drink." His final procession was likewise exemplary, the poor sinner alternately praying aloud and asking those he passed for forgiveness. Most important to Meister Frantz, the condemned man made one final confession and plea for forgiveness before kneeling to recite a Paternoster and other prayers.

In the end, Frantz had decided to rely on both a gunpowder sack and secret strangulation, disregarding his own argument to the magistracy. Perhaps he had a premonition that the secret garroting might fail, but he could not have anticipated that both measures would misfire, producing the agonizing and spectacular failure that we witnessed at the book's outset. True to form, Schmidt does not implicate his Lion, Claus Kohler, for the bungled strangulation, either to his superiors or in his private journal. In a bit of deft revisionism, he in fact records the execution as a successful live burning, effectively denying any mishaps whatsoever. He also does not identify the execution as his last— contrary to later manuscript versions of the journal—and soldiers on, even personally administering a flogging three weeks later and another (his last) on January 8, 1618.

The final punctuation to a forty-five-year career was a decidedly anticlimactic affair. On July 13, 1618, the longtime sacristan Lienhard Paumaister reported to the city council that the venerable Meister Frantz was too infirm to carry out either of the two executions planned for the next week. Paumaister did not specify the nature of the illness, but Schmidt himself carefully annotates that it began nine days earlier. When asked to suggest a "competent person" to replace him "until he is returned to health," Frantz remained markedly noncommittal, replying that he knew of no one to recommend but that "my lords" might make inquiries at nearby Ansbach or Regensburg. If the veteran executioner intended to keep his options open, these hopes were quickly quashed. Anxious to carry out the impending death sentences of a thief and a child murderer, his superiors acted in typically expedient fashion when a week later they received an unsolicited application from Bernhard Schlegel, the executioner of Amberg, a nearby provincial town. After a cursory look at Schlegel's credentials, they offered him 2½ fl. per week salary plus free lodging. The job candidate immediately demanded, with a directness Nuremberg's councilors would come to know well, the same salary as Meister Frantz (3 fl. per week), plus a year's supply of wood and immediate possession of the Hangman's House. Still awaiting a response from Regensburg, the council agreed to Schlegel's terms and had him sworn in as a lifelong employee within two weeks of Meister Frantz's initial message. One week later the new executioner beheaded his first two victims on Nuremberg's Raven Stone.[71] The final entry in Frantz's journal of nearly a half century is typically succinct: *On July 4 [1618] I became ill and on St. Laurence's Day [August 10] gave up my service, having held and exercised the office for forty years.*

The apparent ease of Frantz's retirement belies the onset of a power struggle between the old executioner and his replacement that would continue for years to come. The seemingly unsentimental indifference of Meister Frantz's superiors to his forty years of exemplary service likewise obscures their continuing deference to him in that contest, particularly as the favorable contrast to his successor became increasingly obvious. That loyalty was evident from the time of Schlegel's arrival, when Nuremberg's magistrates made only one qualification to his list of demands: that he give Meister Frantz and his family sufficient time to locate another residence and clean out their current home for him. This seemingly reasonable and innocuous compromise would spawn a bitter lifelong feud between the two executioners and their families that would end only when both men were dead.

Within two days of his first executions in Nuremberg, the newly hired Schlegel complained that his temporary lodging in the former pesthouse was still (!) not ready and that staying in an inn presented a great inconvenience and expense. The council immediately responded with a bonus of 12 fl. (one month's salary) and delicately "made inquiries of Meister Frantz" as to when he expected to vacate the Hangman's House. In the first countersalvo of an extended stalling campaign, Schmidt replied that he fully intended to buy a new house but was unable to undertake the task because of his current infirmity. Unwilling to press the venerated veteran, his superiors instead ordered the acceleration of renovations to a large third-floor apartment for the new, married executioner in a building he and his wife would share with twenty single male renters and the occasional chain gang. As a further concession to an apparently indignant Schlegel, the council granted the new executioner several extended leaves during the next few months "to settle his affairs" as well as an additional 12 fl. for moving expenses.[72]

Over the next year, the councilors' annoyance with their new employee grew steadily, as did their appreciation of his predecessor, the realization gradually dawning that Bernhard Schlegel was no Frantz Schmidt. On the issue of salary alone, Schlegel was unrelenting. Whereas Meister Frantz requested a raise only twice in forty years (the last time in 1584), Meister Bernhard lamented his own inadequate compensation regularly—sometimes several times within a year. Occasionally the council granted him a onetime bonus of 25 fl.; other times they denied his requests outright, with ever more strident language.

One petition for a loan of 60 fl.—likewise refused—suggests that the new executioner was not merely greedy but probably strapped with insurmountable debts, likely brought on by gambling, drinking, or other "frivolous living"—a marked contrast to the sober lifestyle of his esteemed predecessor. Less than a year after his arrival in Nuremberg, Schlegel was summoned before the council: he had taken part in a bar fight at the fencing school, an altercation that began when Schlegel's drinking companion was harassed by fellow craftsmen for sharing a table with the executioner. While dismissing the traditional notion of contagion and reaffirming the respectability of the potter in question, the city fathers also chided Schlegel to "conduct himself more temperately and to not get involved in citizen drinking bouts at public taverns."[73]

Succeeding a venerated icon, famous for his modest living, piety, and sobriety, was bound to be difficult for anyone, but much more so for an outsider widely perceived to be grasping, confrontational, and living beyond his means.[74] The specter of Meister Frantz clearly haunted Meister Bernhard from the day of his arrival in Nuremberg, and the latter was likely dogged by frequent unflattering comparisons to his predecessor that began to erode public confidence in his professional expertise. Within a few weeks of reprimanding Schlegel for his public fraternizing, the city council "fervently admonished" him to do a better job of maintaining order at public executions. Less than a year later he was chided for an especially prolonged hanging, during which Schlegel knocked over the ladders and was stranded on a crossbeam of the gallows while the poor sinner slowly choked in agony, crying out the name of Jesus for several minutes before expiring. Eventually the veteran Lion rescued the bumbling executioner, but only after both received a thorough pelting with frozen mud balls by the outraged crowd.[75]

In 1621, despite grave misgivings, the worn-down city councilors finally conceded the right of citizenship to Schlegel, a privilege that Frantz had won only after fifteen years of service but which Meister Bernhard had requested repeatedly since his arrival in Nuremberg three years earlier.[76] To their dismay, the new executioner's performance on the scaffold showed no improvement. After Schlegel blamed still another bungled execution on the Lion, the council upbraided him and threatened outright dismissal unless he immediately improved his performance and "banish[ed] his gluttonous ways." Aware that his employers were in fact loath to undertake the search for a replacement, Meister Bernhard grudgingly endured their periodic scolding, including humiliating reminders before executions "to take [the matter] earnestly and not to bungle it."[77]

Relentlessly assaulted by unfavorable comparisons to the great Frantz Schmidt, Schlegel took out much of his anger on the former executioner for his continuing resistance to vacating the Hangman's House. Here the new executioner had a legitimate grievance, and it is hard not to sympathize with his frustration about being consistently outmaneuvered by a wilier and better-connected rival. Perhaps because of Schlegel's frequent complaints on so many other issues, his laments over the Schmidt family's continual squatting in the home that had been promised to him fell on deaf ears for nearly seven years. Possibly the magistrates hoped that the matter might eventually be resolved in relatively easy fashion by the elderly Schmidt's death.

Finally, in the summer of 1625, the devastation of war, an influx of refugees, and the arrival of yet another epidemic triggered a severe housing crisis that forced the city councilors to act against the still vital seventy-one-year-old Meister Frantz. Desperate for emergency hospital space, the councilors evacuated the former pesthouse where Schlegel and his wife had been residing and began the eviction of his predecessor from the Hangman's House, offering to pay all the Schmidt family's moving expenses. Again Frantz repeatedly demurred, claiming that he had been promised the house for life—a dubious assertion that contradicted his own declared intentions to relocate seven years earlier. The tactic nevertheless appeared to work and the councilors directed Schlegel to find alternate housing on his own. When a clerk from the criminal bureau subsequently reported that he found no trace of any such promise in the official records, Schmidt fluently switched tactics. He now claimed to have identified a suitable new house two blocks away, on Obere Wöhrdstrasse, but required financial help from the council to cover its yearly mortgage of 75 fl. The residence itself— actually two conjoined houses, owned for the last six decades by a prominent goldsmith—had a steep purchase price of 3,000 fl. and also required a sizable down payment of over 12.5 percent. Desperate for resolution, the council did not blanch at the cost but merely verified that the former executioner's investments earned a yearly interest of only 12 fl. before agreeing to grant him an annual stipend of 60 fl. in perpetuity. Shortly after Walpurgis Day (May 1) 1626, Frantz Schmidt finally vacated his home of nearly fifty years and the jubilant Bernhard Schlegel moved in.[78]

Fresh from this victory, Schlegel turned his resentment of the revered Meister Frantz to their competition in the medical sphere. Until then, the new executioner's conflicts had been mostly with local barber-surgeons, who early on complained about his aggressiveness in pursuing their clients.[79] At one point the council admonished him for consulting on a case involving magic and mental illness, reminding him that he was to confine his medical work to "external injuries."[80] Again, Schlegel clearly lacked his predecessor's diplomatic skills, and his professional reputation suffered as a result. On a few occasions, he even suffered the humiliation of having his prognoses formally second-guessed by Meister Frantz.[81] Within a year after taking possession of the Hangman's House, Schlegel complained to the city council that the former executioner was taking away too many of his clients and demanded both a formal sanctioning of Schmidt and the construction of a new entrance for his own patients, away from the dishonorable pig market. Both requests were denied and Schlegel was reminded that "since Frantz Schmidt helped him for many years, he should be able to tolerate him."[82] Rebuffed yet again, the exasperated executioner lodged no more formal complaints against his venerated predecessor but no doubt looked with anticipation toward the old man's imminent demise.

A father's legacy

The single greatest indignity suffered by Schlegel was the moment of ultimate triumph for Meister Frantz and his children. In late spring 1624, while still ensconced in the Hangman's House, Meister Frantz Schmidt wrote to the emperor Ferdinand II (r. 1618–37), requesting a formal restitution of his family's honor. Direct appeals to the imperial court were not unheard-of, but why did Frantz choose this particular moment to seek the final completion of his quest? Perhaps the retired executioner needed such an endorsement to purchase a new house or his sons had requested help in obtaining honorable craft positions. It's possible that Meister Frantz was even thinking of his eleven-year-old granddaughter, who had just moved in with him and his adult children. An even more intriguing question is why he waited six years after his retirement to write such an appeal. Given how important the restoration of family honor was to Schmidt, it's likely that he had been trying to draft and send the missive for some time, but that forces beyond his control—reluctance on the part of his patrician backers or some other local political issue—had until then thwarted him.

Whatever the reason for its timing, this remarkable document—no more than fifteen pages long in its original form—provides not just an old man's summary of his life's work but also a final, telling illustration of the personal networking and powers of persuasion that had made that life such a success. Frantz's petition is a model of rhetorical finesse, skillfully alternating his many accomplishments on behalf of the emperor and his subjects with a personal plea for sympathy over the misfortune suffered by him and his family. Like his *Meisterlied* on the healing of King Abgar, the petition was without a doubt composed with help, probably from a professional notary. The reasoning and sentiments, however, are pure Meister Frantz. After the formulaic obeisance, he begins his appeal by invoking *the responsibility imposed on secular authorities by God Himself to protect the pious [and] law-abiding from all violence and fear [as well as] to punish the unruly and evil with the appropriate severe punishment, so that peace, calm, and unity might be preserved.* Meister Frantz goes on to establish the divine origin of the office of executioner, citing the Old Testament account of the Israelites and their ritualistic execution by stoning as well as the imperial dictates of the *Carolina.* And yet, he writes, despite the legitimacy and necessity of his work, the profession of executioner represented a vocation thrust upon him by an unfortunate incident, *which I cannot refrain from recounting.*

Frantz's subsequent appeal to the emperor's compassion contains the most introspective and personally revealing lines he ever wrote. Finally out of the public spotlight, he is surprisingly frank about the deep shame that has haunted his family ever since Margrave Albrecht callously forced Heinrich Schmidt to perform those long-ago executions on the market square in Hof. Just as unfair, *and as much as I would have liked to shake free of it,* he writes, the family dishonor forced him into the office of executioner as well, a cruel contradiction of his own natural calling to medicine. And now Meister Frantz turns to the final reason his restitution request should be granted: Medicine, he writes, is the vocation he has managed to practice for forty-six years, *next to my difficult profession, helping with my healing over fifteen thousand people in Nuremberg and the surrounding lands—with the help of the most high and eternal God.* Healing is also the trade he has taught to his own children, he writes, *out of true paternal responsibility with good discipline . . . just as my father taught me, despite the difficult and universally despised office forced upon both of us.* Moreover, he has always applied his medicinal learning *in useful and honorable ways,* including the healing of certain highly placed imperial representatives, whom he names in an appendix, together with nearly fifty noble and patrician clients, more than a third of them women.

Only at this point does Meister Frantz return to his forty years of service to the emperor and his Nuremberg representatives in the role of executioner, *which I undertook and administered without the slightest concern for the danger to my life. During that entire time, there were no complaints about me or my executions and I voluntarily left office about* *six years ago on good terms, on account of my age and infirmity.* An attached recommendation from the Nuremberg city council confirms that Schmidt was *well-known for his calm, retiring life and behavior as* *well as his thriving medical practice . . . and his enforcement of imperial* *law.* In consideration of his many years of service in both law enforcement and medicine, as well as his thirty-one years as a Nuremberg citizen, Frantz Schmidt closes by humbly requesting the restoration of his family name, which will finally lift the stigma he has known all his life and open all honorable professions to his own sons.

Sometime after June 9, 1624, Frantz paid a private courier to carry the sealed petition to the imperial court in Vienna, possibly as part of the city council's regular diplomatic pouch. After only three months, an ornately inscribed and wax-sealed reply arrived at the Hangman's House, also delivered by private courier. The original of Frantz's petition has not survived, but this formal response to it remains preserved in Nuremberg's Staatsarchiv (thanks to Schmidt's immediately filing it with the city's chancery on September 10).[83] Ferdinand himself had probably never even seen the former executioner's appeal, and the entire affair was likely handled at least a few levels of bureaucracy below the emperor, possibly including the imperial signature itself. Following a reiteration of Frantz's request, though, the brief document culminated in the words he had longed to hear his entire life:

> On account of the subservient petition to us from the highly esteemed mayor and council of the city of Nuremberg, the inherited shame of Frantz Schmidt that prevents him and his heirs from being considered upright or presents other barriers is, out of imperial might and clemency, hereby abolished and dissolved and his honorable status among other reputable people declared and restored.[84]

Little matter that in the end the decision was less influenced by the executioner's heartfelt plea or his long service than by the dignitaries in his corner: Meister Frantz knew the ways of his status-obsessed society. He had achieved his goal; his father's dishonor had been transformed into his sons' honor. It was not the executioner's sword that he would pass on to them but the physician's scalpel.

When the victorious Frantz Schmidt moved into the large new house on nearby Obere Wöhrdstrasse two years later, the seventy-two-year-old paterfamilias brought with him all his surviving progeny—five in total plus one or two servants. Rosina, the oldest and the only child to marry thus far, was now a thirty-nine-year-old widow with a thirteen-year-old daughter. Rosina's wedding fifteen years earlier to Wolf Jacob Pickel, a respectable printer from Frankfurt, had involved a significant dowry and possibly other financial concessions on the part of her executioner father. Two years after their private ceremony, the couple presented Meister Frantz with his first grandchild, Elisabeth, bringing his dream of establishing a line of honorable descendants that much closer to fulfillment.[85] Yet despite Pickel's artisanal standing and financial backing, the foreigner from Frankfurt consistently failed to establish himself in his new home, instead suffering a series of professional setbacks. Shortly after the new grandchild's birth, a loan of 20 fl. from his father-in-law was either squandered or stolen by a would-be business partner and, to Meister Frantz's still greater shame, both Wolf and Rosina were imprisoned for fraud. Only the executioner's direct intervention cleared up the matter, and the young couple was released after five days' incarceration.[86] Four years later, Pickel was still struggling financially and complained to the city council that the local printers refused to accept him because he had married the executioner's daughter. After hearing both sides, the magistrates consulted with the jurists about whether Pickel "can be considered respectable [redlich]," and upon receiving word of his good reputation among the printers of Frankfurt, they ordered the Nuremberg printers to accept the newcomer on a probationary basis.[87] Such mandates could still be ignored, but Pickel did not lodge any more formal complaints. However, by 1624 he had either died or absconded. That same year, Rosina herself once again landed in prison on allegedly spurious charges of fornication. After a brief stay she was rescued, as she had been before, through her embarrassed father's intervention.[88] Shortly afterward, she and her daughter rejoined the Schmidt household.

Meister Frantz's two surviving sons, Frantz Steffan (age thirty-five) and Frantzenhans (age thirty-one) also continued to live with their father and siblings in the reconstituted household. Their occupations are unclear. We know that their father decided early on that neither would follow him into his own dishonorable profession, despite its lucrativeness and his own ability to ensure their placement in Nuremberg or elsewhere. One later source refers to Frantz Steffan as "an upright [ersam] young journeyman with no property," but neither his craft nor any actual employment is specified. Given his achievement of journeyman status, it's unlikely that he was hindered by any physical or mental disability. He may well have been simply unable to find gainful employment because of his family background.[89]

Frantzenhans, the baby of the family, also apparently suffered from continued discrimination on the part of Nuremberg's artisans, despite both his father's formal restitution of honor and a 1548 imperial proclamation that had specifically given executioners' sons the right to pursue an honorable craft. Instead, he sought to follow his father into the profession of healing. Just one generation later, a few sons of German executioners would actually be admitted to medical schools and still more would become successful surgeons or physicians during the eighteenth century.[90] This honorable option was not yet open to the sons of Frantz Schmidt, however, so Frantzenhans built on the expertise and client base of his highly respected father, treating broken bones and external wounds, as well as sick or injured animals.

Frantz's daughter Maria, thirty-eight in 1626, had been running the Schmidt household for more than fifteen years—ever since her older sister had left home to marry. The return of Rosina with her daughter probably challenged Maria's dominant role, especially since the older sister had already led her own household as a married woman and mother. We can only wonder if this was a factor in Frantz's decision to purchase two adjoining residences.

As he settled into the house on Obere Wöhrdstrasse, Meister Frantz Schmidt must have felt a great sense of achievement. After years of work and sacrifice—and not a little political maneuvering—he had finally managed to provide for his family not only an unimpeachably honorable name but also a large and comfortable home in which to enjoy the fruits of their new status. Unfortunately, less than two years later, a tragedy befell the family, one that even the resourceful Frantz could do nothing to prevent. On January 10, 1628, the date of her sixteenth birthday, Schmidt's granddaughter, Elisabeth, died of causes that were not recorded. She was precisely the same age that her uncle Jörg had

been when he died, almost three decades earlier. We can only imagine
how this loss must have devastated the entire household. Deprived of
the one youthful presence in their midst, the aged Frantz Schmidt and
his four adult children accompanied her cortege to the family plot the
next morning, Elisabeth's small casket carried by two sacristans and
followed by an unknown number of fellow mourners.[91]

Meister Frantz's last years were brightened by one final accomplishment, nearly on a par with his imperial restitution. On February 6,
1632, forty-four-year-old Maria married forty-four-year-old Hans Ammon in a private ceremony at the Schmidt house. Despite Ammon's
own modest roots—and his memorable stint as an actor under the
name of Peter Leberwurst (Liverwurst)—the groom had by then succeeded in building an enviable reputation for himself among the city's
many artists and engravers. For Frantz's daughter to marry such a man
marked a greater social achievement than many would have thought
possible for the former executioner. As a public symbol that the family
had finally been accepted into honorable society, the wedding represented the crowning moment of Frantz's lifelong quest and a definitive
reversal of the shame that four generations of Schmidts had been forced
to endure.

Yet even this victory was tragically short-lived. Despite its significance, the wedding had taken place quietly. But this time, the absence
of a large church ceremony was dictated not by any lingering dishonor
of the bride but by the fragile health of the bridegroom. Perhaps the
artist suspected that he did not have much time remaining and was
mostly intent on passing his inheritance to the personal physician he
had come to consider a cherished friend and mentor. After all, the former actor and the retired executioner were both outsiders who had overcome formidable obstacles and ultimately succeeded in their respective
quests. Whatever the motivation for Ammon's decision, he never again
left the house on Obere Wöhrdstrasse; nineteen days later he was
dead.[92] Maria was left with the famous artist's name and property, but
no progeny, no grandchildren for her aged father.

The next month, the Swedish king Gustavus II Adolphus and a regi-
ment of his troops marched into Nuremberg's marketplace, cheered by
sympathetic Protestant crowds. Since 1618 most German lands had
been convulsed by what later became known as the Thirty Years

War—a series of armed conflicts spawned by a toxic mix of religious fervor, dynastic ambition, and self-perpetuating violence. The Swedish intervention of 1630 initially portended a reversal of imperial Catholic gains and an imminent end to nearly a dozen years of warfare and suffering. Instead, the prematurely triumphant entry of Gustavus Adolphus into Nuremberg marked the beginning of the most devastating five years in the city's history and a further extension of the war. Over the months to come, the twenty thousand Swedish troops encamped outside the city walls demanded exorbitant "contributions" from municipal coffers. Still worse, from the magistrates' point of view, Gustavus Adolphus himself was slain in battle at Lützen before the year was out, robbing Protestant forces of their most charismatic leader and bringing the war to a deadlock that doomed central Europe to another sixteen years of bloody conflict. At the same time, Nuremberg itself was struck by the first of three waves of plague, this one killing more than fifteen thousand residents and refugees, among them forty-one-

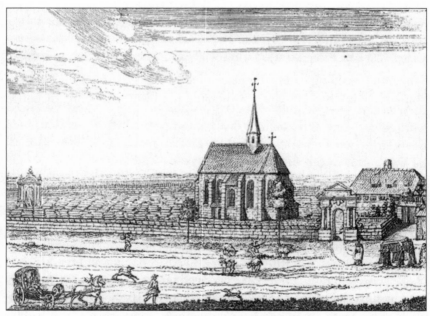

A funeral procession to the Saint Rochus Cemetery, just southwest of the city's walls. Frantz's grave lies about fifty feet to the left of the cemetery's chapel in the foreground (c. 1700).

year-old Frantz Steffan Schmidt, who died on January 11, 1633.[93] He had never married and had resided until his death in the family home. He left behind no children.

Like all Nurembergers, Frantz and his three remaining adult children—Rosina, Maria, and Frantzenhans—welcomed the brief respite from mass graves and quarantines that finally came in the summer of 1633, only to be assaulted the following winter by a still more virulent outbreak of the plague and other epidemics. The year 1634 turned out to be the deadliest in Nuremberg's history, with at least twenty thousand adults and children succumbing to the deadly diseases that thrived in the severely overcrowded city. Appropriately, perhaps, the man who had killed more people with his own hands than any other in the city—possibly in the entire empire—was himself finally consumed by the death around him on Friday, June 13, 1634, at the age of eighty.[94]

The funeral of Meister Frantz Schmidt, which in calmer times might have been a significant local event, passed barely noticed amid the widespread suffering of that annus horribilis. We know little about the venerated executioner's burial itself, only that the city council unanimously declared that "in view of the imperial restitution of honorable birth," Meister Frantz was allowed to be fully recognized as "respectable" (*kunstreich*). He was buried the day after he died, in the Saint Rochus family plot he had purchased half a century earlier, next to his long-deceased Maria and four dead children. Most important, he was designated in all official records as "Honorable Frantz Schmidt, Physician, in Obere Wöhrd[strasse]," with no reference whatsoever to the more infamous profession of forty-five years that had in the end secured this status.[95] The seemingly impossible dream that had animated his life was at last, in death, a reality, engraved for all posterity to see on his still legible gravestone.

EPILOGUE

How peaceful in its steadfast ways,
content in deed and work,
lies nestled in Germany's center,
my dear Nuremberg!
    —Richard Wagner, *Die Meistersinger von Nürnberg*,
        act 3, scene 1 (1868)

If society really believed what it said [about capital punishment as a deterrent],
it would exhibit the heads.
    —Albert Camus, "Reflections on the Guillotine" (1957)[1]

The year of Frantz Schmidt's death, 1634, marked the nadir of a particularly tumultuous decade in Nuremberg. Following the peak of prosperity the city reached during the middle years of Schmidt's life, Nuremberg entered a period of gradual, then precipitous decline. The rise of global trade presented an escalating challenge for the city's merchants and bankers, as did increased competition in high-quality manufacturing from the Netherlands and France. But the resulting rise in inflation and unemployment, while dire, was quickly dwarfed in magnitude by the devastating impact of the Thirty Years War. By the time of the Peace of Westphalia in 1648, more than fifty thousand residents of Nuremberg had died from epidemics or starvation during the previous fifteen years, the municipal government was 7,500,000 fl. in debt, and the celebrated city of Nuremberg had slipped into the decline that would relegate it to the status of a provincial backwater by the eighteenth century. "Nobody won the Thirty Years War," Mack Walker has written, but indisputably Nuremberg was one of the biggest losers of all—a tragic coda to its previous two centuries of glory.[2]

Frantz's personal legacy did not fare much better. Less than a year after his death, forty-seven-year-old Rosina died, possibly as a result of the same epidemic that had killed her aged father, leaving Maria and Frantzenhans as the late executioner's only surviving children. Frantzenhans continued to support the reduced household through the medical consultancy he had inherited from his father. But within months of Meister Frantz's death, the executioner's successor and longtime nemesis Bernhard Schlegel revived his vendetta against his popular predecessor. This time he complained to the city council that Schmidt's son had left him "no one to cure," depriving him of the opportunity to earn "my little piece of bread" from this side occupation. According to Meister Bernhard, the terms of Frantz's imperial restitution did not extend to his offspring, and if the council did not censure his competitor, it should at least compensate Schlegel for the lost income—"especially during these difficult, troubled times." After quickly consulting both its copy of Meister Frantz's restitution and the city's chief jurist, the council rejected Schlegel's petition but granted him a small bonus. A year later, the relentless Meister Bernhard once more lamented that the sole surviving Schmidt male was leaving him "no patients whatsoever," and he repeated his request for official intervention or an appropriate raise in his own salary. Again rebuffed, Schlegel this time informed his employers that the cities of Regensburg and Linz were both looking for full-time executioners, but that an annual raise of 52 fl.—a 35 percent increase—would keep him in Nuremberg. Exasperated, the city council instructed its criminal bureau either to find another executioner or to settle with the current one, underscoring that "Schmidt's healing cannot be prohibited." Unable to identify an alternate to Schlegel, his employers agreed to a temporary weekly raise "until better times"— albeit considerably less than the always cash-strapped Meister Bernhard had requested. Three years later, in May 1639, Valentin Deuser, "a foreign executioner," was granted permission to heal patients in the city, and before the year was out he had replaced the ailing Bernhard Schlegel on a temporary and then permanent basis as Nuremberg's official executioner. On August 29, 1640, Bernhard Schlegel died and was buried in Saint Rochus Cemetery, not far from the resting place of his reviled predecessor.[3]

Free at last of their longtime persecutor, Frantzenhans and Maria continued their quiet lives in the house on Obere Wöhrdstrasse, with no further appearance in the official record until their deaths. Maria lived until the age of seventy-five, dying in 1664; Frantzenhans persevered alone in the family home for another nineteen years, finally joining his long-deceased siblings and parents at the age of eighty-six.[4] Maria had never remarried, and Frantzenhans remained a bachelor his entire long life. By the time the last of the Schmidt children died, Frantz's only grandchild had been dead for over half a century. There would be no others. The executioner's dream of a line of descendants living respectable, socially unfettered lives, the inspiration of his lifelong struggle for respectability, was never to be.

Meister Frantz's demise also coincided with the end of a golden age for European executioners. The frequency of public executions had already begun to decline during the second half of Schmidt's career, but the destruction and other effects of the Thirty Years War accelerated that process. Everywhere, including in Nuremberg, death sentences became both less common and more likely to be commuted. The rise of discipline houses and workhouses as punishment for habitual nonviolent criminals simultaneously reduced the number of executions for theft from one-third to one-tenth of all capital punishments. By 1700 the overall number of executions in German lands had fallen to one-fifth of what it had been a century earlier, a decline that would be even steeper if seventeenth-century executions for the by then defunct crime of witchcraft were included. The number of corporal punishments, particularly flogging and mutilation, fell just as dramatically, as did the more gruesome traditional punishments of burning alive, drowning, and death by the wheel. Nuremberg saw only six executions by the wheel during the entire seventeenth century—compared to thirty during Meister Frantz's career alone—and only one, which was preceded by decapitation, during the eighteenth century. Hanging and beheading became the two execution methods of choice, both made more humane by the inventions of the drop door and the guillotine, respectively.[5]

Why did such a remarkable social transformation occur? Modern historians have proposed a wide range of theories. Some posit the widespread development of greater empathy among Europeans in general, part of a profound "civilizing process" beginning in the late Middle Ages. Others claim that the emerging states of Europe simply modified their methods of control, replacing capital punishment for nonviolent offenses with incarceration or transportation to an overseas colony. Unfortunately for these theories and their popularizers, there is no evidence whatsoever of a shift in popular mentalities regarding human suffering, nor can the development of workhouses and execution methods that did not become dominant until the eighteenth century or later explain the profound changes that began more than a hundred years earlier (especially in Nuremberg, where a discipline house was not established until 1670).[6] To account for the decline in public execution, we must look, rather, to the reasons it became so popular in the first place.

Nuremberg's city councilors and other secular authorities in Europe did not grow soft on crime during the seventeenth century—to the contrary—but they did finally feel secure enough in their legal authority to rely more on public displays of clemency than on carefully choreographed rituals of brutality. Thanks in large part to the work of Meister Frantz and his fellow enforcers, the authority of the state and its judges was now an established reality, as opposed to the not always convincing assertion it had been a century before. Professional and sober executioners had become the norm, not the exception, and the public redemption ritual of the scaffold was now firmly enough established in the social consciousness that it did not need to be reiterated at such frequent intervals. Crime continued to flourish and wars consumed ever more victims, but governmental control of criminal justice had become an unquestioned reality.[7]

The precipitous drop in public executions after Meister Frantz's time bestowed a mixed blessing on his professional brethren. In the short term, it spelled a decline in both demand and salary for executioners. In the long term, however, it led to the gradual dismantling of many social barriers for these now more legitimate enforcers/enactors of state justice. By the beginning of the eighteenth century, executioners' sons were regularly accepted into medical schools and other professions. Active executioners themselves could finally practice medicine unencumbered, and Frederick I of Prussia (d. 1713) even appointed the

Berlin executioner, Martin Koblentz, as his court physician—despite vigorous opposition from academic circles. Later, the empress Maria Theresa (d. 1780) herself recognized the new social standing of the executioner, in 1731 issuing an imperial decree that reinstated the honor of all executioners' children and that of executioners themselves, once they had completed their service.

Many of the social prejudices against executioners nevertheless persevered well into the nineteenth century, once more thanks mainly to the craft guilds, which endeavored to shore up their declining influence—as they had in the sixteenth century—by limiting the social mobility of those who had historically been beneath them. Consequently, many executioner families remained clannish and continued to intermarry. In fact, just two extended dynasties dominated Nuremberg's office of the executioner from the mid-seventeenth to the early nineteenth century. By then, the insidious stigma that had dominated Frantz Schmidt's life had well and truly begun to fade and would one day vanish altogether.[8]

The 1801 publication of Meister Frantz's journal by a local jurist thus came at the very moment that public executioners were fading from the legal scene and becoming ever more prominent in the popular imagination. Local patrician Johann Martin Friedrich von Endter was one of the most outspoken and passionate reformers of Nuremberg's "outdated and draconian" legal system. His manifesto "Thoughts and Recommendations on Nuremberg's Criminal Justice and Its Administration" (1801) proposed reforms based on his own Enlightenment version of the Golden Rule: "As you wish to be judged, so should others be judged." Coming across a manuscript copy of Meister Frantz's "long-forgotten journal" in the city archive, Endter recognized the perfect foil for his soon-to-be-published manifesto. In bringing the work to print, Endter sought "to rescue [Schmidt's book] from obscurity" and in the process reveal how brutally "the misfortunate [were punished] at the hands of our rustic Frantz." His principal target, though, remained the cruelties of the old regime—not "old, honorable Frantz, [who] acted not according to his own feeling and instinct but at the orders of those who put the sword in his hand." After overcoming municipal censors, who feared the journal would present the city in a bad light, the impassioned editor made his final corrections to the text, then abruptly died at the age of thirty-seven, never to know the subsequent success of his proposed legal reforms or his edition of Meister Frantz's journal.[9]

The most vocal admirers of the new publication—in hindsight predictably so—were neither the jurists nor the academics Endter envisioned, but men of letters. Romantic authors in particular embraced the melodramatic figure of the "medieval hangman," an entertaining anachronism in an age of mechanical guillotines and gallows with trapdoors. In an 1810 letter to the folklorists and academics Jacob and Wilhelm Grimm, the poet Ludwig Achim von Arnim wrote enthusiastically of "the well-known annals of the Nuremberg skinner who executed five hundred people."[10] Clearly an object of interest for those celebrated collectors of often grisly folktales, the printed version of Schmidt's journal rapidly made the rounds in the salons and literary circles of German intelligentsia. A certain "Meister Franz" even made an appearance in Clemens Brentano's popular play *The Story of the Sturdy Kasperl and the Beautiful Annerl* (1817), in which the executioner both heals a sick dog and beheads the female protagonist for infanticide. Even Johann Wolfgang von Goethe, the most celebrated German author of the day, embraced the long-shunned figure of the hangman, entering into a lengthy personal friendship with the executioner of Eger, Karl Huss, who shared the poet's geological interests.[11]

Nowhere was the romantic figure of the medieval hangman more fervently embraced than in the revitalized Nuremberg of the nineteenth century. After more than two centuries of obscurity, the old imperial city had been annexed by the prosperous and relatively progressive duchy of Bavaria in 1806. This much-lamented end to Nuremberg's seven centuries of independence had in fact spurred a dramatic economic revival that simultaneously jolted the city out of its old-regime turpitude and unleashed the series of criminal justice reforms long sought by Endter. That the newly progressive city would embrace Meister Frantz's journal is in some ways ironic. Even before the Bavarian Occupation (as it is jokingly still known in Nuremberg), city fathers had abolished judicial torture and public execution and marked the retirement of the last executioner, Albanus Friedrich Deubler, in 1805. Four years later, the municipal discipline- and workhouse was closed and the site converted into the House of Society, a venue for public concerts, lectures, and balls. That same year, the gallows outside the Ladies'

Gate finally collapsed and the entire surrounding area was converted to a park. Even the warden's residence at the formerly dreaded Hole was transformed into a popular pub known as the Green Frog.

How did a sixteenth-century executioner and his not entirely forgotten journal fit into the new Nuremberg? By the middle of the nineteenth century, the city had become internationally famous not just as a manufacturing dynamo but also as a popular tourist destination. Thanks to the efforts of local folk poets such as Johann Konrad Grübel and Johann Heinrich Witschel, the hometown of Albrecht Dürer and Hans Sachs became a powerful symbol of traditional German culture at its most idealized. City fathers lost no time in capitalizing on this proto-nationalist cultural windfall for the city on the Pegnitz. During the 1830s and 1840s they purchased and restored a number of historic city buildings, including the former home of Albrecht Dürer, which they converted to a museum. In 1857 Nuremberg became home to the Germanisches Nationalmuseum, today a sprawling collection of artworks and other objects illustrating the magnificence of "Germanic" culture and history. By the time of German unification in 1870, the entire old city, including all the surrounding walls and gates, had been completely restored, and Nuremberg stood supreme among cities of the recently proclaimed Second Empire as the embodiment of a proud German past.[12]

Of course that proud past had a seamy underside as well, and Nuremberg's lucrative heritage industry cashed in on it with new tourist destinations, including a "torture chamber" set up by the local antiquarian Georg Friedrich Geuder in the city's old Frog Tower prison. Taking advantage of continuing popular fascination with the figure of the medieval hangman, Geuder's collection most famously included the iron maiden, a supposedly ancient method of torture and execution said to have been used in a secret court. Both the iron maiden and the secret court were complete fabrications, possibly based on a misinterpretation of old texts, but the exhibit proved highly effective in popularizing a Gothic imagining of pre-Enlightenment "justice" and its sinister enforcers. The entire romance of "medieval cruelties" overseen by an executioner in a hood—another nineteenth-century invention—proved irresistible to tourists and novelists alike. Bram Stoker, the author of *Dracula* (1897), visited Nuremberg twice and even incorporated the

Iron Maiden into one of his short stories. The city's torture collection moved to a more prominent location in the so-called Five-Cornered Tower of the imperial castle and later went on an extended tour of Great Britain and North America, prompting even more popular literary works about executioners and a new edition of the Schmidt journal in 1913.[13] Eventually, the Iron Maiden, together with assorted thumbscrews, shackles, executioner swords, and other items—many of them high-quality nineteenth-century forgeries—were auctioned off to private collectors.

By then, the Gothic executioner had become a permanent fixture of modern culture. Only during the past few decades have scholarly accounts fully escaped the gravitational pull of that stereotype, but even the most impressive of these works have been no match in the public arena for the formidable icon created by the Romantics of nearly two centuries ago.[14] Like pirates, witches, and other historical outcasts, executioners have been reclaimed by romance and fantasy writers for

A typical Romantic imagining of medieval criminal justice, including a hooded executioner and his assistants, the Iron Maiden, and a clandestine trial (c. 1860).

dramatic purposes, by cartoonists for comical purposes, and by pur-
veyors of popular culture for commercial gain.[15] The modest tourist
ventures of nineteenth-century Nuremberg pale in comparison to modern enterprises. Cities across Europe boast well-publicized "historical
criminal tours" of dungeons and other sites, and Germany's premier
historical reenactment city, Rothenburg ob der Tauber, features a medieval crime museum. These attractions—and I can't claim to have done
a systematic survey of them all—run the gamut from legitimate historical presentation to harmless amusement to historical vandalism in the
service of profit. The worst of them do no more than exploit the
"pornography of suffering and death" that already saturates modern
culture.[16]

Even the less titillating and more scholarly treatments of the premodern executioner produce a distancing effect. In Nuremberg, Meister Frantz's residence has recently been transformed into a historical
museum of local criminal justice, and the dreaded Hole beneath the
town hall has become the site of daily tours through the dungeon's
dank cells and torture chamber. The documentation provided in both
instances is excellent and the guides are invariably well-informed ra-
conteurs who bravely refrain from passing along the spurious gruesome
detail or ghost story. Yet even scrupulous attention to historical accu-
racy cannot entirely counter the voyeuristic nature of all tourism, the
inescapable reduction of all past triumphs and tragedies to a form of
entertainment, a diversion from our own "real lives." For most of the
smiling tourists who pose in front of the Hangman's House, the emotional and intellectual life of its most famous occupant is not even a
tepid afterthought—it is a non sequitur.

More than most of his contemporaries, Meister Frantz Schmidt remains the victim of modern condescension and disgust. The very symbol of a barbarous and ignorant age, he affirms for us the collective
social progress of our modern world. To this day, allegedly learned and
"scientific" works, such as the social psychologist Steven Pinker's *The
Better Angels of Our Nature*, perpetuate the Gothic fantasy of ancien
régime cruelty in the service of their own modern, secularist agenda.[17]
In distancing Meister Frantz and his fellow executioners from ourselves, we make them safe figures from the world of fairy tales, perpetrators of horrors that cannot touch us, in the process revealing more

about our own fears and dreams than about the world we have inherited from them. We view the hooded caricature of modern popular culture with the same patronizing amusement as adults watching children at play, all the time confident of our own superior rationality and sophistication.

But is such emotional and intellectual distancing justified? Surely it is not edifying, at least in terms of any genuine understanding of past individuals and societies. Contrary to modernist narratives of the civilizing process or gradual conscience formation among later generations, Frantz Schmidt and his contemporaries do not appear to have been more or less prone to cruelty than individuals in the twenty-first century, nor have we seen any evidence of more or less fear, more or less hatred, more or less compassion. It would have surprised the executioner who so closely identified with the victims of crime to hear his society characterized as especially cruel and heartless, particularly once he learned of such unthinkable modern atrocities as genocide, atomic obliteration, and total war. He would admit that the criminal justice of his day could be harsh, but he would recoil at the notion of trials and incarcerations that extended for years, even decades, sometimes involving long periods of isolation. The premodern execution ritual itself, which Michel Foucault characterized as a carnivalesque savoring of human suffering, in fact offers the strongest repudiation of some qualitative shift in popular attitudes, since it was the very cruelty of botched executions—and the suffering they imposed—that was most likely to trigger mob retaliation. There is no defense imaginable today for such abominations as execution with the wheel and judicial torture, but we must recognize that neither was primarily motivated by either mass sadism or pervasive indifference to the suffering of others.

It is not our emotional responses to crime or suffering that separate us from Schmidt's world, but two specific historical developments, one practical and one conceptual. Medieval and early modern judicial mechanisms, as we have seen, were by our standards woefully ineffective. Without modern investigative capabilities, modern technology, and modern alternatives to banishment (i.e., prison), the legal authorities of Frantz Schmidt's day felt compelled to rely on self-incrimination and torture as well as capital punishment for a variety of serious and recidivist offenses. Popular fear and magistrates' concerns about their own authority also required some public punishment of those few perpetrators unlucky enough to get caught; "frontier-style" justice was often the result—preferable to lynch mob actions but prone to coercion and other procedural shortcuts.

The even more fundamental distinction between most developed societies today and Nuremberg in the sixteenth century is the notion of inalienable human rights. This other relatively late development in the public sphere, though still contested, provides at least a theoretical and legal basis for limiting state coercion and violence, even in the pursuit of justice. Authoritarian regimes of the past and present recognize no such externally imposed restrictions, nor do they place the sovereignty of the individual on par with, let alone above, the sovereignty of the state. Meister Frantz would have agreed that even apprehended criminals had a right to due process, but the idea that this right included protection of their bodies following incriminating evidence or conviction for a serious offense would have been an incomprehensible concept. Nuremberg's magistrates and their executioner strove for moderation, consistency, and even religious redemption, all in the face of widespread pressure for simple revenge. Abolishing—rather than moderating and standardizing—state violence was simply too much of an intellectual jump for them.

The leap backward for us, by contrast, is neither long nor inconceivable. Procedural enhancements and technological innovations in law enforcement have produced less of a stable or fundamental gap between premodern and modern justice than we would like to admit. Neither death by the wheel nor burning at the stake appears likely to make a comeback in the near future (we hope), but rises in criminality anywhere—real or perceived—still reliably generate popular calls for less constrained means of investigation and harsher punishments of convicted felons. Many modern regimes still employ systematic torture—without any of the legal constraints of sixteenth-century Nuremberg—and other governments (including my own, the United States) have deliberately blurred the line between acceptable and unacceptable coercion during criminal interrogations. Capital punishment is still practiced in fifty-eight countries, most prolifically in China and Iran (with combined 2011 execution figures in the thousands), but also in self-proclaimed liberal democracies such as the United States and Japan.[18] Fear of violent attack and frustration with inadequate law enforcement—both legitimate reactions in themselves—appear to be not only constant in human history but also ever on the verge of escalating into overwhelming passions. The abstract legal concept of a set of basic human rights, by contrast, remains relatively new and surprisingly vulnerable to characterization as a disposable luxury in difficult times, easily outmatched by older, more entrenched primal urges.

Should we be encouraged by the greater limitations on state violence since Meister Frantz's time or disheartened by the fragility of that achievement? The story of Frantz Schmidt offers little of the self-congratulatory reassurance that we have come to expect from this subject. His life in fact provides no straightforward moral for our time. Instead we are limited to sharing the joys and disappointments of one man within the context of his own world. In the judgment of his contemporaries, Meister Frantz fulfilled his duty to provide Nuremberg's citizens with a sense of order and justice. By his own account, he kept his promise to his father, his children, and himself against seemingly insurmountable odds, bolstered by religious faith and by extraordinary success in his self-professed true vocation of healing. We know much too little of Frantz's personal experiences to say whether his was on balance a happy life. But it can be stated with certainty that it was a singularly purposeful life. Perhaps, in a cruel and capricious world, there is hope to be found in one man defying his fate, overcoming universal hostility, and simply persevering amid a series of personal tragedies. Meister Frantz clearly thought so. And that, we can agree with him, is an act of faith worthy of remembrance.

Notes

Abbreviations Used in Notes

Angstmann: Else Angstmann, *Der Henker in der Volksmeinung: Seine Namen und sein Vorkommen in der mündlichen Volksüberlieferung* (Bonn: Fritz Klopp, 1928).

ASB: Amts- und Standbücher; Staatsarchiv Nürnberg, Bestand 52b.

CCC: *Die Peinliche Gerichtsordnung Kaiser Karl V: Constitutio Criminalis Carolina: Die Carolina und ihre Vorgängerinnen. Text, Erläuterung, Geschichte.* Edited by J. Kohler and Willy Scheel (Halle an der Saale: Verlag Buchhandlung des Waisenhauses, 1900).

FSJ: Frantz Schmidt's journal; Stadtbibliothek Nürnberg, Amb 652.2°.

G&T: Johann Glenzdorf and Fritz Treichel, *Henker, Schinder, und arme Sünder*, 2 vols (Bad Münder am Deister: Wilhelm Rost, 1970).

GNM: Germanisches Nationalmuseum Nürnberg.

JHJ: Journal of prison chaplain Johannes Hagendorn (1563–1624). Germanisches Nationalmuseum Nürnberg, 3857 Hs.

Hampe: Theodor Hampe, *Die Nürnberger Malefizbücher als Quellen der reichsstädtischen Sittengeschichte vom 14. bis zum 18. Jahrhundert* (Bamberg: C. C. Buchner, 1927).

Keller: Albrecht Keller. *Der Scharfrichter in der deutschen Kulturgeschichte* (Bonn: K. Schroeder, 1921).

Knapp, *Kriminalrecht*: Hermann Knapp, *Das alte Nürnberger Kriminalrecht* (Berlin: J. Guttentag, 1896).

Knapp, *Loch*: Hermann Knapp. *Das Lochgefängnis, Tortur, und Richtung in Alt-Nürnberg* (Nuremberg: Heerdengen-Barbeck, 1907).

LKAN: Landeskirchlichesarchiv Nürnberg.

MVGN: *Mitteilungen des Vereins für die Geschichte der Stadt Nürnbergs.*

Nowosadtko: Jutta Nowosadtko, *Scharfrichter und Abdecker: Der Alltag zweier "unehrlicher Berufe" in der Frühen Neuzeit* (Paderborn: Ferdinand Schöningh, 1994).

Restitution: Haus-, Hof-, Staatsarchiv Wien. *Restitutionen.* Fasz. 6/S, Franz Schmidt, 1624.

RV: *Ratsverlaß* (decree of Nuremberg city council). Staatsarchiv Nürnberg, Rep. 60a.

StaatsAB: Staatsarchiv Bamberg.

StaatsAN: Staatsarchiv Nürnberg.

StadtAB: Stadtarchiv Bamberg.
StadtAN: Stadtarchiv Nürnberg.
Stuart: Kathy Stuart, *Defiled Trades and Social Outcasts: Honor and Ritual Pollution in Early Modern Germany* (Cambridge, UK, and New York: Cambridge University Press, 1999).
Wilbertz: Gisela Wilbertz. *Scharfrichter und Abdecker im Hochstift Osnabrück: Untersuchungen zur Sozialgeschichte zweier "unehrlichen" Berufe im nordwesten Raum vom 16. bis zum 19. Jahrhundert* (Osnabrück: Wenner, 1979).

Preface

1. Heinrich Sochaczewsky, *Der Scharfrichter von Berlin* (Berlin: A. Weichert, 1889), 297.

2. *JHJ* Nov 13 1617; see also Theodor Hampe, "Die lezte Amstverrichtung des Nürnberger Scharfrichters Franz Schmidt," in *MVGN* 26 (1926): 321ff.

3. Among twentieth-century historians of early modern executioners, characterizations ranged from sociopathic to emotionless to fellow victims of society; Nowosadtko, 352.

4. *Meister Frantzen Nachrichter alhier in Nürnberg, all sein Richten am Leben, so wohl seine Leibs Straffen, so Er verRicht, alleß hierin Ordentlich beschrieben, aus seinem selbst eigenen Buch abschrieben worden*, ed. J.M.F. von Endter (Nuremberg: J.L.S. Lechner, 1801), reprinted with a commentary by Jürgen C. Jacobs and Heinz Rölleke (Dortmund: Harenberg, 1980). *Maister Franntzn Schmidts Nachrichters inn Nürmberg all sein Richten*, ed. Albrecht Keller (Leipzig: Heims, 1913), reprinted with an introduction by Wolfgang Leiser (Neustadt an der Aisch, P.C.W. Schmidt, 1979). The English translation of the latter is *A Hangman's Diary, Being the Journal of Master Franz Schmidt, Public Executioner of Nuremberg, 1573–1617*, trans. C. V. Calvert and A. W. Gruner (New York: D. Appleton, 1928), reprinted (Montclair, NJ: Patterson Smith, 1973).

5. See, for example, the "journals" of Ansbach's executioners from 1575 to 1603 (StaatsAN Rep 132, Nr. 57); in Reutlingen from 1563–68 (*Württembergische Vierteljahrshefte für Landesgeschichte*, 1 [1878], 85–86); Andreas Tinel of Ohlau, c. 1600 (cited in Keller, 257); Jacob Steinmayer in Haigerloch, 1764–81 (*Württembergische Vierteljahrshefte für Landesgeschichte*, 4 [1881]: 159ff.); Franz Joseph Wohlmuth in Salzburg (*Das Salzburger Scharfrichtertagebuch*, ed. Peter Putzer [Vienna: Österreichischer Kunst- und Kulturverlag, 1985]); Johann Christian Zippel in Stade (Gisela Wilbertz, "Das Notizbuch des Scharfrichters Johann Christian Zippel in Stade [1766–1782]," in *Stader Jahrbuch*, n.s. 65 [1975]: 59–78). For an overview of early modern executioner registers, see Keller, 248–60.

At most, about one in three German males was to some degree literate. Hans Jörg Künast, "Getruckt zu Augspurg": *Buchdruck und Buchhandel in Augsburg zwischen 1468 und 1555* (Tübingen: Max Niemeyer, 1997), 11–13; R. A. Houston, *Literacy in Early Modern Europe: Culture and Education, 1500–1800* (Harlow, UK: Pearson Education, 2002), 125ff.

6. The most famous of these were the memoirs of the Sanson executioner dynasty of Paris, collected by Henri Sanson as *Sept générations d'exécuteurs, 1688–1847,* 6 vols. (Paris: Décembre-Alonnier, 1862–63); translated and published in an abbreviated English version (London: Chatto and Windus, 1876). For British examples of the genre, see John Evelyn, *Diary of John Evelyn* (London: Bickers and Bush, 1879); and Stewart P. Evans, *Executioner: The Chronicles of James Berry, Victorian Hangman* (Stroud, UK: Sutton, 2004).

7. In addition to the beginning and end of the journal, as well as the beginning of Schmidt's tenure in Nuremberg: 1573 (2x); 1576 (3x); 1577 (2x); Mar 6 1578; Apr 10 1578; Jul 21 1578; Mar 19 1579; Jan 26 1580; Feb 20 1583; Oct 16 1584; Aug 4 1586; Jul 4 1588; Apr 19 1591; Mar 11 1598; Sep 14 1602; Jun 7 1603; Mar 4 1606; Dec 23 1606.

8. Friedrich Werner, executed Feb 11 1585. The sole exception is a passing reference to *Hans Spiss, my kinsman, who is whipped out of town here with the rods by the Lion* (for abetting an escaping murderer); *FSJ* Jun 7 1603.

9. Keller concludes that "he never succeeds in the ordering of his thoughts" (252).

10. The 1801 version of Endter was based on an eighteenth-century manuscript in the StaatsAN Rep 25: S II. L 25, no. 12. The version edited by Albrecht Keller in 1913 was derived mainly from the late-seventeenth-century copy of GNM Bibliothek 2° HS Merkel 32. My own translation of the *FSJ* (forthcoming in print) is based on the copy in the 1634 Stadtchronik of Hans Rigel in the StadtBN, 652 2°. Apparently other copies and fragments were produced during the late seventeenth and eighteenth centuries, of which at least two survive in the Staatsbibliothek Bamberg (SH MSC Hist. 70 and MSC Hist. 83) and two in the GNM (Bibliothek 4° HS 187 514; Archiv, Rst Nürnberg, Gerichtswesen Nr. V1/3).

11. This motive is suggested by both Keller (*Maister Franntzn Schmidts Nachrichters,* Introduction, x–xi) and Nowosadtko ("'Und nun alter, ehrlicher Franz': Die Transformation des Scharfrichtermotivs am Beispiel einer Nurnberger Malefizchronik," *Internationales Archiv für Sozialgeschichte der deutschen Literatur* 31, no. 1 [2006]: 223–45), but neither follows through on the implications for the author's life.

12. Marriage, birth, and death registers, located in the LKAN, have allowed me to reconstruct the externals of Schmidt's origins and family life. Interrogation protocols and other criminal court records, found principally in the Staatsarchiv Nürnberg, have filled in considerable context on his professional activity. Decrees of the Nuremberg council, known as *Ratsverläße,* were the most versatile sources, providing a range of revealing information about both aspects of his life. The decrees also helped shed light on his simultaneous work as a medical consultant, particularly in the years following his retirement as Nuremberg's executioner (only fleetingly mentioned in his journal). Finally, I owe much to the valuable bits of biographical information culled by previous scholars, most notably Albrecht Keller, Wolfgang Leiser, Jürgen C. Jacobs, and Ilse Schumann.

13. For a useful overview, see Julius R. Ruff, *Violence in Early Modern Europe, 1500–1800* (Cambridge, UK: Cambridge University Press, 2001).

1. The Apprentice

1. *Collected Works of Erasmus,* vol. 25, *Literary and Educational Writings,* ed. J. K. Sowards (Toronto: University of Toronto Press, 1985), 305.

2. *Essays,* trans. J. M. Cohen (Harmondsworth, UK, and Baltimore: Penguin, 1958), 116.

3. On the apparent premodern indifference to animal suffering, see, most famously, Robert Darnton's *The Great Cat Massacre and Other Episodes in French Cultural History* (New York: Vintage, 1985).

4. This reconstruction is based on the common training experiences of the sons of executioner dynasties, as described in Wilbertz, 120–31. Frantz Schmidt does not provide any account of training with his father in the journal other than the June 1573 beginning of his work as a traveling journeyman.

5. This section is especially indebted to the treatment of Arthur E. Imhof, *Lost Worlds: How Our European Ancestors Coped with Everyday Life and Why Life Is So Hard Today,* trans. Thomas Robisheaux (Charlottesville: University of Virginia Press, 1996), 68–105.

6. For a recent overview, see C. Pfister, "Population of Late Medieval Germany," in *Germany: A New Social and Economic History,* vol. 1, *1450–1630,* ed. Bob Scribner, 213ff.

7. Imhof, *Lost Worlds,* 72.

8. Imhof, *Lost Worlds,* 87–88. See also John D. Post, *The Last Great Subsistence Crisis in the Western World* (Baltimore: Johns Hopkins University Press, 1977). On the Little Ice Age, see Wolfgang Behringer, *Kulturgeschichte des Klimas: Von der Eiszeit bis zur globalen Erwärmung* (Munich: C. H. Beck, 2007), esp. 120–95.

9. Thomas A. Brady, Jr., *German Histories in the Age of Reformations* (Cambridge, UK: Cambridge University Press, 2009), 96–97.

10. Brady, *German Histories,* 97. See also Knapp, *Kriminalrecht,* 155–60.

11. I am persuaded by the argument of Hillay Zmora, *The Feud in Early Modern Germany* (Cambridge, UK: Cambridge University Press, 2011). See also his companion volume, *State and Nobility in Early Modern Franconia, 1440–1567* (Cambridge, UK: Cambridge University Press, 1997).

12. Decree of August 12, 1522, cited in Monika Spicker-Beck, *Räuber, Mordbrenner, umschweifendes Gesind: Zur Kriminalität im 16. Jahrhundert* (Freiburg im Breisgau: Rombach, 1995), 25.

13. Hans Jakob Christoffel von Grimmelshausen, *An Unabridged Translation of Simplicius Simplicissimus,* trans. Monte Adair (Lanham, MD: University Press of America, 1986), 9–10.

14. *FSJ* Feb 14 1596. More than one in three robbers in one sixteenth-century sample was identified as a landsknecht. Spicker-Beck, *Räuber,* 68.

15. See Bob Scribner, "The Mordbrenner Panic in Sixteenth Century Germany," in *The German Underworld: Deviants and Outcasts in German History,* ed. Richard J. Evans (London and New York: Routledge, 1988), 29–56; Gerhard Fritz, *Eine Rotte von allerhandt rauberischem Gesindt: Öffentliche Sicherheit in Südwestdeutschland vom Ende des Dreissigjährigen Krieges bis zum Ende des Alten Reiches* (Ostfildern J. Thorbecke, 2004), 469–500; and Spicker-Beck, *Räuber,* esp. 25ff.

16. Imhof, *Lost Worlds*, 4.

17. Angstmann, 85.

18. Other infamous occupations included barbers, beggars, street cleaners, tanners, court servants and archers, shepherds, sow-gelders, privy cleaners, millers, night watchmen, actors, chimney sweeps, and tollkeepers. Nowosadtko, 12–13 and 24–28.

19. "Der Hurenson der Hencker," in 1276 Augsburg Stadtrecht, Keller, 108. The unfree argument falters on the fact that the most common names among executioners were actually from trades and crafts, including Schmidt (smith), Schneider (tailor), and Schreiner (carpenter). A few hangmen may have been condemned criminals but this too seems to have been the exception more than the rule. Angstmann (74–113) is especially influenced by contemporary anthropological research on this subject during the early twentieth century, as well as her findings in the sagas. Some historians even posited, based on Jungian notions of a sacra-lmagical discourse (and no historical evidence), that medieval executioners were the heirs to pagan Germanic priests who led ritual sacrifices and that their subsequent vilification was part of a Christian conversion campaign. Karl von Amira, *Die germanischen Todesstrafen* (Munich: Verlag der Bayerischen Akademie der Wissenschaften, 1922); see also discussion in Nowosadtko, 21–36, and G&T, 14, 38–39.

20. The most celebrated executioner dynasties in early modern Germany were Brand, Döring, Fahner, Fuchs, Gebhardt, Gutschlag, Hellriegel, Hennings, Kaufmann, Konrad, Kühn, Rathmann, Schwanhardt, and Schwarz, G&T, 46; also Stuart, 69.

21. Frantz's account of his father's disgrace is found in *Restitution*, 201r–v, and confirmed in *Enoch Widmans Chronik der Stadt Hof*, ed. Christian Meyer (Hof: Lion, 1893), 430, which does not mention Heinrich Schmidt by name, however, and specifies that the margrave ordered two servants and one gunmaker hanged. The siege of Hof is described in Friedrich Ebert, *Kleine Geschichte der Stadt Hof* (Hof: Hoermann, 1961), 34ff.; E. Dietlein, *Chronik der Stadt Hof*, vol. 1: *Allgemeine Stadtgeschichte bis zum Jahre 1603* (Hof: Hoermann, 1937), 329–94; Kurt Stierstorfer, *Die Belagerung Hofs, 1553* (Hof: Nordoberfränkischen Vereins für Natur, Geschichts-, und Landeskunde, 2003).

22. Hof's baptismal records from this period are not extant. I have based this dating on the journal entry of chaplain Johannes Hagendorn, who upon Meister Frantz's retirement in early August 1618 noted that the executioner had already celebrated his sixty-fourth birthday (*JHJ* 68r). Since Schmidt's 1624 restitution edict does not mention that Frantz was already born at the time of his father's disgrace, this leaves us with a window of roughly November 1553 to July 1554.

23. Ebert, *Kleine Geschichte der Stadt Hof*, 25–27.

24. *Widmans Chronik*, 180, 188.

25. Dietlein, *Chronik*, 434–35.

26. Ilse Schumann, "Der Bamberger Nachrichter Heinrich Schmidt: Eine Ergänzung zu seinem berühmten Sohn Franz," in *Genealogie* 3 (2001): 596–608.

27. Johannes Looshorn, *Die Geschichte des Bisthums Bamberg*, vol 5: *1556–1622* (Bamberg: Handels-Dr., 1903), 106, 148, 217.

28. StaatsAB A231/a, Nr. 1797, 1–Nr. 1809, 1 (Ämterrechnungen, 1573–1584).
29. StadtAB Rep B5, Nr. 80 (1572/73).
30. Stuart, 54–63; G&T, 23; Keller, 120; Wilbertz, 323–24.
31. Whereas Hof was almost exclusively Lutheran, only 14 percent of Bamberg's population in 1570 was Protestant. Karin Dengler-Schrieber, *Kleine Bamberger Stadtgeschichte* (Regensburg: Friedrich Puslet, 2006), 78.
32. Wilbertz, 319–21.
33. Werner Danckert, *Unehrliche Leute. Die verfemten Berufe*, 2nd ed. (Bern: Francke, 1979), 39ff. On guild moralism, see Mack Walker, *German Home Towns: Community, State, and General Estate, 1648–1871* (Ithaca, NY: Cornell University Press, 1971), 90–107.
34. The Berlin executioner was identified by his gray hat with red trim, and some fourteenth-century executioners apparently wore caps covering their ears but never their faces. In 1543 the city of Frankfurt am Main required its executioner to wear "red, white and green stripes at the top of his vest sleeves" or pay a fine of 20 fl., Keller, 79ff., 121–22; G&T, 26–28; Nowosadtko, 239–48.
35. Wilbertz, 333; Nowosadtko, 266; also Stuart, 3.
36. Carolingian rulers continued to refer to these officials by their Roman name of *carnifices* (literally, flesh-makers) as well as *apparitores* or more simply as knaves (*Knechte*) or lords of the court (*Gerichtsherren*). By the thirteenth century, the chief figure had become the *Fronbote* or beadle (also *Büttel*), called by the *Sachenspiegel* (1224) "a holy emissary" or "knave of God," thereby reinforcing the sacral nature of his duty. There is no mention of a full-time executioner in either the *Sachenspiegel* or *Schwabenspiegel* (1275), G&T, 14. See also Keller, 79–91.
37. *Bambergensis Constitutio Criminalis,* published as *Johann von Schwarzenberg: Bambergische halßgericht und rechtliche Ordnung, Nachdruck der Ausgabe Mainz 1510* (Nuremberg: Verlag Medien & Kultur, 1979), 258b.
38. Stuart, 23–26; Nowosadtko, 50–51, 62; G&T, 9, 15; Keller, 46–47.
39. Stuart, 29ff.
40. *Bambergensis; CCC.*
41. *CCC,* preamble.
42. The term *Nachrichter* was introduced in Nuremberg as early as the thirteenth century but didn't catch on elsewhere until the sixteenth century (cf. articles 86, 96, and 97 of the *CCC*), spreading to the north by the beginning of the seventeenth century. *Scharfrichter,* by contrast, was used early in the sixteenth century in the same way everywhere in German lands. On the multiple regional variations of German names for the executioner, see Angstmann, 4–75, especially 28–31, 36–43, and 45–50; also Keller, 106ff.; and Jacob and Wilhelm Grimm, *Deutsches Wörterbuch* (Leipzig: S. Hirzel, 1877), 4, pt. 2: 990–93; 7: 103–4; and 8: 2196–97.
43. *CCC,* art. 258b.
44. Gerd Schwerhoff, *Köln im Kreuzverhör: Kriminalität, Herrschaft, und Gesellschaft in einer frühneuzeitlichen Stadt* (Bonn: Bouvier, 1991), 155; Schumann, "Heinrich Schmidt Nachrichter," 605; Angstmann, 105.

45. In a late-sixteenth-century sample from Cologne this comprised three-quarters of executions during the period, 85 of 193 executions for theft and 62 for robbery, Schwerhoff, *Köln im Kreuzverhör*, 154.

46. *FSJ* Apr 5 1589.

47. Transportation to foreign colonies was more popular in England during the eighteenth century and France during the nineteenth century. See André Zysberg, "Galley and Hard Labor Convicts in France (1550–1850): From the Galleys to Hard Labor Camps: Essay on a Long Lasting Penal Institution," in *The Emergence of Carceral Institutions: Prisons, Galleys, and Lunatic Asylums, 1550–1900*, ed. Pieter Spierenburg (Rotterdam: Erasmus Universiteit, 1984), esp. 78–85; also Knapp, *Kriminalrecht*, 79–81.

48. On the origin of Nuremberg's discipline- and workhouse, see Joel F. Harrington, "Escape from the Great Confinement: The Genealogy of a German Workhouse," in *Journal of Modern History* 71 (1999): 308–45.

49. *FSJ* Dec 15 1593; Sep 5 1594; Mar 29 1595; May 19 1601; May 28 1595; Nov 22 1603; Aug 17 1599; May 2 1605; Jan 25 1614 (2x); Jul 19 1614; Jan 11 1615; Jan 12 1615. See also Harrington, "Escape from the Great Confinement," 330–32.

50. "Ob Kriegsleute auch in seligem Stande sein können" (1526), in *D. Martin Luthers Werke: Kritische Gesamtausgabe* (Weimar: Herman Böhlau, 1883ff.; reprint, 1964–68), 19:624–26; "Kirchenpostille zum Evangelium am 4. Sonntag nach Trinitatis," ibid., 6:36–42; "Von weltlicher Obrigkeit, wie weit man ihr Gehorsam schuldig sei," ibid., 11:265.

51. *Praxis rerum criminalium, durch den Herrn J. Damhouder, in hoch Teutsche Sprach verwandelt durch M. Beuther von Carlstat* (Frankfurt am Main, 1565), 264ff. Jacob Döpler, *Theatrum poenarum, suppliciorum, et executionum criminalium: oder, Schau-platz derer leibes und lebens-straffen* (Sondershausen, 1693), 1:540.

52. G&T, 23.

53. In Bayreuth on Sep 2 1560; G&T, 5398.

54. *RV* 1313: 14v (Mar 4 1570).

55. Nowosadtko, 196; Wilbertz, 117–20.

56. Keller, 114–15.

57. Keller, 245–46. *Rotwelsch* was a combination of the Latin jargon of wandering monks and students with Hebrew, Yiddish, and Romany (Gypsy). Like English Cockney, the majority of words were created by a change in meaning (through metaphor or "formal techniques such as substitution, affixing, or reversal of consonants, vowels, and syllables"), Robert Jütte, *Poverty and Deviance in Early Modern Europe* (Cambridge, UK: Cambridge University Press, 1995), 182–83; and see also his *Abbild und soziale Wirklichkeit des Bettler- und Gaunertums zu Beginn der Neuzeit: Sozial-, mentalitäts-, und sprachgeschichtliche Studien zum Liber vagatorum (1510)* (Cologne and Vienna: Böhlau, 1988), especially 26–106; also Siegmund A. Wolf, *Wörterbuch des Rotwelschen: Deutsche Gaunersprache* (Mannheim: Bibliographisches Institut, 1956); Ludwig Günther, *Die deutsche Gaunersprache und verwandte Geheim und Berufssprachen* (Wiesbaden: Sändig, 1956).

58. See the fascinating overview of Angstmann, especially 2–73.

59. Jacob Grimm et al., *Weisthümer* (Göttingen: Dieterich, 1840), 1:818–19; Eduard Osenbrüggen, *Studien zur deutschen und schweizerischen Rechtsgeschichte* (Schaffhausen: Fr. Hurter, 1868), 392–403; Keller, 243.
60. Keller, 247–48; G&T, 68–70.
61. *FSJ* 1573; Aug 13 1577; Mar 19 1579.
62. Wilbertz, 123.
63. Based on the 1772 *Meisterbrief* of Johann Michael Edelhäuser, G&T, 99. For the full text of a *Meisterbrief* from 1676, see Keller, 239; also Nowosadtko, 196–97.
64. *Restitution*, 201v–202r.

2. The Journeyman

1. *Essays*, 63.
2. Hollfeld: twice in 1573, once in 1575; Forchheim: four times in 1577, once in 1578; Bamberg: once in 1574, twice in 1577.
3. Harrington, *The Unwanted Child: The Fate of Foundlings, Orphans, and Juvenile Criminals in Early Modern Germany* (Chicago and London: University of Chicago Press, 2009), 78–79. Katherine A. Lynch (*Individuals, Families, and Communities in Europe, 1200–1800: The Urban Foundations of Western Society* [Cambridge, UK: Cambridge University Press, 2003], 38) estimates that migrants constituted 3–8 percent of most German urban populations.
4. Angstmann, especially 2–73.
5. For examples of these symbols, see Spicker-Beck, *Räuber*, 100ff. See also Florike Egmond, *Underworlds: Organized Crime in the Netherlands, 1650–1800* (Cambridge, UK: Polity Press, 1993); and Carsten Küther, *Menschen auf der Strasse: Vagierende Unterschichten in Bayern, Franken, und Schwaben in der zweiten Hälfte des 18. Jahrhunderts* (Göttingen: Vandenhoeck and Ruprecht, 1983), especially 60–73.
6. Two-thirds of all early modern homicides involved stabbings, most commonly in taverns. Julius R. Ruff, *Violence in Early Modern Europe, 1500–1800* (Cambridge, UK: Cambridge University Press, 2001), 123. On the drinking culture of Meister Frantz's day, see B. Ann Tlusty, *Bacchus and Civic Order: The Culture of Drink in Early Modern Germany* (Charlottesville and London: University Press of Virginia, 2001); B. Ann Tlusty and Beat Kümin, eds., *Public Drinking in the Early Modern World: Voices from the Tavern, 1500–1800*, vols. 1 and 2, *The Holy Roman Empire* (London: Pickering and Chatto, 2011); Marc Forster, "Taverns and Inns in the German Countryside: Male Honor and Public Space," in *Politics and Reformations: Communities, Polities, Nations, and Empires: Essays in Honor of Thomas A. Brady, Jr.*, ed. Christopher Ocker et al. (Leiden: Brill, 2007), 230–50.
7. For a typical reference that Meister Frantz "drank neither wine nor beer," see ASB 210: 248v.
8. *FSJ* Nov 18 1617; Dec 3 1612; Mar 15 1597; Nov 14 1598.
9. In one 1549 account from Nuremberg, a suspected child murderer was confronted with the corpse of a newborn found in the household's common toilet: "When the master of the house said, 'Oh! You innocent baby, if one among us here is guilty [of your murder], then give us a sign,' then supposedly the left arm

of the child immediately lifted up," whereupon the accused maid immediately fainted, ASB 226a: 32v; *FSJ* May 3 1597; StaatsAN 52a, 447: 1155; Ulinka Rublack finds references to the *Bahrprobe* in some seventeenth-century criminal records (*The Crimes of Women in Early Modern Germany* [Oxford, UK: Clarendon Press, 1999], 58) and Robert Zagolla claims that the practice continued in some locations even later (*Folter und Hexenprozess: Die strafrechtliche Spruchpraxis der Juristenfakultät Rostock im 17. Jahrhundert* [Bielefeld: Verlag für Regionalgeschichte, 2007], 220).

10. *FSJ* Jul 6 1592; Jan 16 1616; also *JHJ* Jan 16 1616. Johann Christian Siebenkees, ed. (*Materialien zur nürnbergischen Geschichte* [Nuremberg, 1792], 2:593–98) records two instances of the bier test in sixteenth-century Nuremberg, one in 1576 and one in 1599.

11. E.g., *RV* 1419: 26v. See also Knapp, *Loch*, 25ff.; Zagolla, *Folter und Hexenprozess*, 327–28.

12. Christian Ulrich Grupen, *Observationes Juris Criminalis* (1754), quoted in Keller, 200.

13. Only 1 to 2 percent of criminal suspects in late-sixteenth-century Cologne were tortured, the great majority of them professional robbers and thieves. Schwerhoff, *Köln im Kreuzverhör*, 109–15; also Stuart, 141–42.

14. G&T, 86–88; Zagolla, *Folter und Hexenprozess*, 399–400.

15. See *CCC*, art. 131, para. 36, on sufficient grounds for torture in infanticide cases; also Rublack, *Crimes of Women*, 54; Wilbertz, 80; and Nowosadtko, 164.

16. *FSJ* May 10 1599; Knapp, *Loch*, 37.

17. *FSJ* Dec 4 1599; Dec 23 1605. See also *RV* 2551: 23r–v (Oct 10 1663).

18. *JHJ* 88v–89r (Feb 8 1614). The interrogators of both Helena Nusslerin (*RV* 1309: 16v [Nov 12 1569]) and of Barbara Schwenderin (*RV* 1142: 31v; 1143: 8r [May 8 1557]) were ordered to wait eight days before further torture. Similarly, Margaretha Voglin was allowed two weeks to grow stronger before her execution was carried out (*RV* 2249: 24v [Feb 19 1641]).

19. StadtAN F1-2/VII (1586).

20. ASB 215: 18.

21. Magistrates accused Kreuzmayer of "many hundred sacramental curses." ASB 212: 121r–122v, 125v–126r; *FSJ* Sep 5 1594.

22. For a detailed analysis of Mayr's case, see Harrington, *Unwanted Child*, 177–227.

23. ASB 215: 332r.

24. It is difficult to estimate how many torture sessions Schmidt took part in per year. Contemporary Ansbach executioners (1575–1600) had an average rate of about one per week, Angstmann, 105.

25. *FSJ* Apr 21 1602.

26. See, for instance, *FSJ* May 25 1581; Feb 20 1582; Aug 4 1586 (2x); Jul 11 1598.

27. *FSJ* Jul 6 1592. On widespread questioning of torture's reliability among contemporary jurists, see Zagolla, *Folter und Hexenprozess*, 34ff.

28. 1588 and 1591, cited in Knapp, *Loch*, 33. On the latitude of executioners in this respect, see Zagolla, *Folter und Hexenprozess*, 367–73; also Joel F. Harrington, "Tortured Truths: The Self-Expositions of a Career Juvenile Criminal in Early Modern Nuremberg," in *German History* 23, no. 2 (2005): 143–71.

29. Based on a sample of 114 torture outcomes from Cologne, 1549–1675, Schwer- hoff, *Köln im Kreuzverhör*, 114–17. In Cologne and Rostock, for instance, six in ten robbers were tortured versus only one in ten homicides, Zagolla, *Folter und Hexenprozess*, 48, 61–63.

30. Jacob Grimm, "Von der Poesie im Recht," first published in 1815.

31. Knapp, *Kriminalrecht*, 60.

32. *FSJ* Aug 13 1578; Oct 9 1578; Nov 9 1579; Feb 7 1581; May 6 1581; Apr 22, 1585; Jun 25 1586; Aug 23 1593; Sep 25 1595; Oct 24 1597; Feb 23 1609; Nov 25 1612; Jan 30 1614. See Jütte, *Poverty and Deviance*, 164ff., on the branding of vagrants during this period. The ear-clippings were on Jan 29 1583; Sep 4 1583; Jan 22 1600; Aug 4 1601; and Dec 9 1600. The sole tongue-trimming was on Apr 19 1591.

    The young journeyman does not record the number or nature of corporal punishments administered during these early years, but he witnessed or assisted his father cutting off at least six ears and two fingers, as well as administering two brandings. In 1576 he notes of the executed Hans Peyhel, *Two years ago at Herzogenaurach I cut off his ears and flogged him with rods.* During the period 1572–1585, Heinrich (or occasionally Frantz Schmidt before 1578) administered 85 floggings, 11 ear-clippings, 3 finger-choppings, and 2 brandings. Schumann, "Heinrich Schmidt Nachrichter," 605.

33. StaatsAB A231/a, Nr. 1797, 1–Nr. 1803,1.

34. Jason P. Coy, *Strangers and Misfits: Banishment, Social Control, and Authority in Early Modern Germany* (Leiden: Brill, 2008), 2–3; Schwerhoff, *Köln im Kreuz- verhör*, 148–53. The use of banishment overall appears to have peaked in Ger- man lands during the second half of the sixteenth century. In addition to the unrecorded floggings before 1578, journal references to other whippings are found in *FSJ* Feb 29 1580; Jun 7 1603; and Aug 4 1586.

35. *FSJ* Oct 24 1597.

36. *FSJ* Jan 10 1583.

37. One flogging by Schmidt's predecessor in 1573 resulted in a fatality the next day, Knapp, *Kriminalrecht*, 63.

38. Stuart, 143.

39. Keller, 100.

40. Siebenkees, *Materialien*, 1:543ff; Keller, 189–96; Knapp, *Kriminalrecht*, 52–53. Both traditions continued in some German localities into the eighteenth cen- tury.

41. Keller, 7.

42. Siebenkees, *Materialien*, 2:599–600. A 1513 case is cited in Keller, 160. See also G&T, 55–56; Richard van Dülmen, *Theatre of Horror: Crime and Punishment in Early Modern Germany*, trans. Elisabeth Neu (Cambridge, UK: Polity Press, 1990), 88–89; and *CCC*, arts. 124, 130, and 133.

43. Keller, 185; Knapp, *Kriminalrecht*, 58.

44. *FSJ* Mar 6 1578. For a fuller account of Apollonia Vöglin's ordeal, see Har- rington, *Unwanted Child*, 21–71.

45. *FSJ* Jan 26 1580; jurist opinions cited in Knapp, *Kriminalrecht*, 58.

46. *FSJ* Jul 17 1582; Aug 11 1582; Jul 11 1598; Mar 5 1611; Jul 19 1595; Aug 10 1581; Oct 26 1581; Jun 8 1587; Oct 11 1593.

47. *FSJ* Jan 18 1588.
48. *FSJ* 1573; 1576; Aug 6 1579; Jan 26 1580; Mar 3 1580; Aug 16 1580; Jul 27 1582; Aug 11 1582; Aug 14 1582; Nov 9 1586; Jan 2 1588; May 28 1588; May 5 1590; Jul 7 1590; May 25 1591; Jun 30 1593; Jan 2 1595; Mar 15 1597; Oct 26 1602; Aug 13 1604; Dec 7 1615.
49. *RV* 1551: 5v (Jan 2 1588).
50. *FSJ* Jul 27 1582; Nov 9 1586; Jan 2 1595; Feb 10 1597; Mar 15 1597; Dec 7 1615.
51. *FSJ* Mar 29 1595. Frantz Schmidt only specifies the number of nips four times in his journal: 2 nips: Feb 11 1585; 3 nips: Aug 16 1580 and Oct 23 1589; 4 nips: Mar 5 1612. Again, drawing and quartering for treason, made infamous by Foucault and others, remained an extremely rare form of execution in the early modern era, too much of an anomaly to be useful in any social historical context.
52. *FSJ* May 10 1599; *JHJ* Aug 4 1612.
53. *FSJ* Feb 11 1584; Feb 12 1584; Oct 21 1585; Dec 19 1615. See also above, pages 173–79. The first woman was not hanged in Hamburg until 1619, Aachen in 1662, and Breslau in 1750. Keller, 171; G&T, 55.
54. Cited in Keller, 170. See also *CCC*, arts. 159 and 162; Wilbertz, 86–87.
55. *FSJ* Sep 23 1590; Jul 10 1593; also Knapp, *Kriminalrecht*, 136.
56. *FSJ*: 187 *executions with the sword*; 172 *executions with the rope*. During Heinrich Schmidt's tenure in Bamberg, from late 1572 to early 1585, 105 of 106 executions were either hanging (67) or decapitation (38). Schumann, "Heinrich Schmidt Nachrichter," 605.
57. Overall, decapitations constituted 47.5 percent (187 of 394) of Frantz Schmidt's capital punishments.
58. *FSJ* Jun 5 1573; 1573; 1576. For Schmidt's references to himself as the *Nachrichter* (never *Henker*), see *Restitution*, 201v–202v.
59. Knapp, *Kriminalrecht*, 52–53; Wilbertz, 87–88.
60. *FSJ* Mar 19 1579; Aug 16 1580; Jul 17 1582; Aug 11 1582; Jul 7 1584.
61. Keller, 157, 160–65.
62. Dülmen, *Theatre of Horror*, especially 5–42.
63. *JHJ* Mar 5 1612, quoted in Hampe, 73.
64. *JHJ* 97r–v (Mar 7 1615); *FSJ* Mar 7 1615. See also Stuart, 175ff., on the importance of a good death on the scaffold.
65. Hampe, 73.
66. Hampe, 69, 75.
67. Hampe, 19; also Richard J. Evans, *Rituals of Retribution: Capital Punishment in Germany, 1600–1987* (Oxford, UK, and New York: Oxford University Press, 1996), 69–70.
68. *FSJ* Feb 9 1598.
69. ASB 226a: 58v; *FSJ* Sep 23 1590.
70. *FSJ* Feb 18 1585; Sep 16 1580; also Dec 19 1615. "Wenn mein Stündlein vorhanden ist" (1562) and "Was mein Gott will" (1554), Jürgen C. Jacobs and Heinz Rölleke, commentary to 1801 version of Schmidt journal, 230.
71. *JHJ* Mar 5 1611.
72. *FSJ* Mar 11 1597; *JHJ* Mar 11 1597. See also Dec 18 1600; Mar 18 1616.
73. *FSJ* Nov 6 1595; Jan 10 1581; 1576; Jul 1 1616; *JHJ* Jul 1 1616.

74. *FSJ* Mar 9 1609; Dec 23 1600; Jul 8 1613.

75. *FSJ* Jul 11 1598.

76. *FSJ* Jan 28 1613; *JHJ* Jan 28 1613; ASB 226: 56r–57v.

77. *FSJ* Aug 16 1580.

78. *JHJ* Feb 28 1611; *FSJ* Feb 28 1611.

79. 1506, 1509, 1540, and Jul 20 1587. *FSJ* Feb 12 1596; Sep 2 1600; Jan 19 1602; Feb 28 1611. Two additional notations of *putzen*, which appear only in the Bamberg manuscript (Dec 17 1612; Feb 8 1614), were clearly the interpolations of a later editor, based on chronicle descriptions, since Schmidt is referred to in the third person. Hampe, 31; also G&T, 73–74.

80. Angstmann, 109–10; Wilbertz, 127–28; Dülmen, *Theatre of Horror*, 231–40; Keller, 230.

81. StaatsAN 52b, 226a: 176; Hampe, 79; *RV* 2250:13r–v, 15r–v (Mar 16 1641), 29r–v (Mar 30 1641), 59r (Apr 1 1641); StadtAN FI-14/IV: 2106–7.

82. *Restitution*, 202v. At another point, Schmidt records that *I executed at some risk* (*FSJ* Jan 12 1591). The stoning of Simon Schiller and his wife took place on Jun 7 1612.

83. G&T, 68; also Angstmann, 109.

84. *RV* 1222: 5r (Apr 14 1563); *RV* 1224: 5r (Jun 28 1563); *RV* 1230: 29v (Dec 9 1563), 38r (Dec 16 1563); *RV* 1250: 31v (Jun 19 1565); *RV* 1263: 20r (Jun 4 1566).

85. *RV* 1264: 17v (Jun 28 1566); *RV* 1268: 8v (Oct 10 1566); *RV* 1274: 2r (Apr 14 1567); *RV* 1275: 14r (Apr 14 1567); *RV* 1280: 24r (Sep 10 1567); *RV* 1280: 25v (Sep 12 1567). The seven children of Lienhardt and Kunigunda Lippert were Michael (baptized Oct 25 1568), Lorentz (Nov 8 1569), Jobst (Dec 27 1570), Conrad (Jul 17 1572), Barbara (Jul 10 1573), Margarethe (Feb 13 1575), and Magdalena (Dec 6 1577). LKAN Taufungen St. Sebaldus.

86. *RV* 1310: 24r–v (Dec 3 1569), 29r–v (Dec 7 1569); *RV* 1402: 22r (Oct 24 1576); *RV* 1404: 1r (Dec 6 1576), 39v (Dec 28 1576).

87. *RV* 1405: 24v (Jan 14 1577).

88. ASB 222: 75v (23 Oct 1577).

89. *RV* 1421: 14v (Mar 21 1578); *RV* 1422: 24v (Apr 5 1578), 58r–v (Apr 25 1578), 68r (Apr 29 1578).

90. *RV* 1423: 33v (May 16 1578).

3. The Master

1. *Essays*, 76.

2. Baltasar Gracián, *The Art of Worldly Wisdom: A Pocket Oracle*, trans. Christopher Maurer (New York: Doubleday, 1991), 73.

3. *FSJ* Oct 11 1593.

4. StaatsAB A245/I, Nr. 146, 124–125r. For other especially scandalous examples of fraud, see *FSJ* Feb 9 1598; Dec 3 1605; Jul 12 1614; also Knapp, *Kriminalrecht*, 247ff.

5. Stuart Carroll, *Blood and Violence in Early Modern France* (Oxford, UK: Oxford University Press, 2006), 49.

6. *Brevis Germaniae Descriptio*, 74; cited in Klaus Leder, *Kirche und Jugend in Nürnberg und seinem Landgebiet: 1400–1800* (Neustadt an der Aisch: Degener, 1973), 1. My brief description of Nuremberg's appearance is greatly indebted to Gerald Strauss's much more lyrical and evocative description in *Nuremberg in the Sixteenth Century* (New York: John Wiley, 1966), 9–35, which remains the single best English-language overview of daily life in early modern Nuremberg. I have also found the following surveys particularly helpful: Emil Reicke, *Geschichte der Reichsstadt Nürnberg* (Nuremberg: Joh. Phil. Rawschen, 1896; reprint, Neustadt an der Aisch: P.C.W. Schmidt, 1983); Werner Schultheiß, *Kleine Geschichte Nürnbergs*, 3rd ed. (Nuremberg: Lorenz Spindler, 1997); *Nürnberg: Eine europäische Stadt in Mittelalter und Neuzeit*, ed. Helmut Neuhaus (Nuremberg: Selbstverlag des Vereins für Geschichte der Stadt Nürnberg, 2000); and the indispensable reference work *Stadtlexikon Nürnberg*, ed. Michael Diefenbacher and Rudolf Endres (Nuremberg: W. Tümmels Verlag, 2000).

7. Reicke, *Geschichte der Reichsstadt Nürnberg*, 998.

8. Andrea Bendlage, *Henkers Hertzbruder. Das Strafverfolgungspersonal der Reichsstadt Nürnberg im 15. und 16. Jahrhundert* (Constance: UVK, 2003), 28–31.

9. William Smith, "A Description of the Cittie of Nuremberg" (1590), *MVGN* 48 (1958), 222. For information on the informers (*Kundschaftler*) employed by the city, see Bendlage, *Henkers Hertzbruder*, 127–37.

10. During his thirteen years in Bamberg, Heinrich Schmidt's annual income—paid by the execution, not by the week—averaged 50 fl., with a peak of 87 fl. from 1574 to 1575 and a low of 29 fl. the following year. StaatsAB A231/1, Nr. 1797/1. For the details of Frantz's contract, see *RV* 1422: 68r (Apr 29 1578); also Knapp, *Loch*, 61–62. The Bregenz executioner had a base salary of 52 fl. annually plus 1–2 fl. per execution; the Munich executioner was paid 83 fl. annually until 1697; while their Osnabrück counterpart received 2 thaler (1.7 fl.) per execution. Nowosadtko, 65–67; Wilbertz, 101.

11. *RV* 1119: 9v, 11v, 12r, 17r–v, 18r, 20r (Nov 13–15 1554); Knapp, *Loch*, 56–57.

12. StaatsAN 62, 54–79; LKAN Beerdigungen St. Lorenz, 57v: "Jorg Peck Pallenpinder bey dem [sh]onnetbadt Sep 16 1560." At least two of the nine children born to Jorg and Margareta Peck died in childhood, possibly others. LKAN Taufungen, St. Sebaldus: 93v (Magdalena; Jul 24 1544), 95r (Maria; Sep 20 1545), 96r (Jorg; May 26 1546), 97r (Gertraud; Mar 14 1547), 99r (Sebastian; Aug 10 1549), 104v (Georgius; Dec 1 1551), 105v (Barbara; Oct 6 1552), 107v (Magdalena; Aug 30 1554), 110v (Philipus; Nov 29 1555).

13. LKAN Trauungen, St. Sebaldus 1579, 70; *RV* 1430: 34r (Dec 7 1579).

14. *Stadtlexikon Nürnberg*, 437.

15. Ernst Mummenhoff, "Die öffentliche Gesundheits- und Krankenpflege im alten Nürnberg: Das Spital zum Heilige Geist," in *Festschrift zur Eröffnung des Neuen Krankenhauses der Stadt Nürnberg* (Nuremberg, 1898), 6–8; Stuart, 103.

16. G&T, 92. In the late sixteenth century, the Nuremberg Lion earned a base annual salary of 52 fl., Bendlage, *Henkers Hertzbruder*, 36–37, 89.

17. *RV* 1576: 6v, 10v (Nov 11 and 18 1589); StaatsAN 62, 82–145.

18. *FSJ* Aug 16 1597.
19. Knapp, *Loch*, 67.
20. Schwerhoff, *Köln im Kreuzverhör*, 103.
21. Knapp, *Kriminalrecht*, 64–81. On the incarceration of the insane during this period in German history, see H. C. Erik Midelfort, *A History of Madness in Sixteenth-Century Germany* (Stanford, CA: Stanford University Press, 1999), especially 322–84.
22. For instance, a stay of eleven weeks and three days in 1588 cost Christoph Greisdörffer 13 fl., 2 d. 8 H; paid in full at his release, StaatsAN 54a, II: 340.
23. Öhler was appointed *Lochhirt* on Oct 26 1557 and at a salary of 2 fl. per week was almost as well paid as Frantz Schmidt, *RV* 1148: 24v–25r (Oct 26 1557). On the duties of Nuremberg wardens, see Bendlage, *Henkers Hertzbruder*, 37–42.
24. StaatsAN 52a, 447: 1002 (Jun 23 1578); Knapp, *Loch*, 145–47.
25. Knapp, *Loch*, 20–21.
26. Knapp, *Loch*, 20. *FSJ* Jul 3 1593; Nov 22 1603, Sep 15 1604. See also prison suicides recorded for 1580, 1604, 1611, and 1615, as well as attempted suicides mentioned by Frantz Schmidt, StadtAN F1, 47: 8314, 876r; *FSJ* Jul 11 1598; May 10 1599. In 1604 a convicted murderer stabbed an accused rustler to death in prison (ASB 226: 17r–v).
27. StaatsAN 52a, 447: 1009–10; ASB 226: 23v; *RV* 1775: 13r–v (March 1605). The collective rebuilding of the gallows was prescribed in *CCC*, art. 215. See also Keller, 209ff.; Knapp, *Loch*, 69–70; Dülmen, *Theatre of Horror*, 70–73.
28. *FSJ* Sep 3 1588; Nov 5 1588; Dec 22 1586.
29. *FSJ* Jun 15 1591. Jacobs, commentary to 1801 Schmidt journal, 212.
30. William Ian Miller, *Humiliation: And Other Essays on Honor, Social Discomfort, and Violence* (Ithaca, NY: Cornell University Press, 1993), 16.
31. *FSJ* Dec 16 1594; Jun 21 1593.
32. *FSJ* Nov 10 1596; Jan 12 1583.
33. *FSJ* Aug 16 1580.
34. *FSJ* Jan 4 1582; Jul 24 1585; Oct 5 1597.
35. *FSJ* Jul 10 1593; and see, e.g., Dec 23 1605.
36. *FSJ* Oct 11 1593; Feb 9 1598; Jul 12 1614.
37. *FSJ* May 12 1584.
38. Knapp, *Kriminalrecht*, 100. For a fuller account, see Wilhelm Fürst, "Der Prozess gegen Nikolaus von Gülchen, Ratskonsulenten und Advokaten zu Nürnberg, 1605," *MVGN* 20 (1913): 139ff.
39. *FSJ* Dec 23 1605.
40. *FSJ* Apr 10 1578; Aug 12 1578; 1576.
41. *FSJ* Apr 15 1578; 1576; Dec 22 1586; Jun 1 1587; Feb 18 1585; May 29 1582. See also Nov 17 1582; Sep 12 1583.
42. *FSJ* Mar 6 1578; Jan 26 1580; Aug 10 1581; Jul 17 1582, Jun 8 1587; Jul 20 1587; Mar 5 1612.
43. ASB 210: 74vff., 112 r; ASB 210: 106r–v. See also Norbert Schindler, "The World of Nicknames: On the Logic of Popular Nomenclature," in *Rebellion, Community, and Custom in Early Modern Germany*, trans. Pamela E. Selwyn (Cambridge,

UK: Cambridge University Press, 2002), especially 57–62; also F. Bock, "Nürnberger Spitzname von 1200 bis 1800," *MVGN* 45 (1954): 1–147, and Bock, "Nürnberger Spitzname von 1200 bis 1800—Nachlese," *MVGN* 49 (1959): 1–33. The same naming tendencies were evident in contemporary England: Paul Griffiths, *Lost Londons: Change, Crime, and Control in the Capital City, 1550–1660* (Cambridge, UK: Cambridge University Press, 2008), 179–92.

44. *JHJ* 39v.
45. *FSJ* Jul 19 1614; Jun 22 1616; Sep 16 1580; Aug 4 1612; Aug 23 1594; Nov 21 1589; Aug 16 1587; Apr 30 1596; Jul 4 and Jul 7 1584.
46. Schmidt frequently mentions punishments elsewhere in Franconia that suggest more than word-of-mouth news, for instance, he identifies one condemned thief as *Hans Weber from Neuenstadt, . . . whom I saw whipped with rods out of Neuenkirchen ten years ago* (*FSJ* Aug 4 1586). See also Jan 29 1583; Feb 9 1585; Jun 20 1588; Nov 6 1588; Jan 15 1594; Mar 6 1604.
47. *FSJ* May 29 1582; Nov 17 1582; Sep 12 1583; Dec 4 1583; Jan 9 1581; Jul 23 1583. See also archer Georg Mayr whipped out of town for theft (Aug 11 1586); and Nov 18 1589; Mar 3 1597; Aug 16 1597; May 2 1605; Feb 10 1609; Dec 15 1611. For details on the frequent disciplining of such employees, see Bendlage, *Henkers Hertzbruder*, 165–201, 226–33.
48. *FSJ* Mar 3 1597; Aug 16 1597; May 25 1591.
49. *FSJ* Feb 10 1596; Mar 24 1590.
50. Griffiths, *Lost Londons*, 138; see also 196ff. on contemporary English terms for men of ill repute.
51. *FSJ* May 21 1611; Nov 24 1585.
52. *FSJ* May 24 1580; Apr 15 1581; Dec 20 1582; Nov 19 1584; Aug 14 1584; Mar 16 1585; Nov 17 1586; Nov 21 1586; Jul 14 1593; Jul 26 1593; Oct 9 1593; Nov 10 1597; Dec 14 1601; Mar 3 1604; Feb 12 1605; Nov 11 1615; Dec 8 1615. See also corporal punishments of Sep 8 1590; Jan 18 1588; Dec 9 1600; Apr 21 1601; Jan 27 1586.
53. *FSJ* Oct 9 1578; Oct 15 1579; Oct 31 1579; Oct 20 1580; Jan 9 1581; Jan 31 1581; Feb 7 1581; Feb 21 1581; May 6 1581; Sep 26 1581; Nov 25 1581; Dec 20 1582; Jan 10 1583; Jan 11 1583; Jul 15 1583; Aug 29 1583; Sep 4 1583; Nov 26 1583.
54. *FSJ* Oct 20 1580; Jan 10 1583; Jan 31 1581; Apr 2 1589; Jan 2 1588; Jan 18 1588. See also May 5 1590; Jun 11 1594; Jan 3 1595; Jun 8 1596.
55. On overall criminal pattern for female crime and executions, see Rublack, *Crimes of Women*; Otto Ulbricht, ed., *Von Huren und Rabenmüttern: Weibliche Kriminalität in der frühen Neuzeit* (Vienna, Cologne, and Weimar: Böhlau, 1995); Joel F. Harrington, *Reordering Marriage and Society in Reformation Germany* (Cambridge, UK, and New York: Cambridge University Press, 1995), 228–40; and Schwerhoff, *Köln im Kreuzverhör*, 178–79.
56. *FSJ* Feb 9 1581; Mar 27 1587; Jan 29 1599.
57. *FSJ* Jul 7 1584.
58. *FSJ* Nov 6 1610; Jul 19 1588. See also Laura Gowing, *Domestic Dangers: Women, Words, and Sex in Early Modern London* (Oxford, UK: Oxford University Press, 1996).
59. *FSJ* Jul 3 1593; Dec 4 1599; May 7 1603; Mar 9 1609.

60. *FSJ* Jul 20 1587; Sep 15 1604.
61. Cf. accounts of annual tributes required of Hof's Jews and frequent break-ins to Jewish homes, often leaving bits of pork behind. Dietlein, *Chronik der Stadt Hof,* 267–68; *FSJ* Sep 23 1590; Aug 3 1598; Oct 26 1602.
62. *FSJ* Sep 23 1590; Aug 25 1592; Jul 10 1592; and Jul 10 1593.
63. On this question of fluid early modern identity, see Natalie Zemon Davis, *The Return of Martin Guerre* (Cambridge, MA: Harvard University Press, 1983), and Valentin Groebner, *Who Are You? Identification, Deception, and Surveillance in Early Modern Europe,* trans. Mark Kyburz and John Peck (Cambridge, MA: Zone, 2007).
64. *FSJ* Dec 2 1613; see also Jul 3 1593; Jul 12 1614.
65. *FSJ* Jan 23 1610.
66. *FSJ* Feb 23 1593; May 3 1596; Jul 27 1594; Sep 8 1590.
67. *FSJ* Aug 12 1579; Jul 28 1590; Apr 21 1601. See also Apr 18 1598; Feb 9 1581; Feb 12 1600.
68. *FSJ* Jan 29 1588.
69. *FSJ* Jul 4 1588; Jul 30 1588; Dec 16 1594; Jul 4 1588; Feb 10 1597.
70. *FSJ* May 28 1588.
71. *FSJ* Feb 12 1596; Jul 11 1598; Nov 18 1617; Nov 13 1617.
72. *FSJ* Jan 16 1616. See also Jul 17 1582.
73. *FSJ* Jan 23 1595; Mar 4 1606; May 23 1615; Jun 25 1617; Jan 23 1610; Nov 14 1598.
74. *FSJ* Oct 16 1584; Oct 23 1589; Mar 8 1614. See also Oct 27 1584.
75. *FSJ* Mar 3 1580; Nov 17 1580; Jul 3 1593; Mar 30 1598; Jan 18 1603; Nov 20 1611; Nov 2 1615. See also Apr 29 1600.
76. *FSJ* May 27 1603.
77. *FSJ* Jul 2 1606.
78. *FSJ* Jul 23 1578; Jun 23 1612. See also May 2 1579; Apr 10 1582; Jun 4 1599.
79. *FSJ* Apr 28 1579; Jun 21 1593. See also Feb 28 1615.
80. *FSJ* Nov 18 1589. See also Apr 10 1582; Nov 1 1578; Sep 2 1598.
81. *FSJ* Jul 12 1614; Jan 22 1611.
82. *FSJ* Mar 6 1578; Jul 13 1579; Jan 26 1580; Feb 29 1580; Aug 14 1582; May 5 1590; Jul 7 1590; Mar 15 1597; May 20 1600; Apr 21 1601; Aug 4 1607; Mar 5 1616.
83. *FSJ* Jan 26 1580; May 5 1590; Jul 7 1590; Jun 26 1606; Feb 8 1614.
84. *FSJ* May 17 1606; Aug 4 1607; Dec 6 1580; Nov 17 1584.
85. *FSJ* Jun 11 1585. See also Jun 21 1593; Dec 23 1601; Sep 15 1604; Jul 9 1605; Nov 20 1611; Mar 5 1612; Nov 19 1613.
86. *FSJ* Oct 15 1585; Oct 21 1585; Apr 14 1586; Apr 25 1587; Jul 15 1589.
87. *FSJ* Nov 11 1585.
88. *FSJ* Jun 1 1581; Jul 27 1582; Oct 3 1587.
89. The popular stereotypes of spousal murder in early modern Germany typically contrasted the cool and calculating murdering wife with the violent and passionate husband. See Silke Göttsch, "'Vielmahls aber hätte sie gewünscht einen anderen Mann zu haben,' Gattenmord im 18. Jahrhundert," in Ulbricht, *Von Huren und Rabenmüttern,* 313–34.

90. Two wives: *FSJ* Feb 15 1580; Apr 27 1583; Jul 9 1583; Mar 26 1584; Oct 29 1584; Jun 6 1586; Jul 14 1590. Three wives: Dec 1 1580; Apr 3 1585. Four wives: Apr 3 1585; May 29 1588. Five wives: Nov 5 1595.

91. *FSJ* Jul 28 1590. See also Feb 20 1582; Oct 16 1582; Apr 27 1583; Jul 9 1583; Mar 16 1585; Sep 20 1586; Oct 4 1587; Jul 10 1592; Jul 23 1605; Dec 6 1609.

92. *FSJ* Jul 28 1590. See also Feb 20 1582; Oct 16 1582; Apr 27 1583; Jul 9 1583; Mar 16 1585; Sep 20 1586; Oct 4 1587; Jul 10 1592; Jul 23 1605; Dec 6 1609.

93. *FSJ* Feb 28 1611; Jun 7 1612.

94. *RV* 1431: 37v (Dec 29 1579); *RV* 1456: 46r (Nov 8 1580); *RV* 1458: 25v (Dec 28 1580).

95. StaatsAN 44a, Rst Nbg Losungamt, 35 neue Laden, Nr. 1979; StaatsAN 60c, Nr. 1, 181r; also *RV* 1507: 9v–10r (Aug 19 1584); *RV* 1508: 32r (Sep 25 1584).

96. Shortly after Easter 1582 Frantz requested and received permission to visit his ailing father in Bamberg. *RV* 1475: 23v (Apr 10 1582).

97. ASB 210: 154; also *RV* 1523: 8r–v, 23r, 25r, 31r (Feb 1, 8, 9, 10, 1585). StaatsAN 52a, 447: 1076.

98. *FSJ* Feb 11 1585. See also Jul 23 1584.

99. StaatsAB A245/I, Nr. 146, 106v–107v; StaatsAN 52a, 447: 1076–77. In another passage, Schmidt not only identifies a culprit as a kinsman but also relegates the flogging to his assistant, *FSJ* Jun 7 1603.

100. StaatsAB A231/1, Nr. 1809, 1.

101. StadtsAB B7, Nr. 84 (May 1 1585); StadtsAB B4, Nr. 35, 102r–v (1586); *RV* 1517: 21v–22r (May 25 1585).

102. StadtAN F1–2/VII: 682.

103. St. Rochus Planquadrat H5, #654; Ilse Schumann, "Neues zum Nürnberger Nachrichter Franz Schmidt," in *Genealogie* 25, nos. 9–10 (Sep–Oct 2001): 686.

104. Hilpoltstein (*FSJ* Jul 20 1580; Aug 20 1584; Mar 6 1589; Sep 19 1593; Feb 28 1594); Lauf (*FSJ* Aug 4 1590; Jun 8 1596; Jun 4 1599); Sulzbach (*FSJ* Feb 23 1593; Mar 11 1597); Hersbruck (*FSJ* Jul 19 1595; Dec 18 1595; Feb 10 1596; Sep 2 1598); Lichtenau (*FSJ* Apr 18 1598). See also *RV* 1706: 38r (Jan 12 1600).

105. LKAN St. Sebaldus, 49v, 50v, 70v.

106. One local study from the period, for instance, found that only one in six poor families had more than three children resident at the same town, while nearly three in four upper-middle-class and wealthy families enjoyed this privilege. On the other hand, based on a sample of 782 executioner families during the early modern period, three boys and three girls was the average among executioner families, Jürgen Schlumbohm, *Lebensläufe, Familien, Höfe: Die Bauern und Heuerleute des osnabrückischen Kirchspiels Belm in proto-industrieller Zeit, 1650–1850* (Göttingen: Vandenhoeck and Ruprecht, 1994), 201, 297; G&T, 45–50.

107. *RV* 1621: 3v, 10v (Jul 14 1593); ASB 308 (Bürgerbuch 1534–1631): 128v.

4. The Sage

1. *Essays*, 398.

2. *FSJ* Mar 15 1597.

3. *RV* 2122: 23r–v (May 19 1631). StaatsAN Rep 65 (Mikrofilm S 0735). The plague and winter of 1600 are recounted in StaatsAN 52b, 226a: 1256–57.

4. See especially the excellent overview of Joy Wiltenburg, *Crime and Culture in Early Modern Germany* (Charlottesville: University of Virginia Press, 2012).

5. *FSJ* 1573; Nov 9 1586; Nov 17 1580; Mar 3 1580; Aug 16 1580; Dec 14 1579.

6. *FSJ* Oct 11 1604; Apr 18 1598.

7. *FSJ* Mar 29 1595.

8. Knapp, *Kriminalrecht*, 179–80.

9. *FSJ* Apr 28 1579; Dec 6 1580; Jul 27 1582.

10. *FSJ* Oct 23 1589. See also Oct 16 1584; Mar 13 1602; Oct 11 1604.

11. *FSJ* Apr 28 1579; Mar 5 1612; Jan 16 1616; Jan 27 1586; Sep 23 1590; May 18 1591; Dec 17 1612. See also 1574; May 25 1581; Feb 20 1582; Aug 4 1586; Dec 22 1587; Jan 5 1587; May 30 1587; Apr 11 1592; Jun 21 1593. On the vulnerability of nighttime, see Craig Koslofsky, *Evening's Empire: A History of the Night in Early Modern Europe* (Cambridge, UK: Cambridge University Press, 2011).

12. *FSJ* Aug 29 1587; Oct 16 1584.

13. *FSJ* Jun 30 1593.

14. *FSJ* Sep 18 1604; Aug 13 1604. See also Jan 2 1588; Jul 10 1593; Feb 28 1615.

15. *FSJ* Jan 16 1616.

16. *FSJ* Jun 4 1599.

17. Four of these included violent robbery (Dülmen, *Theatre of Horror*, appendix, table 5), as did several cases from the sixteenth century. In three instances, the rape of minors resulted in executions (*FSJ* Jul 3 1578; Apr 10 1583; Jun 23, 1612).

18. *FSJ* Mar 13 1602; Aug 22 1587. See also Nov 19 1612; Jun 2 1612; Dec 7 1615.

19. *FSJ* Jun 4 1596; Nov 28 1583; Nov 13 1599.

20. *FSJ* Jul 17 1582; Aug 11 1582; May 27 1603; May 8 1598; May 17 1611; Oct 11 1608.

21. *FSJ* Oct 13 1604.

22. *FSJ* Jul 15 1580.

23. *FSJ* 1578; Jul 15 1580; May 25 1581; Feb 20 1582; Mar 14 1584; Aug 4 1586; Jan 2 1588; Jul 4 1588; Jun 21 1593; Feb 10 1596; Jul 22 1596; Jul 11 1598; Jan 20 1601; Apr 21 1601.

24. *FSJ* May 25 1581.

25. *FSJ* Jul 21 1593. See also three cases in 1573; Jul 15 1580; May 25 1581; Feb 20 1582; Aug 4 1586; Dec 8 1587; Feb 10 1596; Jul 22 1596; Apr 21 1601.

26. *FSJ* 1574.

27. *FSJ* Oct 11 1603. Other examples of corpse desecration are 1574; May 25 1591; Aug 28 1599; Jul 15 1580; Jan 2 1588; Mar 13 1602; Dec 2 1596; Mar 15 1597; Mar 5 1612.

28. *FSJ* May 2 1605; Jul 29 1600; Nov 12 1601; Dec 2 1596; Feb 18 1591; Jun 21 1593; Jul 11 1598. See also 1573; 1574; Feb 11 1585; May 4 1585; May 2 1605.

29. *FSJ* Mar 3 1597; Jul 29 1600; Feb 10 1596; Jan 17 1611; Feb 20 1582; Jul 27 1582.

30. *FSJ*: 300 of 394 capital punishments; 301 of 384 corporal punishments.

31. On the "Code of the West," see especially Richard Maxwell Brown, "Violence," in *The Oxford History of the American West*, ed. Clyde A. Milner II et al. (Ox-

ford, UK: Oxford University Press, 1994), 393–95. I am indebted to my colleague Dan Usner for this citation.

32. Knapp, *Kriminalrecht*, 170–77, 191–95.
33. *FSJ* Oct 26 1602; Mar 17 1609; May 4 1585. See also Apr 28 1586.
34. *FSJ* 1577; Apr 10 1578; Oct 6 1579; Nov 28 1583; Apr 28 1586; Feb 18 1591; Jun 1 1587; Oct 13 1588; Aug 11 1600; Aug 11 1606. Knapp, *Kriminalrecht*, 31–37. See also Schwerhoff, *Köln im Kreuzverhör*, 265–322.
35. *FSJ* Oct 13 1588.
36. *FSJ* Aug 7 1599.
37. *FSJ* Apr 20 1587.
38. *FSJ* Apr 11 1592.
39. *FSJ* Sep 20 1587; Mar 6 1604.
40. Harrington, *Unwanted Child*, 30–34.
41. *FSJ* Oct 5 1597; Jul 8 1609; also Jul 1 1609.
42. *FSJ* Jan 9 1583; Jul 18 1583; Sep 1 1586; Jul 4 1584; also Jun 16 1585.
43. *FSJ* Jun 28 1614.
44. *FSJ* Feb 22 1611.
45. *FSJ* Jul 20 1587.
46. See Ulinka Rublack "'Viehisch, frech vnd onverschämpt': Inzest in Südwestdeutschland, ca. 1530–1700," in Ulbricht, *Von Huren und Rabenmüttern*, 171–213; also David Warren Sabean, Simon Teuscher, and Jon Mathieu, eds., *Kinship in Europe: Approaches to the Long-Term Development (1300–1900)* (New York: Berghahn, 2007).
47. *FSJ* Jul 23 1605; Jan 29 1599; Mar 5 1611; Feb 28 1611; Jul 7 1584. See also Mar 27 1587; Apr 23 1588; Apr 2 1589; Jun 26 1594; Jun 17 1609.
48. The best work on this subject is Helmut Puff, *Sodomy in Reformation Germany and Switzerland, 1400–1600* (London and Chicago: University of Chicago Press, 2003).
49. *FSJ* Aug 13 1594.
50. *FSJ* Mar 11 1596.
51. *FSJ* Mar 11 1596; Aug 10 1581.
52. *FSJ* Jul 3 1596. For evidence of a surprisingly tolerant atmosphere in this respect, see Maria R. Boes, "On Trial for Sodomy in Early Modern Germany," in *Sodomy in Early Modern Europe*, ed. Tom Betteridge (Manchester, UK: Manchester University Press, 2002), 27–45.
53. *FSJ* Apr 19 1591. See also Jul 15 1584; Oct 13 1587; May 17 1583; Jul 15 1585. On the fear of divine retribution for blasphemy, see Knapp, *Kriminalrecht*, 277–79.
54. *FSJ* Jan 5 1587; Jun 25 1590; Jul 29 1600. See also Aug 12 1600; Jan 19 1602; Apr 21 1601.
55. *FSJ* Feb 10 1609; Mar 9 1609; Jan 23 1610; Jan 19 1602.
56. *FSJ* Oct 1 1605.
57. *FSJ* Jan 27 1586. See also Aug 4 1586; Jan 2 1588; Mar 4 1589; Sep 23 1590.
58. Knapp, *Kriminalrecht*, 119–22. See also 233ff., on the "diebliche Behalten" identified by executing magistrates.
59. *FSJ* Dec 29 1611; Jul 19 1588.

60. *FSJ* Jan 12 1615; Sep 12 1583; Jul 23 1584; Aug 3 1598; Aug 26 1609.
61. *FSJ* Nov 14 1598.
62. *FSJ* Nov 18 1617.
63. *FSJ* Dec 13 1588; Nov 18 1597; Oct 13 1601.
64. *FSJ* Sep 15 1604.
65. *FSJ* Apr 29 1600. See also Jul 1 1616.
66. *FSJ* Oct 25 1597. See also Jun 1 1587.
67. *FSJ* Mar 9 1609.
68. *FSJ* Nov 18 1617; Sep 2 1600. See also Jul 23 1594; Jul 13 1613.
69. *FSJ* Oct 17 1587; Sep 7 1611; Sep 14 1602; Sep 16 1595.
70. *FSJ* Oct 1 1612; Jul 8 1613.
71. *FSJ* Oct 11 1593; Feb 9 1598; Mar 20 1606; Feb 23 1609; Jul 12 1614.
72. *FSJ* May 4 1585; Nov 17 1584; Oct 5 1588; May 7 1603. Explicitly "good deaths" included Jan 10 1581; Nov 6 1595; Dec 23 1600; Sep 15 1605; Sep 18 1605; Jul 8 1613.
73. *JHJ*, quoted in Hampe, 71; *FSJ* Jul 19 1614. See also May 17 1611.
74. *JHJ* 39v.
75. *JHJ*, quoted in Hampe, 19.
76. *JHJ*, quoted in Hampe, 17–18.
77. *FSJ* Jan 11 1588.
78. *FSJ* Jan 28 1613; Jul 8 1613.
79. *FSJ* Feb 20 1582; Sep 18 1604. See also Aug 11 1582; Oct 9 1593.
80. *JHJ* Mar 10 1614.
81. Dülmen, *Theatre of Horror*, 28–32; Schwerhoff, *Köln im Kreuzverhör*, 166ff.
82. StaatsAN 226a, 40v, 77r.; *JHJ* 153r; *FSJ* Mar 15 1610.
83. Hampe, 14–16.
84. Ibid., 83.
85. *FSJ* Oct 3 1588. See also Jul 12 1614; Jun 15 1588; May 23 1597; Dec 18 1593.
86. *JHJ* Mar 10 1614, quoted in Hampe, 16.
87. Quoted in Hampe., 83.
88. *FSJ* Feb 10 1609.
89. Keller, 144–45, 148.
90. *FSJ* Jan 10 1581; also Oct 16 1585.
91. *FSJ* Apr 11 1592; Mar 4 1606; Oct 11 1593; Aug 11 1606; Mar 5 1612. See also Mar 17 1609; Sep 5 1611.
92. See Harrington, *Unwanted Child*, 195–214.
93. CCC, art. 179 and art. 14.
94. Harrington, *Unwanted Child*, 221–25.
95. StadtAN F1–14/IV: 1634.
96. *FSJ* May 16 1594; Jul 22 1593; Jun 4 1600; Nov 29 1582.
97. *FSJ* Oct 1 1612.
98. Hampe, 84. The five boys in the first group were forced to watch the execution of their eighteen-year-old leader, Heinrich Lind, before they were publicly flogged and banished. A group of thirteen boys the same year, "of whom none was over twelve years old," was also banished after flogging. StadtAN F1–2/VII: 529; Knapp, *Kriminalrecht*, 9.

99. *FSJ* Jan 25 1614; StaatsAB A245/I Nr. 146, 82v; ASB 210: 86v.
100. *FSJ* Oct 7 1578; Mar 19 1579; Apr 28 1580; Aug 2 1580; Oct 4 1580; Feb 11 1584; Feb 12 1584; Jul 20 1587; May 15 1587; Sep 5 1594; May 3 1597; Jun 16 1604; Jan 12 1615; Dec 19 1615; also ASB 226a: 49r–52v.
101. ASB 226a: 48r; *FSJ* Jan 25 1614.
102. *FSJ* Feb 11 1584; Feb 12 1584.
103. *FSJ* Sep 5 1594; May 3 1597; Jun 16 1604; Feb 28 1615; Dec 14 1615.
104. *FSJ* Jan 12 1615. See also Dec 14 1615.
105. *FSJ* Dec 19 1615; ASB 218: 72vff.
106. *FSJ* Jan 29 1588; Jan 13 1592. See also Feb 11 1584; Feb 12 1584; Jun 5 1593; Jan 12 1615; Dec 14 1615; Dec 19 1615.
107. *FSJ* Oct 25 1615.
108. *FSJ* May 19 1601.
109. Joel F. Harrington, "Bad Parents, the State, and the Early Modern Civilizing Process," in *German History* 16, no. 1 (1998): 16–28.
110. *FSJ* Jan 8 1582; 1574; Apr 15 1578; Mar 6 1606; Apr 2 1590; Jan 14 1584.
111. *FSJ* Dec 12 1598; Mar 6 1606; Jul 18 1583; Sep 1 1586; Jun 7 1612. *RV* 1800: 48v–49r (Mar 14 1607).
112. *FSJ* Jan 14 1584; also Jan 8 1582.
113. ASB 213: 214v.
114. *FSJ* May 2 1605.
115. *FSJ* Jun 16 1604.
116. ASB 210: 154r. *FSJ* Feb 11 1585.
117. Dieter Merzbacher, "Der Nürnberger Scharfrichter Frantz Schmidt—Autor eines Meisterliedes?," in *MVGN* 73 (1986): 63–75.
118. Stuart, 179–80.
119. *FSJ* Apr 2 1590.
120. *FSJ* Sep 15 1604. On the theme of the good and bad thieves in fifteenth- and sixteenth-century art, see Mitchell Merback, *The Thief, the Cross, and the Wheel: Pain and the Spectacle of Punishment in Medieval and Renaissance Europe* (Chicago: University of Chicago Press, 1999), 218–65.

5. The Healer

1. *Essays*, 174.
2. *FSJ* Jan 2 1588; Jan 11 1588; Jan 18 1588.
3. Geoffrey Abbott, *Lords of the Scaffold: A History of the Executioner* (London: Eric Dobby, 1991), 104ff.
4. ASB 210: 289r–v, 292v–293v.
5. *Restitution*, 201v.
6. *RV* 1119: 13r (Jul 22 1555); G&T, 104–6.
7. Nowosadtko, 163. In 1533, Augsburg's retired executioner was unable to support himself as a full-time medical consultant and was forced to ask for his old job back. Stuart, 154.
8. Robert Jütte, *Ärzte, Heiler, und Patienten: Medizinischer Alltag in der frühen Neuzeit* (Munich: Artemis & Winkler, 1991), 18–19.

9. Angstmann, 92; Keller, 226. Paracelsus, *Von dem Fleisch und Mumia*, cited in Stuart, 160.

10. Matthew Ramsey, *Professional and Popular Medicine in France, 1770–1830: The Social World of Medical Practice* (Cambridge, UK: Cambridge University Press, 1988), 27; Nowosadtko, 165.

11. On the proliferation of general medical knowledge among artisanal families, see Michael Hackenberg, "Books in Artisan Homes of Sixteenth-Century Germany," *Journal of Library History* 21 (1986): 72–91.

12. *Artzney Buch: Von etlichen biß anher unbekandten unnd unbeschriebenen Kranckheiten/deren Verzeichnuß im folgenden Blat zu finden* (Frankfurt am Main, 1583).

13. The edition I consulted was *Feldtbuch der Wundartzney, newlich getruckt und gebessert* (Strasbourg, 1528).

14. One popular work, the 1532 *Spiegel der Artzney* of Lorenz Fries, was in fact structured around questions during the consultation. See Claudia Stein, *Negotiating the French Pox in Early Modern Germany* (Farnham, UK: Ashgate, 2009), 48–49.

15. Jütte, *Ärzte*, 108. See also David Gentilcore, *Medical Charlatanism in Early Modern Italy* (Oxford, UK: Oxford University Press, 2006).

16. In a sample of 2,179 cases, 36.6 percent of the injuries were treated by wound doctors in late-sixteenth-century Cologne. Jütte, *Ärzte*, table 6; G&T, 111.

17. Nowosadtko, 163–66.

18. *Restitution*, 202r.

19. Valentin Deuser was able to obtain an imperial privilege in 1641 that allowed him "to make house calls in any location and practice without hindrance as a wound doctor and barber," G&T, 41.

20. *Restitution*, 203r–v.

21. *RV* 1726: 58r–v (Jul 7 1601).

22. *RV* 1835: 25r (Oct 14 1609).

23. Mummenhoff, "Die öffentliche Gesundheits," 15; L.W.B. Brockliss and Colin Jones, *The Medical World of Early Modern France* (Oxford, UK: Clarendon Press, 1997), 13–14.

24. In 1661 the Nuremberg council answered an angry query from Augsburg physicians about their own executioner's wide-ranging medical activities, stating that such activities were acceptable for executioners, Stuart, 163.

25. G&T, 41. For accounts of conflicts elsewhere, see Wilbertz, 70ff.; Stuart, 164–72; G&T, 109ff.

26. In Nuremberg this was usually Saint Peter's, although sometimes on land within the cemetery that was not consecrated, Knapp, *Loch*, 77.

27. Karl H. Dannenfeldt, "Egyptian Mumia: The Sixteenth Century Experience and Debate," in *Sixteenth Century Journal* 16, no. 2 (1985): 163–80.

28. Stuart, 158–59; Stuart compares the distributing of blood and occasionally body parts to Christian communion, 180.

29. Markwart Herzog, "Scharfrichterliches Medizin. Zu den Beziehungen zwischen Henker und Arzt, Schafott und Medizin," in *Medizinhistorisches Journal* 29 (1994), 330–31; Stuart, 155–60; Nowosadtko, 169–70.

30. Nowosadtko, 179.

31. Stuart, 162; Angstmann, 93.
32. For a different interpretation of the intersection of art and anatomy, see Andrea Carlino, *Books of the Body: Anatomical Ritual and Renaissance Learning*, trans. John Tedeschi and Anne C. Tedeschi (Chicago: University of Chicago Press, 2009).
33. Roy Porter, *Blood and Guts: A Short History of Medicine* (London: Allen Lane, 2002), 53–58.
34. Nowosadtko, 168–69.
35. G&T, 67.
36. Hampe, 79–81.
37. Cited in Knapp, *Kriminalrecht*, 64.
38. *FSJ* Jul 21 1578; *RV* 1425: 48r (Jul 17 1578).
39. *FSJ* Jun 1 1581; Oct 16 1584; Dec 8 1590; Dec 18 1593. Pessler was still dissecting executed criminals in 1641. Knapp, *Kriminalrecht*, 100.
40. *FSJ* Jun 26 1578; Aug 22 1587.
41. *FSJ* Jan 20 1601; Aug 29 1587.
42. *FSJ* Jun 4 1596; Mar 21 1615; Oct 1 1605.
43. *FSJ* Sep 14 1602.
44. Angstmann, 99–101; StaatsAN 42a, 447: 1063 (Aug 7 1583).
45. Döpler, *Theatrum poenarum*, 1:596; Nowosadtko; 183–89; *RV* 2176: 56r (Jul 15 1635); Hartmut H. Kunstmann, *Zauberwahn und Hexenprozess in der Reichsstadt Nürnberg* (Nuremberg: Nürnberg Stadtarchiv, 1970), 94–97.
46. Nowosadtko, 98–117; Zagolla, *Folter und Hexenprozess*, 368; Wolfgang Behringer, *Witchcraft Persecutions in Bavaria: Popular Magic, Religious Zealotry, and Reason of State in Early Modern Europe*, trans. by J. C. Grayson and David Lederer (Cambridge, UK, and New York: Cambridge University Press, 1997), 401, table 13. On the witch craze elsewhere in Franconia, see also Susanne Kleinöder-Strobel, *Die Verfolgung von Zauberei und Hexerei in den fränkischen Markgraftümern im 16. Jahrhundert* (Tübingen: J.C.B. Mohr Siebeck, 2002).
47. Kunstmann, *Zauberwahn*, 39–44.
48. *FSJ* Jul 28 1590.
49. ASB 211: 111r–114r; see also Kunstmann, *Zauberwahn*, 69–78.
50. ASB 211: 111r.
51. *FSJ* Jul 28 1590.
52. Kunstmann, *Zauberwahn*, 78–86. Later in the century, Nuremberg too would succumb to the surrounding mania and execute three men and two women for witchcraft (compared to 4,500 for surrounding Franconia).
53. *FSJ* Nov 13 1617; ASB 217: 326r–v.
54. *FSJ* Oct 13 1604.
55. *FSJ* May 2 1605; Dec 23 1600.
56. *FSJ* Dec 13 1588.
57. *FSJ* Jul 8 1613; *JHJ* Jul 8 1613.
58. *FSJ* May 10 1599.
59. *FSJ* Mar 6 1604; ASB 215, cited in Hampe, 59–60.
60. ASB 218: 324r–342r.
61. *FSJ* Mar 7 1604; Aug 17 1599; Mar 20 1606; Feb 18 1585.

62. *FSJ* Sep 25 1595; Nov 26 1586.
63. *FSJ* Feb 9 1598. On this topic, see the fascinating book by Johannes Dillinger, *Magical Treasure Hunting in Europe and North America: A History* (New York: Palgrave Macmillan, 2011).
64. Between 1601 and 1606, Schmidt traveled at least once a year, and often twice, for executions in Hilpoltstein, Altdorf, Lauf, Salzburg, Lichtenau, and Gräfenberg (*FSJ* Jun 20 1601; Jul 8 1601; Mar 3 1602; May 7 1603; May 27 1603; Jun 16 1604; Aug 13 1604; May 6 1605; May 17 1606). He journeyed to Heroldsberg and Hersbruck in 1609 (Feb 10 and Mar 17), then once to Eschenau on Jan 17 1611. Meister Frantz averaged only two floggings annually during the following seven years, even though there were demonstrably other such corporal punishments administered.
65. ASB 226: 43r–v; *FSJ* Feb 28 1611.
66. StaatsAN 52a, 447: 1413–14; *RV* 1871: 7v, 22v–23v, 25v, 31v–32r.
67. StaatsAN 52a, 447: 1493.
68. Siebenkees, *Materialen,* 4:552; *FSJ* Jul 29 1617.
69. *RV* 1943: 12v, 18r–v, 24v (Nov 10, 12, 13 1617).
70. *JHJ* Nov 13 1617.
71. *RV* 1943: 37v, 58r, 80r, 85r–v (Jul 13, 17, 24, 27 1618); 1953: 10v, 41r, 47r (Aug 1, 10, 12 1618).
72. *RV* 1953: 55v–56r, 72v, 80r (Aug 14, 20, 22 1618); 1954: 33v, 74r (Sep 7 and 21 1618); 1957: 42r (Dec 4 1618).
73. *RV* 1963: 4v, 27r–v, 39r (Apr 29, May 8 and 13 1619).
74. *RV* 2005: 104r–v (Jul 17 1622); 2018: 45v (Jun 23 1623); 2037: 17r (Nov 16 1624); 2038: 32r (Dec 12 1624); 2068: 117r (Apr 17 1627); 2189: 30r–v (Jul 22 1636); 2194: 25r–v (Dec 7 1636); 2214: 36r (May 31 1638).
75. Keller, 174.
76. *RV* 1969: 29v (Oct 22 1619); 1977: 54v (Jun 7 1620); 1991: 35v (Jun 8 1621).
77. *RV* 2052: 92v (Feb 21 1626).
78. *RV* 2044: 29v–30r, 64r–v (Jun 23 and Jul 4 1625); 2045: 13r–v, 41r–v, 71v (Jul 18 and 26, Aug 3 1625); 2047: 16r (Sep 13 1625); 2048: 1v (Oct 6 1625); StadtAN B 14/1 138, 108v–110r: down payment of 373 fl. 27¼ kr.; remainder paid after cleaning of house (Sep 22 1625), StadtAN B1/II, no. 74 (c. 1626).
79. *RV* 1959: 37v–38r (Jan 23 1619); *RV* 1968: 9r (Sep 18 1619).
80. *RV* 2040: 29v–30r (Feb 10 1625).
81. *RV* 2002: 2r (Apr 4 1622); *RV* 2046: 7r–v (Aug 13 1625).
82. *RV* 2071: 25v (Jun 26 1627); StaatsAN B1/III, Nr. VIa/88.
83. StaatsAN 54a II: Nr. 728.
84. *Restitution,* 209r–211r.; *RV* 2039: 34v (Jan 17 1625).
85. LKAN St. Lorenz Taufungen 910 (Jan 4 1612); Schumann, "Franz Schmidt," 678–79.
86. *RV* 1877: 15r, 21r, 31v–32r (Dec 2, 4, and 7 1612).
87. *RV* 1929: 64r (Nov 13 1616); 1931: 49v–49r (Dec 30 1616); 1933: 8v–9r (Feb 8 1617).
88. *RV* 2025: 25v, 37r (Jan 8 and 14 1624). She is initially listed as Rosina Schmidin and later as Rosina Bückhlin; there is no reference to her husband.
89. StaatsAN Rep 65, Nr. 34: 42r, 56r.

90. Between 1680 and 1770, at least nine at University of Ingolstadt alone, G&T, 17–20, 111–12; Nowosadtko, 321ff.
91. *RV* 2122: 23r–v (May 19 1631).
92. *RV* 2131: 74v (Feb 3 1632); LKAN Lorenz 512. *Nürnberger Kunstlerlexikon*, ed. Manfred H. Grieb (Munich: Saur, 2007), 1:24; StaatsAN 65, 20 (Feb 24 1632).
93. LKAN Lorenz 109; StaatsAN Rep 65, Nr. 34: 56.
94. LKAN Lorenz L80, 129; *RV* 2162: 49v (Jun 13 1634).
95. StaatsAN 65, 32: 244.

Epilogue

1. In *Resistance, Rebellion, and Death*, trans. Justin O'Brien (New York: Vintage Books, 1974), 180.
2. Walker, *German Home Towns*, 12.
3. StaatsAN 54a II: Nr. 728; also *RV* 2189: 30r–v (Jul 22 1636); 2194: 25r–v (Dec 7 1636); 2225: 97r (May 10 1639); 2232: 10v–11v (Nov 2 1639); 2243: 91v (Sep 23 1640). By Schlegel's own estimate, he had only ninety-seven clients in Nuremberg, as contrasted with over fifteen hundred in his previous position.
4. Maria died on Apr 12 1664; Frantzenhans on Feb 26 1683 (LKAN Beerditgungen St. Lorenz, fol. 311, 328).
5. Evans, *Rituals of Retribution*, 109–49.
6. I am strongly swayed by Richard Evans's devastating criticisms of the teleological and otherwise flawed arguments of Michel Foucault and Philippe Ariès in this respect, although a bit more sympathetic to Norbert Elias, whose "civilizing process" remains valuable in other cultural contexts (*Rituals of Retribution*, 880ff.). Steven Pinker's recent popularization of the latter, however, unfortunately amplifies one of the weakest components of Elias's theory, namely the alleged rise of empathy during the eighteenth century on. According to Pinker, for instance, "Medieval Christendom was a culture of cruelty," and only with the advent of Enlightenment "humanism" did "people beg[i]n to sympathize with more of their fellow human beings," Steven Pinker, *The Better Angels of Our Nature: Why Violence Has Declined* (New York: Viking, 2011), 132–33. For more nuanced analyses of changes in popular sensibilities regarding public executions, see Pieter Spierenburg, *The Spectacle of Suffering: Executions and the Evolution of Repression* (Cambridge: Cambridge University Press, 1984), and Paul Friedland, *Seeing Justice Done: The Age of Spectacular, Punishment in France* (Oxford: Oxford University Press, 2012), especially 119–91. I am grateful to my colleague Lauren Clay for bringing the second work to my attention.
7. Cf. similar conclusions of Dülmen, *Theatre of Horror*, 133–37.
8. Keller, 262–79; Stuart, 75–82, 227–39; Nowosadtko, 305–16, 333–36; Knapp, *Loch*, 60–61.
9. This section is especially indebted to the excellent treatment of Nowosadtko, "'Und nun alter, ehrlicher Franz.'"
10. Letter dated Sep 3 1810; *Achim von Arnim und Jacob und Wilhelm Grimm*, ed. R. Steig (Stuttgart: J. G. Cotta, 1904), 69–70.

11. G&T, 49; Nowosadtko, "'Und nun alter, ehrlicher Franz,'" 238–41.

12. See especially Stephen Brockmann, *Nuremberg: The Imaginary Capital* (Rochester, NY: Camden House, 2006).

13. See the fascinating historical excursion in Wolfgang Schild, *Die Eiserne Jungfrau: Dichtung und Wahrheit*, Schriftenreiche des Mittelalterlichen Kriminalmuseums Rothenburg ob der Tauber (2001). I thank Dr. Hartmut Frommer for bringing this publication to my attention.

14. For discussions of the twentieth-century historiography of the early modern executioner in Germany, see Wilbertz, 1ff.; Nowosadtko, 3–8; and Stuart, 2–5.

15. Among the multitude of literary works incorporating the "medieval hangman" as a central character, the most successful have been Wilhelm Raabe's *Das letzte Recht* (1862) and *Zum wilden Mann* (written in 1873, published in 1884); and the plays of Gerhart Hauptmann (*Magnus Garbe*, 1914; second version, 1942) and Ruth Schaumann (*Die Zwiebel*, 1943). More recently the figure has become the subject of popular romance novels such as Oliver Pötzsch's *The Hangman's Daughter* (English translation by Lee Chadeayne; Seattle: AmazonCrossing, 2011) or *Der Henker von Nürnberg* (Mannheim: Wellhöfer, 2010), a collection of imaginative short stories edited by Anne Hassel and Ursula Schmid-Spreer.

16. I take this term from Evans, *Rituals of Retribution*, xiii.

17. Pinker, *Better Angels of Our Nature*, especially 129–88.

18. www.amnesty.org/en/death-penalty/numbers.

Acknowledgments

I began writing this book during a blissful fall semester at the American Academy in Berlin and cannot imagine a more ideal incubator for a nascent project. Director Gary Smith and his staff have realized a Platonic ideal of intellectual vitality, providing fellows with long hours of contemplative serenity in a stunning Wannsee villa, incomparable support services, and countless opportunities for intellectual interaction, all topped off by the nightly dining extravaganzas of chef Reinold Kegel. Among the many Academy staff members who contributed to this idyllic environment, Gary Smith, R. Jay Magill, Alissa Burmeister, Malte Mau, and Yolande Korb all deserve special thanks. My family and I were also blessed by an exceptionally convivial cohort of resident fellows, all of whom shared in many hours of lively conversation, urban adventures, and fierce Ping-Pong games (Jochen Hellbeck still owes me a rematch). I am particularly grateful for the friendship and inspiration of Nathan Englander, Rachel Silver, George Packer, and Laura Secor. This book owes a lot as well to the generosity of the universally admired Rick Atkinson, who not only shared with me some wise advice on constructing a narrative, but also the names of his excellent literary agent and his cartographer (but held on to all of those Pulitzers).

During the course of archival work, I benefited considerably from the expert guidance of Dr. Stefan Nöth and Dr. Klaus Rupprecht at the Staatsarchiv Bamberg, Dr. Arnd Kluge of the Hof Stadtarchiv, Dr. Gerhard Rechter and Dr. Gunther Friedrich at the Staatsarchiv Nürnberg, Dr. Andrea Schwarz of the Landeskirchlichesarchiv Nürnberg, Dr. Christine Sauer of the Stadtbibliothek Nürnberg, and

Dr. Horst-Dieter Beyerstedt of the Stadtarchiv Nürnberg. Dr. Martin Baumeister of the Germanisches Nationalmuseum Nürnberg generously devoted an entire morning to discussing and showing me various execution swords, even allowing me to examine closely and wield (at a safe distance) one specimen that might have belonged to Meister Frantz himself. Michaela Ott likewise indulged me with an extended private tour of Nuremberg's *Lochgefängnis* (dungeon), patiently answering my most arcane queries and allowing me to make measurements and take photos of this still chilling venue. Dr. Hartmut Frommer, who has overseen a remarkable transformation of the Hangman's House into an exemplary museum of criminal legal history, has welcomed me repeatedly into his study at the top of the house's tower, shared his vast knowledge of Nuremberg's legal past and Franconian geography, and introduced me to the finer points of Nuremberg's famed sausages.

Back in Nashville, numerous friends and colleagues have helped me see the book to completion. Steve Pryor was the first to read the manuscript as a whole and Holly Tucker braved large chunks at an early stage. Their suggestions improved both the clarity and flow of the narrative considerably. The legal scholar and gifted author Dan Scharfstein lent his keen editorial eye to several chapters and Ellen Fanning gave me a molecular biologist's take on it all. My greatest intellectual debts continue to be to my remarkable colleagues in Vanderbilt's history department, whose breadth of knowledge and unstinting generosity continue to amaze me. By rights I should list them all by name, but in the interest of brevity I will single out Michael Bess, Bill Caferro, Marshall Eakin, Jim Epstein, Peter Lake, Jane Landers, Catherine Molineux, Matt Ramsey, Helmut Smith, and Frank Wcislo. Graduate students Christopher Mapes, Frances Kolb, and Sean Bortz each helped immensely with various editing and illustration tasks. Despite my best efforts, I have been unable to stump Jim Toplon and his crack team at Vanderbilt Interlibrary Loan—and that is no empty boast. I thank my provost, Richard McCarty, and my dean, Carolyn Dever, for their consistent moral and financial support of this project.

Many other friends have contributed to the book in diverse ways. I am particularly grateful to Wolfgang Behringer, Jennifer Bevington, Tom Brady, Joyce Chaplin, Jason Coy, Heiko Droste, Sigrun Haude, Claudia Jarzebowski, Mark Kramer, Paul Kramer and his Narrative

History Workshop, Wendy Lesser, Mary Lindemann, Gary Morsches, Hannah Murphy, Tom Robisheaux, Ulinka Rublack, Thomas Schnalke, Gerd Schwerhoff, Tom Seeman, Richard Sieburth, Phil Soergel, and Jeff Watt. Kathy Stuart, whose work on executioners has guided and inspired me more than any other, saved me a trip to Vienna (not a terrible fate in itself) by sharing her copy of Frantz Schmidt's 1624 imperial restitution. I also wish to acknowledge my great debt to previous scholars of early modern German executioners, evident throughout the endnotes, including authors of a century ago—Albrecht Keller, Theodor Hampe, Else Angstmann, and Hermann Knapp—as well as those of today, especially Jutta Nowosadtko, Richard J. Evans, Wolfgang Schild, Gisela Wilbertz, Ilse Schumann, and the late Richard van Dülmen.

My agent, Rafe Sagalyn, showed faith in me and this project early on and has gently introduced an academic historian to the brave new world of trade publishing. Thomas LeBien, my initial editor at Hill and Wang, likewise reassured me of this book's potential with his enthusiastic encouragement and sage advice. Courtney Hodell, who has seen the work through to press, has been a mentor *sans pareil* (although she has urged me to cut down on the foreign terms). Thanks to the welcoming spirit and creativity of Courtney and her colleagues—particularly Jeff Seroy, Jonathan Lippincott, Debra Helfand, Nick Courage, and Mark Krotov—my experience at Farrar, Straus and Giroux has been an author's dream. The meticulous eye and judicious red pencil of Stephen Wagley elevated my text to a new level of clarity, and the excellent maps of Gene Thorp provide the perfect visual introduction to Frantz Schmidt's world.

Like all my books so far, this one—to my own surprise—ended up being about family as much as anything else. I can only hope that Frantz Schmidt enjoyed a fraction of the love and support from his kin that I have come to rely on from mine. My wife, Beth Monin Harrington, remains my most unsparing editor and most unflagging supporter. Her relentless campaign against the passive voice saw some impressive victories this time around, but mistakes continue to be made (and loving gratitude sincerely expressed). Our children, George and Charlotte, have come to consider Meister Frantz a member of the household and in the process become the country's most knowledgeable middle schoolers on early modern crime and punishment (to the delight of their friends and classmates). The other members of my family have likewise indulged my obsession with this topic and shown no signs of being less than fascinated with my associated discourses. For their kind forbearance, I thank the Lebanon Filloons and Tampa Harringtons as well as the Monins of Sparta, Jonesborough, and Tulsa. Finally, for their lifelong example of selfless love and encouragement, I thank my parents, Jack and Marilyn Harrington. This book is dedicated to my father, with admiration and gratitude for planting and nurturing the seeds of a writing vocation in his oldest son.

Index

Page numbers in *italics* refer to illustrations.

Illustration Credits

A NOTE ABOUT THE AUTHOR

Joel F. Harrington is a professor of history at Vanderbilt University. He is the author of *The Unwanted Child*, winner of the 2010 Roland H. Bainton Prize for History, as well as *Reordering Marriage and Society in Reformation Germany* and *A Cloud of Witnesses*. He lives with his wife and two children in Nashville.